Microsoft
Power BI Dashboards
Step by Step

By Errin O'Connor

Microsoft Power BI Dashboards Step by Step
Published with the authorization of Microsoft Corporation by:
Pearson Education, Inc.

ISBN-13: 978-1-509-30803-3
ISBN-10: 1-509-30803-2

Library of Congress Control Number: 2018957364

1 18

Trademarks
Microsoft and the trademarks listed at http://www.microsoft.com on the "Trademarks" webpage are trademarks of the Microsoft group of companies. All other marks are property of their respective owners.

Warning and Disclaimer
Every effort has been made to make this book as complete and as accurate as possible, but no warranty or fitness is implied. The information provided is on an "as is" basis. The author, the publisher, and Microsoft Corporation shall have neither liability nor responsibility to any person or entity with respect to any loss or damages arising from the information contained in this book.

Special Sales
For information about buying this title in bulk quantities, or for special sales opportunities (which may include electronic versions; custom cover designs; and content particular to your business, training goals, marketing focus, or branding interests), please contact our corporate sales department at corpsales@pearsoned.com or (800) 382-3419.

For government sales inquiries, please contact governmentsales@pearsoned.com. For questions about sales outside the U.S., please contact intlcs@pearson.com.

Editor-in-Chief
Brett Bartow

Acquisitions Editor
Trina MacDonald

Development Editor
Songlin Qiu

Managing Editor
Sandra Schroeder

Senior Project Editor
Tracey Croom

Copy Editor
Kate Shoup

Production Editor
Dan Foster

Indexer
Valerie Haynes Perry

Proofreader
Dan Foster

Technical Editor
Pierstefano Tucci

Editorial Assistant
Cindy Teeters

Cover Designer
Twist Creative, Seattle

Compositor
Danielle Foster

Graphics
Vived Graphics

I would like to dedicate this book to my wife, Linda,
and my two boys, Carter and Owen.
You guys are my whole world,
and I couldn't have done this without your support.

Contents

Acknowledgments

I would like to thank my wonderful wife, Linda, and my two amazing boys, Carter and Owen, for all their support. This book would not have been possible without you.

I appreciate the time and efforts of Tracey Croom, Kate Shoup, and the entire team at Microsoft Press—past and present—who made this and so many other books possible.

I would also like to thank my team at EPC Group for all their support and their contributions.

About the Author

Errin O'Connor is the founder and chief architect of EPC Group. O'Connor focuses his efforts on implementing technologies in organizations throughout the country and around the globe.

For more than 20 years, O'Connor has assisted in managing EPC Group's corporate strategy and architects the proven methodologies around business intelligence, collaboration, enterprise content management, and custom application development that have set EPC Group apart from its competitors.

EPC Group has completed more than 5,000 Power BI, SharePoint, Office 365, and Microsoft stack-related implementations, including efforts around business intelligence (BI), custom application development, hybrid cloud strategy, Microsoft Azure, Office 365, SQL Server, Microsoft Intune, Amazon Web Services (AWS), and Microsoft Project Server. Founded in 1997, EPC Group has pioneered the way organizations implement BI platforms and collaborate.

In addition to this book, O'Connor is also the author or co-author of three other books: *SharePoint 2013 Field Guide: Advice from the Consulting Trenches* (Sams Publishing, 2014), *Microsoft SharePoint Foundation 2010: Inside Out* (Microsoft Press, 2011), and *Windows SharePoint Services 3.0: Inside Out* (Microsoft Press, 2007).

O'Connor is a frequent speaker at Microsoft Power BI, Office 365, and Microsoft SharePoint events throughout the United States and Canada.

For more information about O'Connor and EPC Group, visit www.epcgroup.net or contact the company at contact@epcgroup.net.

Introduction

Welcome! This *Step by Step* book has been designed so you can read it from the beginning to learn about Microsoft Power BI and then build your skills as you learn to perform increasingly specialized procedures. If you prefer, you can jump in wherever you need guidance to perform Power BI–related tasks. The how-to-steps are delivered in a concise manner. You will find full-color graphics that support the instructional content in this book.

Who this book is for

Microsoft Power BI Dashboards Step by Step is designed for use as a learning and reference resource by home and business users who want to create world-class business analysis dashboards that integrate today's most widely used data sources. The content of this book is designed to be useful for people who have previously used Power BI as well as for people who are discovering Power BI for the first time. This full-color, hands-on guide walks you through the key decisions analysts and developers need to make up front, and introduces all the concepts, skills, and techniques you'll need to achieve your goals.

The Step by Step approach

The book's coverage is divided into several parts representing general Power BI skill sets. Each part is divided into chapters representing skill set areas, and each chapter is divided into topics that group related skills. Each topic includes expository information followed by generic procedures. At the end of the chapters, you'll find a series of practice tasks you can complete on your own by using the skills taught in the chapters. You can use the practice files available from this book's website to work through the practice tasks.

Features and conventions

This book has been designed to lead you step by step through all the tasks you're most likely to want to perform in Microsoft Power BI. If you start at the beginning and work your way through all the procedures, you'll have the information you need to use the program effectively.

However, the topics are self-contained, so you can reference them independently. If you have worked with a previous version of Power BI, or if you complete all the exercises and later need help remembering how to perform a procedure, the following features of this book will help you locate specific information.

- **Detailed table of contents** Search the listing of the topics, sections, and side-bars within each chapter.

- **Chapter thumb tabs and running heads** Identify the pages of each chapter by the colored thumb tabs on the book's open fore edge. Find a specific chapter by number or title by looking at the running heads at the top of even-numbered (verso) pages.

- **Topic-specific running heads** Within a chapter, quickly locate the topic you want by looking at the running heads at the top of odd-numbered (recto) pages.

- **Practice tasks page tabs** Easily locate the practice tasks sections at the end of each chapter by looking for the full-page colored stripe on the book's fore edge.

- **Detailed index** Look up specific tasks and features in the index, which has been carefully crafted with the reader in mind.

You can save time when reading this book by understanding how the *Step by Step* series provides procedural instructions and auxiliary information and identifies on-screen and physical elements that you interact with. The following table lists content formatting conventions used in this book.

Convention Meaning

TIP	This reader aid provides a helpful hint or shortcut to simplify a task.
IMPORTANT	This reader aid alerts you to a common problem or provides information that is necessary to successfully complete a procedure.
SEE ALSO	This reader aid directs you to more information about a topic in this book or elsewhere.
1. Numbered steps 2. 3.	Numbered steps guide you through generic procedures in each topic and hands-on practice tasks at the end of each chapter.
▪ Bulleted lists	Bulleted lists indicate single-step procedures and sets of multiple alternative concepts or procedures.
Interface objects	In procedures and practice tasks, bold black text indicates on-screen elements that you should select (click or tap).
Ctrl+P	A plus sign between two keys indicates that you must press those keys at the same time. For example, "press Ctrl+P" directs you to hold down the Ctrl key while you press the P key.
Emphasis and *URLs*	In expository text, italic formatting identifies web addresses and words or phrases we want to emphasize.

Download the practice files

Although you can complete the practice tasks in this book by using your own instance of Power BI, for your convenience we have provided practice files for some of the tasks. You can download these practice files to your computer from *https://aka.ms/ PowerBIDash/downloads*. Follow the instructions on the webpage to install the files on your computer in the default practice file folder structure.

Chapter	Folder	File
1: Introduction to Power BI	Ch01	PBEI_Dashboard.pbix
2: Power BI architecture and administration	None	None
3: Visuals in Power BI	None	None
4: Power BI report development	Ch04	IT Spend Analysis Sample.xlsx
		IT Spend Analysis Report 01.pbix
		IT Spend Analysis Report 02 - Formatted.pbix
5: Use DAX in Power BI	None	None
6: Develop Power BI reports from Excel	Ch06	Retail Analysis Sample.xlsx
		Retail Analysis Sample Report.pbix
7: Develop Power BI reports from SharePoint Online	Ch07	Expense Budgets.stp
		Expense.stp
		SharePoint Online.pbix
		SharePoint Folder.pbix
8: Develop Power BI reports from SharePoint On-Premises	Ch08	Expense Budget.stp
		Expense.stp
		Expense - SharePoint On Premises.pbix
9: Develop Power BI reports from SQL	Ch09	SQLSERVER - Sample Report for HR.pbix
		Sample Report with RLS.pbix
10: Develop Power BI reports from SSAS cube	Ch10	SSAS SampleCube.pbix

11: Develop Power BI reports from Azure SQL	Ch11	SampleReportAzureSQL.pbix
12: Develop Power BI reports from Oracle	Ch12	SampleReport - Oracle.pbix
13: Develop Power BI reports from Dynamics 365	Ch13	Sample-Dynamics 365 Sales Report.pbix

Ebook edition

If you're reading the ebook edition of this book, you can do the following:

- Search the full text
- Print
- Copy and paste

You can purchase and download the ebook edition from the Microsoft Press Store at: *https://www.microsoftpressstore.com/store/microsoft-power-bi-dashboards-step-by-step-9781509308033.*

Get support and give feedback

This section provides information about getting help with this book and contacting us to provide feedback or report errors.

Errata and support

We've made every effort to ensure the accuracy of this book and its companion content. If you discover an error, please submit it to us at *https://aka.ms/PowerBIDash/errata.*

If you need to contact the Microsoft Press Support team, please send an email message to *microsoftpresscs@pearson.com.*

Introduction to Power BI

In today's competitive marketplace, data is very important for any organization, and it is more important than ever to "know your numbers." If data is represented in an effective manner, it will help organizations make decisions in a timely manner.

Power BI is a powerful business intelligence (BI) tool that enables users to drill into the key metrics of an organization. Businesses use this tool, which generates BI visualizations from specified datasets, to gain key business insights.

When users start working with Power BI, a lot of questions arise about the various licensing options available and the features associated with each version. Selecting the optimal license is key to ensuring success when using Power BI.

This chapter reviews the basics of Power BI and the capabilities supported by the Power BI interface. This includes what Power BI offers, the various Power BI services, the licensing models available, and the process of setting up the environment.

In this chapter:

- Introduction to Power BI
- Power BI services
- Power BI platforms and licensing models
- Set up Power BI
- Prepare a dashboard in Power BI
- Best practices for Power BI security

Practice files

As you work through this chapter, you'll use one practice file, which you can access from the MSPBIDashboards\ch01 folder on the book's companion website at *https://aka.ms/PowerBIDash/downloads*. The file is as follows:

- **PBEI_Dashboard.pbix** This file contains a sample Power BI report used to prepare a dashboard in Power BI service. You'll use this file in the section "Prepare a dashboard in Power BI service" later in this chapter.

An introduction to Power BI

Using business intelligence provides a wider scope for gathering and analyzing data. In this section you will explore what BI is and see a real-world scenario that outlines its possibilities in a general sense. Then you'll get a general overview of Power BI and the different features it offers to users according to their needs.

What is business intelligence?

BI technology enables us to drive meaningful insights from data that can be viewed at various levels of the organization, and to use these insights to drive optimal results. BI consists of theories and methodologies that users can study and apply to make meaningful decisions.

Technologies associated with BI, including Power BI, enable users to easily transform raw unstructured data into more meaningful charts and graphs, making BI a popular tool for transforming business. For example, consider a large organization in which historical data is stored and represented in a form that is difficult for decision-makers to understand. With BI, this data can be converted into a more meaningful form, providing answers to critical questions across the organization.

Real-world scenario

Suppose you work for a popular watch-manufacturing company, and you want to view its historical growth data across the last 30 years. Without BI, the following tasks associated with this effort would have proved difficult:

- Reviewing performance data for each year

- Finding and reviewing the available data to match the customer trend analysis

- Creating interactive visualizations to convey customer-centric goals

With the rise of tools like Power BI, the organization could present the available data into a powerful dashboard with graphs, visualizations, and sales charts, making it easy for members of executive teams to study and drill down on the data. This makes Power BI extremely useful in this critical era of analytics.

What is Power BI?

Power BI is a BI tool developed by Microsoft to present data in a more meaningful way, such as a dashboard, graph, visualization, or report. These are then used to analyze the data to better understand the needs of the organization.

Power BI includes the following capabilities:

- The capability to wrangle data from large databases—even the ones that can read 1 million rows per hour per user

- Dashboards, related visualizations, and reports to present data in a meaningful way for analysis by the end user

- The capability to readily connect faults and errors to provide a corrected methodology and approach for the end user

There are many real-world examples explaining the use of Power BI to spur business growth and transformation. In particular, dashboards and reports generated in Power BI provide actionable analysis to improve the decision-making process and reduce costs.

Who uses Power BI?

Different kinds of people use Power BI in different ways. A general representation is provided in Figure 1-1. For example, one user who studies BI reports might prefer a more enhanced representation of data—for example, with color contrasts and features that affect its look and feel. Another user—for example, a data analyst who studies analytics more often as part of their day-to-day activities—might prefer things the other way around, focusing on the underlying numbers rather than how it is presented in dashboards and related reports.

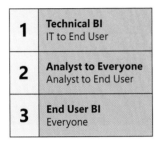

FIGURE 1-1 *The three main users of BI.*

Using Power BI effectively to streamline organizational growth

One way for an organization to gain insights for better understanding and collective decision-making is to collect relevant data and streamline it into reports. Consider an engineering firm with expertise in manufacturing precise metal products. A live data update for higher-level staff will provide insight into several aspects of the manufacturing process. The detection of defects in the metal, the percentage of processes that produce these defects, the number of corrections applied to rectify the defects, and so on are just some of the parameters considered for analysis. This dataset can be fed live into the Power BI server to generate meaningful dashboards and reports based upon regular refreshes.

Power BI features

Power BI offers several features. This section reviews these services and discusses how they are used.

Power BI dashboards

Power BI dashboards provide powerful visualizations of datasets in the form of graphs and charts. These can be analyzed in real-time from a live data feed, making them more interactive for users, and enabling them to surface relevant insights quickly.

Power BI dashboards include links, or tiles, to related reports, which helps users navigate from one report to another. These tiles can be easily customized according to user preference. In addition to adding images to these tiles, users can modify how they are laid out on the dashboard.

A word on datasets

A dataset gathers data from various data sources. Generally, there are two types of datasets in Power BI:

- **Dynamic** These datasets refresh automatically according to a set schedule.
- **Static** These datasets do not refresh automatically.

Natural query processing

Power BI users can use a special Question and Answer box in the dashboard to enter a query in plain English. Power BI will then filter, sort, and group data to return a list of visualizations that match the query. For example, suppose a user wants to analyze sales data for their organization. In this case the user could enter queries like, "How many leads have been converted to sales?" and "How many leads have gone cold?" Power BI can quickly provide useful visualizations to answer the user's questions.

User-friendly reports with data visualization

You can use Power BI to generate reports that contain detailed data in eye-catching visual form, along with easy-to-understand analysis of that data. Visualizations in Power BI reports make it easier to comprehend the analysis and arrive at a specific conclusion or decision. Users generate these reports by pinning different parameters to a Power BI dashboard and applying different filters to those parameters to drill down for deeper insights.

A Power BI report might include visuals such as charts with geographical information, bubble charts (which focus on relationships), comparison charts (including bar charts, line charts, waterfall charts, and so on), and many others. You can also consider adding comparison charts and other visuals—for example, to generate tree maps and pie charts.

> ⚠️ **IMPORTANT** To help users create custom Power BI visuals, Microsoft has publicly released the code for these visuals. For more information, see *https://github.com/ Microsoft/PowerBI-visuals*.

Sharing with others

All data, reports, and visualizations created by a specific user remain private unless that user decides to share it. Sharing within Power BI is easy. For example, to share a Power BI dashboard with other Power BI users, simply select the sharing option under the Actions category on the dashboard page. Or, to share a report, choose the Share with Others option. Then enter the email address(es) of the desired recipient(s) and specify what permissions they should be granted.

Users can share reports with annotated text and highlights to help end users in the decision-making process. Also, any changes made to a shared report are simultaneously reflected on the dashboard of each person granted access to the report. Users with read-only access can apply different filters for different scenarios to a report, but they cannot alter the report or apply different formatting to it.

> ⚠️ **IMPORTANT** You can only share reports with other users who have purchased or been assigned a Power BI Pro license in the same organization. In other words, the free version of Power BI does not allow sharing. (You'll learn more about the various Power BI licenses later in this chapter.)

Power BI Report Server

Power BI Report Server is an on-premises enterprise reporting and self-service BI feature that provides accurate reporting across organization levels. Users can directly publish Power BI reports on Report Server, thereby enabling other members of the organization to view, manage, edit, or update the reports.

> ⚠️ **IMPORTANT** When you publish a report, you place it on a personal or group workspace where others inside your organization with appropriate permissions can access it. When you share a report, you share it with specific people inside or outside your organization.

Power BI Report Server offers editing tools that enable users to create reports with a modern look and feel. Report Server also generates cloud-ready solutions compatible with SQL Server Reporting Services (SSRS).

> ⚠️ **IMPORTANT** On-premises reporting through Power BI Report Server is available only with the Power BI Premium license. You'll learn more about this license shortly.

Power BI Embedded

Power BI Embedded is a useful feature that enables you to embed Power BI reports into materials generated by third-party apps or in emails to share them with non–Power BI users. In addition, data in the form of graphs or other visuals can be rendered in any browser, irrespective of the dataset chosen. End users receive up-to-date analysis of data developed and/or stored within the Microsoft Azure framework. Microsoft suggests that in the near future, Power BI Embedded will become a preferred method for users using a Premium license. (License options are discussed later in this chapter.)

According to Microsoft, Power BI Embedded has some limitations:

- It cannot be used with any on-premises data gateway. This becomes difficult for developers working on specific requirements or customizations.

- Users who have access to Power BI cannot work on the same namespace, as Power BI Embedded runs on a completely different premium capacity model.

Mobile support

The Power BI mobile app enables you to access Power BI dashboards and reports using a mobile device such as an Android or iOS device. In some scenarios analysts can use the mobile app to address minute changes while tracking data in real-time and notify users of a possible solution.

Note that it is sometimes difficult to view BI reports on smaller screens; fortunately, Power BI allows for optimal display at correct resolutions. You can also zoom in and out and drill down to see relevant information feeds within the charts and graphs.

Power BI platforms

Power BI offers users the ability to choose from various platforms depending on their needs:

- Power BI service
- Power BI Desktop
- Power BI Premium

Power BI service

Power BI service is a free, cloud-based platform that works on Microsoft Azure. This version of Power BI is not available on a private cloud or as an internal service.

Power BI service includes the following capabilities and features:

- The capability to connect with hundreds of data sources
- An online dashboard with analytics information including graphs and reports
- Customizable dashboards
- Customizable reports
- The capability to edit reports online
- The capability to easily share reports
- Navigation controls that allow easy access to datasets
- Workspaces to collaborate with others on dashboards, reports, and datasets to create apps

- Home, Help, and Feedback buttons
- An Office 365 app launcher
- A Question and Answer box that enables users to search for data using plain English

Power BI Desktop

Power BI Desktop is like Power BI service except that it lives on the user's desktop machine and not in the cloud. This free tool integrates seamlessly with queries, data modelling, and visualizations for effective and accurate reporting of data, and offers a wide range of features to enable users to create appealing visualizations and detailed reports that can be published directly to other apps, to the web, or for mobile view. Note, however, that Desktop users cannot share reports.

Advantages of using Power BI Desktop include the following:

- Power BI Desktop supports various data sources, which is helpful in adapting to complex business requirements.
- Power BI Desktop includes an auto-detect relationship option for loaded datasets to help users gain understanding and insights.
- A user-friendly interface facilitates the creation and editing of custom visuals.
- Users can save reports for easy access. Reports that are saved have a PBIX extension.
- Users can create and publish reports from a single Power BI Desktop dashboard.

Power BI Premium

Power BI Premium provides greater capabilities and performance by increasing capacity-based offerings to end users. These act as dedicated resources to run the Power BI service for any organization. This dedicated capacity provides better support and stability.

Power BI Premium enables widespread distribution of data across the enterprise—without requiring additional licenses for users within the organization. A Premium workspace is a dedicated workspace allocated within the organization. It works on dedicated hardware handled by Microsoft for bulk data interaction per hour. The workload and number of users change based on specific factors and dictate how many users can access and edit data for reports. In this way, the capacity-based resources work in coordination to handle reports, graphs, and visualizations across the entire enterprise level.

Embedded analytics can be accessed from the Azure API, which offers the flexibility to obtain live data. The Power BI Report Server helps in maintaining BI assets on-premises. The Power BI Premium Report Server supports compatibility with SQL Server Reporting Services (SSRS) to provide interactive visualizations and paginated reports that can be analyzed on-premises. Report Server, which is a part of Power BI Premium, continuously deploys data from the dataset for better graphical analysis of reports, which can later be moved to the cloud.

> ⚠️ **IMPORTANT** Premium removes the down limits for refreshes and dataset sizes, which thereby increases the stability and performance for isolation with a dedicated hardware.

Power BI licensing models

Microsoft offers three types of licenses for Power BI:

- Power BI Free
- Power BI Pro
- Power BI Premium

The features of each license vary. The one you choose depends on your business requirements, including how much storage you need and the total number of users. The following sections consider the various Power BI licensing models.

Power BI Free

Power BI Free enables users to create any number dashboards and reports. However, they cannot share these with others.

Power BI Pro

Power BI Pro offers features that are not available in the free version platform. Most notably, Power BI Pro enables users to share dashboards, enabling multiple users to access them at the same time. Users can also collaborate to create any number of graphs and reports.

Other advantages of using Power BI Pro include the following:

- Users can connect to more than 70 data sources.
- Users can analyze data in the Power BI dashboard or in an Excel file.
- Users can synchronize content across Office 365 teams.
- Users can customize views according to their preferences.
- Users can develop personal dashboards, which they can save and even pin to their Power BI home page.
- Users can access dashboards shared by other members of the Office 365 community (assuming they have appropriate permissions) for collaboration purposes.
- Users can share workspaces.
- Users can subscribe to email alerts to notify them of changes to shared content.
- Users can embed APIs into Power BI visuals and reports.
- Users can publish reports and visuals to a web platform.

Here are a few examples of scenarios that require a Power BI Pro license:

- To publish content in Power BI Premium
- To share and receive content from other users
- To collaborate with other users on a dashboard or report
- To publish reports on Power BI Report Server

Power BI Premium

Power BI Premium is similar to Power BI Pro but can be scaled for larger organizations to accommodate more users or to provide users with more storage or a higher stream rate.

Power BI Premium offers the following advantages:

- Power BI Premium unlocks larger data limits and higher capacity offerings to accommodate large-scale deployments.
- Power BI Premium allows you to embed reports in other applications. (Note that for REST APIs to work with embedded graphs and reports, they will use a service account, which is available in Power BI Premium.)

- The Power BI Premium Report Server allows for the publication of reports on-premises.

- Dedicated servers allow for enhanced performance, with data refreshing 48 times per day.

Comparing the Free, Pro, and Premium licenses

Table 1-1 outlines key differences between the Power BI Free, Pro, and Premium licenses.

Table 1-1 *Power BI Free and Pro versus Power BI Premium*

Power BI Free and Power BI Pro	Power BI Premium
Storage is limited to 1 GB per user (Free) or 10 GB per user (Pro).	Ability to publish at premium capacity.
Data is refreshed 8 times per day.	Data is refreshed 48 times per day.
Data can be handled on-premises and in the cloud.	Data is secured with organizational content packs.
Data streaming occurs at a rate of 1 million rows per hour.	The data-streaming rate depends on the capacity defined for the report or workspace.
Necessary service requests are supported.	Row Level Security (RLS) is available for all users.
Data can be sourced from live datasets.	Data is available in the form of data catalogs.

Set up Power BI

Power BI is an effective reporting and visualization tool that enables you to generate dynamic dashboards and reports. There are numerous options available to you when you sign up for Power BI. You can sign up for a free version or purchase a subscription for Power BI Pro. (You can also sign up for a free 60-day trial of Power BI Pro.) The free account provides all the functionality of Power BI Pro except for sharing and collaboration features.

> ⚠ **IMPORTANT** There are no options within the free trial to upgrade to a Power BI Premium license. Users opting for this setup will need to purchase it directly from the official Microsoft Power BI link.

IMPORTANT You must use a work email address to sign up for Power BI. Personal email addresses aren't allowed.

1

Set up Power BI service

To set up Power BI service, follow these steps:

1. Type *https://powerbi.microsoft.com* in your web browser's address bar to open Microsoft's Power BI page.

2. Click the **Sign Up Free** link in the top-right corner of the screen.

3. Click the **Try Free** button under the Power BI heading.

4. When prompted, enter your work email address. Microsoft will send a verification code to that email address.

5. A Create Your Account dialog box opens. Enter your first name and last name, set and confirm a password, and type the verification code sent to the email address you provided in step 4. (See Figure 1-2.) Then click the **Start** button.

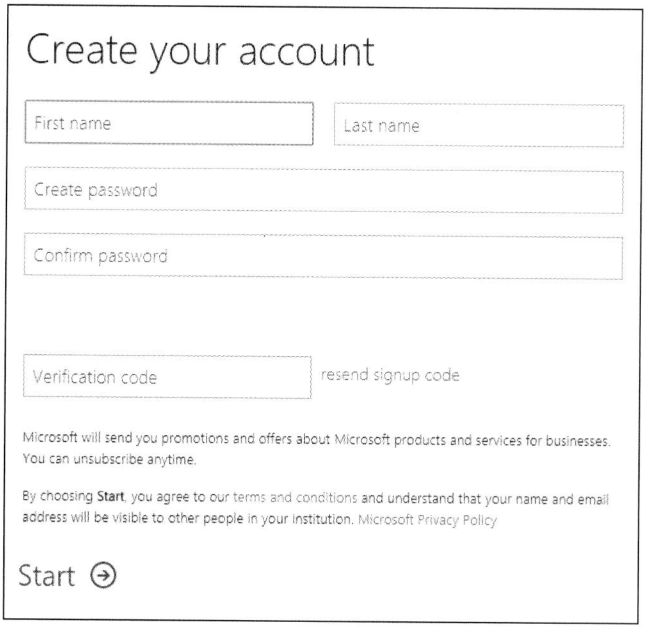

Create your account

First name	Last name

Create password

Confirm password

Verification code	resend signup code

Microsoft will send you promotions and offers about Microsoft products and services for businesses. You can unsubscribe anytime.

By choosing **Start**, you agree to our terms and conditions and understand that your name and email address will be visible to other people in your institution. Microsoft Privacy Policy

Start ⊕

FIGURE 1-2 *Signing up for Power BI service.*

6. A message appears instructing you to invite more members of your organization to create Power BI accounts. If desired, enter the email addresses of anyone you'd like to invite and click **Send Invitations**. Alternatively, click **Skip** for now.

Power BI service opens, displaying the dashboard with a welcome message. (See Figure 1-3.)

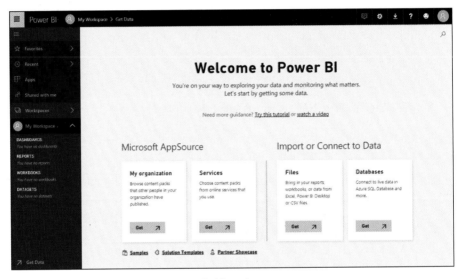

FIGURE 1-3 *The Power BI service welcome dashboard.*

Set up Power BI Desktop

To run Power BI Desktop, your system must meet certain minimum requirements. These appear in Table 1-2.

Table 1-2 *Minimum requirements to install Power BI Desktop*

Operating System	Windows 7/Windows Server 2008 R2 or later
.NET Framework	.NET 4.5
Browser	Internet Explorer 9 or later
RAM	At least 1 GB; 1.5 GB or more recommended
Display	At least 1440x900 or 1600x900 (16:9) recommended
CPU	1 GHz or faster; x86- or x64-bit processor recommended

To download and install Power BI Desktop, follow these steps:

1. Type *https://app.powerbi.com* in your web browser's address bar.

2. Click the **Sign In** button and sign in using your work email credentials.

3. Click the **Download** button in the top-right corner of the screen and select **Power BI Desktop** from the menu that appears. (See Figure 1-4.)

FIGURE 1-4 *Downloading Power BI Desktop.*

>  **TIP** Another way to start the download process is to direct your web browser to *https://powerbi.microsoft.com/en-us/downloads/* and click the **Download** button under Microsoft Power BI Desktop.

4. After the installation file is downloaded, right-click and choose **Run as Administrator** to begin the setup process.

5. The Microsoft Power BI Desktop wizard starts. Click the **Next** button. (See numeral 1 of Figure 1-5.)

6. Select the **Terms and Conditions** checkbox and click **Next**. (See numeral 2 of Figure 1-5.)

7. Leave the file path set to the default. Then click **Next**. (See numeral 3 of Figure 1-5.)

8. If you like, select the **Create a Desktop Shortcut** checkbox. Then click **Install**. (See numeral 4 of Figure 1-5.)

9. Optionally, after the installation is complete, select the **Launch Microsoft Power BI Desktop** checkbox. Then click **Finish**. (See numeral 5 of Figure 1-5.)

10. The Power BI Desktop Sign In page appears (See numeral 6 of Figure 1-5.) Click the **Sign In** button and sign in to open Power BI Desktop.

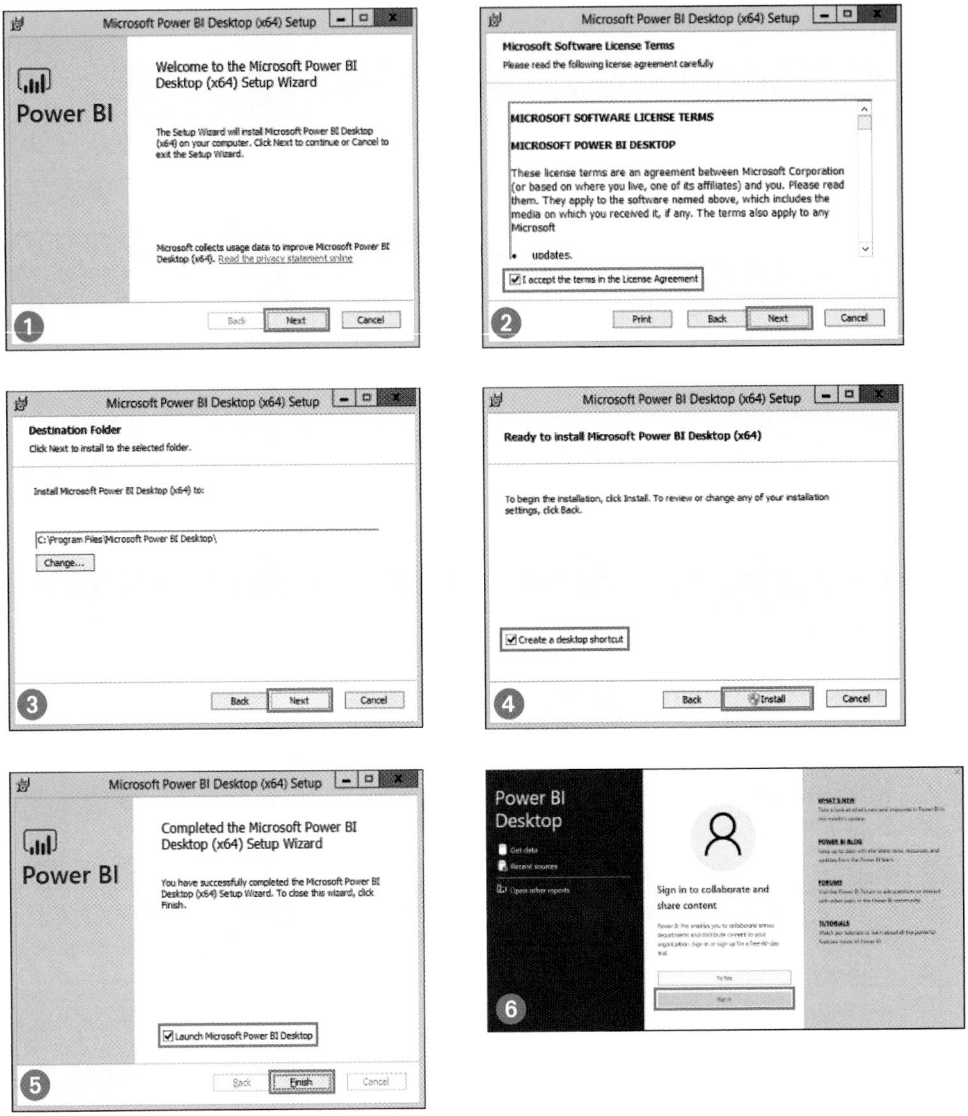

FIGURE 1-5 *Installing Power BI Desktop.*

Set up Power BI on your mobile device

In addition to using Power BI on a desktop machine, you can also use it on your mobile phone, thanks to the Power BI mobile app. This app is available for the following mobile platforms:

- Windows (Windows Store)
- Android (Google Play Store)
- iOS (Apple App Store)

To install Power BI on an Android device, follow these steps. (The steps to install the app on a Windows or iOS device are similar.)

1. Depending on what type of mobile device you have, open the Windows store, the Google Play store, or the Apple App store on your device.

2. Search for the Microsoft Power BI app.

3. Tap the Install button to install the Power BI app on your phone. (See numeral 1 of Figure 1-6.)

4. Open the app. As shown in numeral 2 of Figure 1-6, you'll see two options:

   - Power BI
   - Report Server (part of Power BI Premium)

5. Tap **Power BI**.

6. Enter your work email address and your password and tap **Sign In**. (See numeral 3 of Figure 1-6.) A dashboard will open.

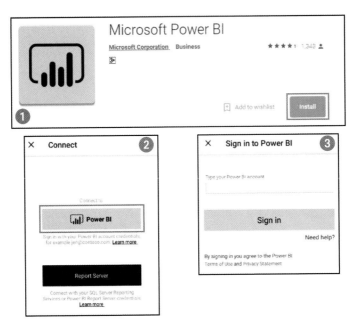

FIGURE 1-6 *Setting up Power BI on a mobile application.*

Prepare a dashboard in Power BI service

Power BI users can prepare custom dashboards. This section shows you how to prepare a simple custom dashboard based on a report prepared and published in Power BI service that uses various out-of-the-box visuals available in Power BI service. (You'll explore a detailed step-by-step approach to preparing reports using different data sources later in this book.)

> ⚠️ **IMPORTANT** Before you can prepare a dashboard based on a Power BI report, you must publish the report. To find out how to publish a report, see Chapter 4. Once you've published a report, you can follow the steps in this section.

Follow these steps to build a dashboard in Power BI service:

1. Type *https://app.powerbi.com* in your web browser's address bar.

2. Click the **Sign In** button and sign in using your work email address. As shown in Figure 1-7, Power BI service opens with an empty workspace displayed. (You'll learn more about workspaces in Chapter 2.)

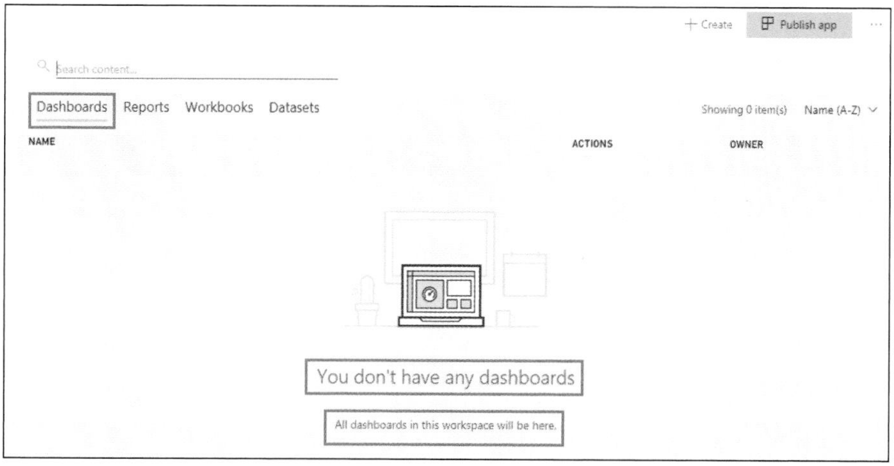

FIGURE 1-7 *An empty Power BI workspace.*

3. To view reports that have been prepared and published in Power BI service, click the **Reports** option in the workspace and select the report from which you want to build a dashboard.

4. Open the report you want to use. (In this example, I used the sample file I mentioned at the beginning of the chapter, PBEI_Dashboard.pbix.)

   As shown in Figure 1-8, this report contains two visuals: PTQ Trend and Sales by Device Type.

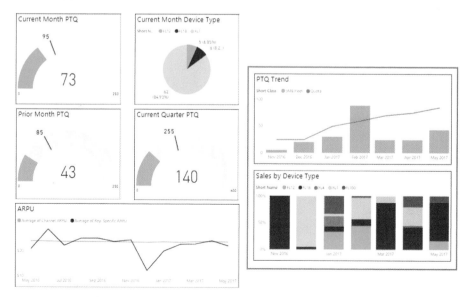

FIGURE 1-8 *Sample Power BI report.*

5. Click the **Pin Visual** button in the upper-right corner of the PTQ Trend visual to pin it to the dashboard. (See Figure 1-9.)

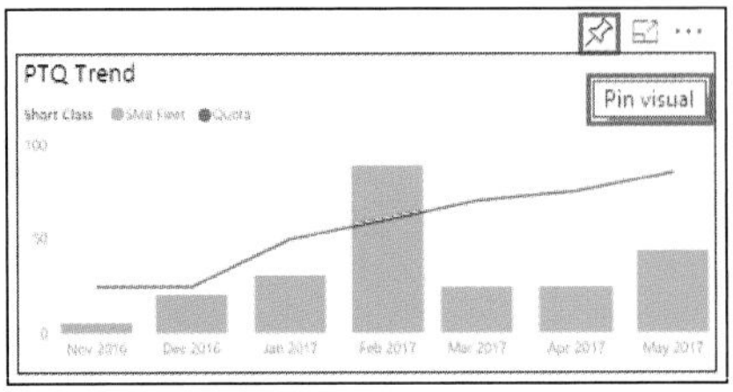

FIGURE 1-9 *A sample Power BI visual with an option to pin the visual to a dashboard.*

A Pin to Dashboard dialog box opens. (See Figure 1-10.)

6. Select the **New Dashboard** option button, type a name for the new dashboard, and click the **Pin button**. Power BI notifies you that the visualization was successfully pinned.

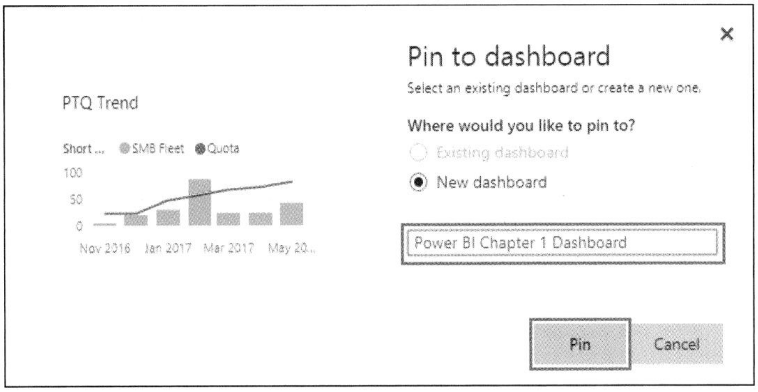

FIGURE 1-10 *The Pin to Dashboard dialog box.*

7. Repeat these steps to add more visualizations to the dashboard, such as the **Sales by Device Type** visualization. This time, however, choose **Existing Dashboard** in the Pin to Dashboard dialog box and select the desired dashboard. (See Figure 1-11.) Figure 1-12 shows a dashboard with several visuals added.

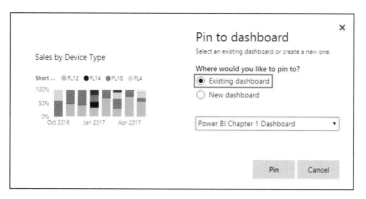

FIGURE 1-11 *Pinning a visualization to an existing dashboard.*

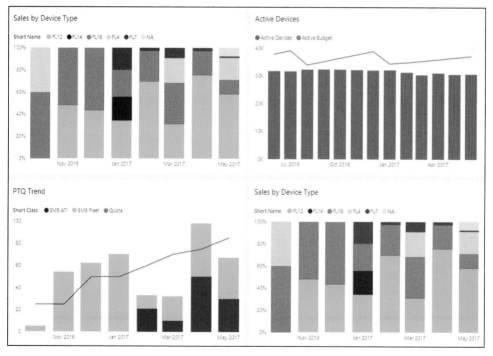

FIGURE 1-12 *The new Power BI dynamic dashboard.*

General note for Power BI security

Microsoft Azure is a cloud-based software as a service (SaaS) platform that empowers users to easily build and manage cloud-based integrations online. Because Power BI is built on the Azure framework, it's fairly easy to secure it from unauthorized users.

In general, Power BI security services depend on two clusters: the web front end (WFE) and the back-end cluster. Using the WFE, the user enters their login credentials. Power BI then uses Azure Active Directory (AAD) to authenticate the user. After the user is authenticated, the back-end cluster takes over. It handles data reporting, manages dashboard data, takes care of data connections, and manages live datasets. Basically, it handles everything from the time the user enters a request until the Power BI service responds to that request.

Skills review

In this chapter, you learned about:

- Business intelligence (BI)

- How Power BI effectively streamlines organizational growth

- Features of Power BI

- Power BI platforms and licensing models

- Procedures for setting up Power BI service, Power BI Desktop, and Power BI for mobile devices

- The procedure for building a dashboard in Power BI

Practice tasks

This section provides a simple case study for you to study and solve using information from this chapter. This section also contains a series of practice questions for you to answer.

Case study

Consider a large finance company in which an IT project manager is charged with deciding which version of Power BI to adopt. Here's the scenario:

- The finance organization has millions of rows of data.

- Thousands of new rows are added to the database every hour.

- Employees have various roles, according to their professions.

- Some employees act only as end users, viewing reports containing this data.

- Some employees are analysts and require the ability to share Power BI dashboards.

- Some employees focus on high-precision data to improve their understanding of performance.

- The finance company wants to set up an on-premises environment within the organization.

Based on these points, decide whether the finance company should select the Power BI Pro version or the Premium package.

Practice questions

1. What is the difference between Power BI Pro and Power BI Premium?

2. What services does Power BI support?

3. Describe the natural query processing capabilities in Power BI.

4. What Power BI feature supports an on-premises environment?

5. What is Power BI Report Server?

6. What is Power BI Embedded?

7. What kind of license do you need to share your Power BI dashboard with other team members?

8. Why are visuals used in Power BI Desktop?

9. How do you set up Power BI Desktop?

10. How do you set up a dynamic dashboard in Power BI?

Power BI architecture and administration

Power BI is one of the most valuable tools available for organizations that seek to gain key insights from their data. Power BI enhances end user efficiency, improves data analysis, and facilitates the overall decision-making process.

This chapter covers the architecture and the underlying services of Power BI, including the internal and external working structures. It also takes a look at Power BI administration processes, in which an assigned user has specific roles to monitor and control the use of Power BI.

This chapter then explains data modeling functionality in detail—the process of converting raw data into a simpler form that can be read by Power BI servers—as well as the report-development process in Power BI Desktop and Power BI service (including workspace functionality).

In this chapter:

- Power BI architecture
- The Power BI Admin Portal
- Power BI data models and report development

Power BI architecture

To better understand Power BI operations, it's important to have a grasp of its architecture from both a technical and an internal standpoint. That's the focus of this section. This section also provides an overview of the Power BI data-processing model.

Power BI technical architecture

By Power BI technical architecture, we mean the manner in which Power BI ingests data, processes it, and spits it back out for analysis. Figure 2-1 illustrates this architecture.

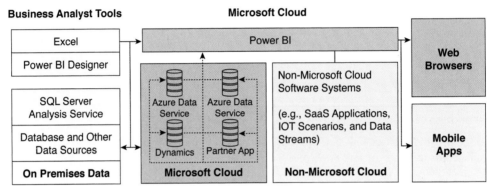

FIGURE 2-1 *Power BI technical architecture.*

As shown in Figure 2-1, the architecture operates as follows:

1. Power BI servers compile raw data from various sources, including Excel, Power BI Designer, SQL Server, and other database servers, as well as Microsoft Cloud sources such as Azure data services, Microsoft Dynamics, non-Microsoft SaaS apps, and others.

2. Power BI looks for direct relationships among the data fed into the system to develop a sequential data model. (Correlations can also be made manually.)

3. Power BI transforms the data model into visualizations and reports for end users. These users can publish the reports and visualizations online or on various desktop or mobile applications for consumption by other users. Depending on what licensing model of Power BI is used, they may also be able to share them with other users for collaboration purposes.

Power BI internal architecture

The internal architecture of Power BI revolves around the sources of data it ingests. For example, suppose you have an on-premises database that contains SharePoint content, which is fed directly into Power BI Desktop. You also have data sources such as on-premises data files, data on OneDrive for Business, data in Excel files, data in Azure, and more, which enter your system through a personal gateway, after which they are filtered for use by Power BI. The Power BI system can use all the data in available datasets to generate dashboards and reports. Users can pin these reports on their Power BI dashboard and (depending on what licensing model of Power BI they use) share them with others. They can also consume these reports online using Power BI service or via the Power BI Windows Phone, Android, or iPhone app. (See Figure 2-2.)

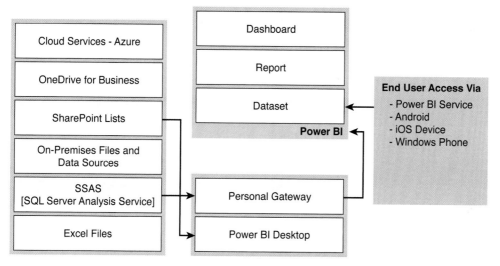

FIGURE 2-2 *Power BI internal architecture.*

> ⚠ **IMPORTANT** The process by which data sources, in the form of datasets, interact with Power BI is called the conception data flow. The interaction between end users and Power BI is called the visualization data flow. The simultaneous process that occurs between datasets, Power BI, and user-generated reports is called the refresh flow.

Data processing in Power BI

The data ingested by Power BI goes through various processes to ensure its integrity. This is an important part of Power BI analysis. Figure 2-3 outlines these processes.

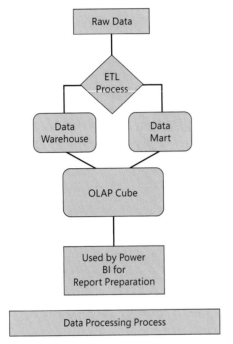

FIGURE 2-3 *Data-processing in Power BI.*

As you can see in Figure 2-3, the processes are as follows:

1. Raw data passes through the extract, transform, load (ETL) process, during which the data is read and assigned a specific data type.

2. The data types rearrange themselves to provide meaningful information in the form of a data warehouse or data mart.

3. The data warehouse and data mart create online analytical processing (OLAP) cubes. An OLAP cube is an array of multidimensional time-specific information that is stored and processed for generating reports and analytical visualizations.

4. The OLAP cubes are fed into Power BI, and their data is converted into maps, histograms, graphs, charts, and other visuals to generate reports.

> **IMPORTANT** Throughout these processes, the integrity and accuracy of the data are maintained—meaning you get near-perfect data in Power BI reports.

These processes—and by extension the Power BI architecture—can be divided into three main phases, or layers. (See Figure 2-4.)

- **Data preparation layer** In this phase, or layer, the system data sources synchronize data. At first, the data sourced from the system exists in different file formats. To read these various sources of information, Power BI first employs a gateway to process the data and then integrates it into a dataset.

- **Data warehouse layer** In this layer, a data warehouse applies filters to the dataset to process it. To maintain accuracy, the data warehouse also uses ETL processes to identify flaws and make corrections as needed. It then forwards the processed data to a Power BI OLAP storage unit.

- **Data presentation layer** After the dataset has been processed by the data warehouse and stored in an OLAP storage unit, it is ready to be converted into reports and visualizations by Power BI. Users can access these visualizations on their dashboard.

Architecture of Power BI

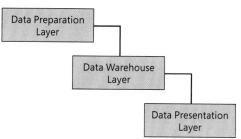

FIGURE 2-4 *Three main phases of Power BI architecture.*

The Power BI Admin Portal

You can use the Power BI Admin Portal to perform various administrative tasks. To access the Admin Portal, follow these steps. (Note that these steps assume you are signed into your Office 365 account.)

1. Type *https://app.powerbi.com* in your web browser's address bar.

2. Click the **Sign In** button and sign in using your registered work email address.

3. Click the **Settings** icon (the one with the gear) in the top-right corner of Power BI service dashboard and choose **Admin Portal** in the menu that appears. (See screen 1 in Figure 2-5.) The Admin Portal opens. (See screen 2 in Figure 2-5.)

FIGURE 2-5 *Accessing the Power BI Admin Portal.*

> ⚠️ **IMPORTANT** To understand various modes of Power BI administration, you need to configure and view the Office 365 Admin Portal. This allows admin roles to be assigned to different users.

Assign the admin role to another user

To assign the Power BI administrative role to different users, follow these steps:

1. Type *https://portal.office.com/adminportal/home#/homepage* in your web browser's address bar.

2. The Admin Portal opens. In the pane on the left, click **Users** and select **Active Users**. (See screen 1 in Figure 2-6.)

3. Select the user to whom you want to assign a specific role.

4. Click the **Edit** button. (See screen 2 in Figure 2-6.)

5. Select the **Customized Administrator** option button. Then select the **Power BI Service Administrator** checkbox. (See screen 3 in Figure 2-6.) Then save your changes.

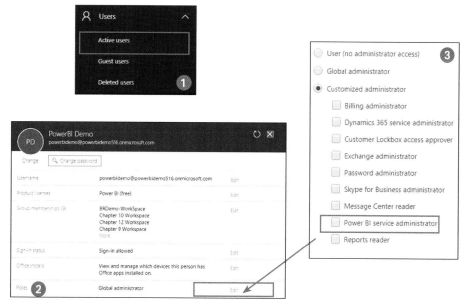

FIGURE 2-6 *Assigning the administrator role to a different user.*

Explore Admin Portal features

The Power BI Admin Portal consists of several features. These include the following:

- Usage Metrics

- Users

- Audit Logs

- Tenant Settings

- Capacity Settings

- Embed Codes

- Organization Visuals

You access these features from links in the navigation pane on the left side of the Admin Portal. (Refer to Figure 2-5.)

Chapter 2: Power BI architecture and administration

Usage Metrics

The Admin Portal's Usage Metrics page shows a rich dashboard composed of different reports from throughout the organization. The purpose of this page is to provide analysis and insight into a Power BI report.

The Usage Metrics page enables you to see which users and groups are most active within the organization. As shown in Figure 2-7, available usage data for individual users includes the following:

- **Number of User Dashboards** This shows the number of dashboards in the user's workspace. (See tile 1 in Figure 2-7.)

- **Number of User Reports** This shows the number of reports in the user's workspace. (See tile 2 in Figure 2-7.)

- **Number of User Datasets** This shows the number of datasets in the user's workspace. (See tile 3 in Figure 2-7.)

- **Most Consumed Dashboards by Users** This shows which dashboards have been consumed by the most users. (See tile 4 in Figure 2-7.) For example, if someone builds a dashboard, and 15 other people in an organization share it, and 10 more people share its content pack, then the total number of users who have consumed that dashboard is 26 (1+15+10). (A content pack is a collection of dashboards, reports, datasets, and workbooks that are combined together within an organization.)

- **Most Consumed Packages by Users** This shows the most popular content with which the user is associated. These packages can be anything from SaaS content packs, to organizational packs, to files, to a database. (See tile 5 in Figure 2-7.)

- **Top Users with Most Dashboards** This lists the users who have created (or consumed through sharing) the most dashboards. (See tile 6 in Figure 2-7.)

- **Top Users with Most Reports** This lists which users have created (or consumed through sharing) the most reports. (See tile 7 in Figure 2-7.)

32

FIGURE 2-7 *Usage metrics for individual users.*

In addition, you can view the following usage data for groups. (See Figure 2-8.)

- **Number of Group Dashboards** This shows the number of dashboards in the group's workspace. (See tile 1 in Figure 2-8.)

- **Number of Group Reports** This shows the number of reports in the group's workspace. (See tile 2 in Figure 2-8.)

- **Number of Group Datasets** This shows the number of datasets in the group's workspace. (See tile 3 in Figure 2-8.)

- **Most Consumed Dashboards by Groups** This shows which dashboards have been consumed by the most groups. (See tile 4 in Figure 2-8.)

- **Most Consumed Packages by Groups** This shows which packages have been consumed by the most groups. (See tile 5 in Figure 2-8.)

- **Top Groups with Most Dashboards** This lists the groups that have created (or consumed through sharing) the most dashboards. (See tile 6 in Figure 2-8.)

- **Top Groups with Most Reports** This lists the groups that have created and viewed the most reports. (See tile 7 in Figure 2-8.)

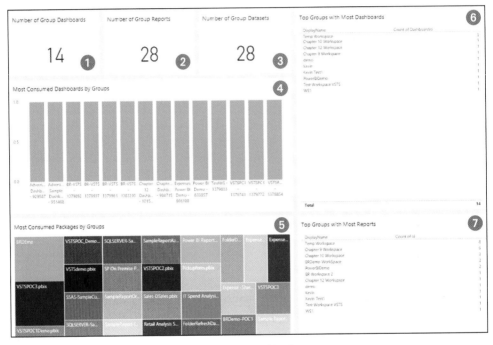

FIGURE 2-8 *Usage metrics data for individual groups combined.*

Users

The Users page provides access to tools to manage users, administrators, and groups in the Office 365 Admin Center. To access these tools, simply click the **Go to O365 Admin Center** button in the Users page. (See screen 1 in Figure 2-9.) This opens a page in the Office 365 Admin Center that shows all active users with proper administration controls for Power BI. (See screen 2 in Figure 2-9.)

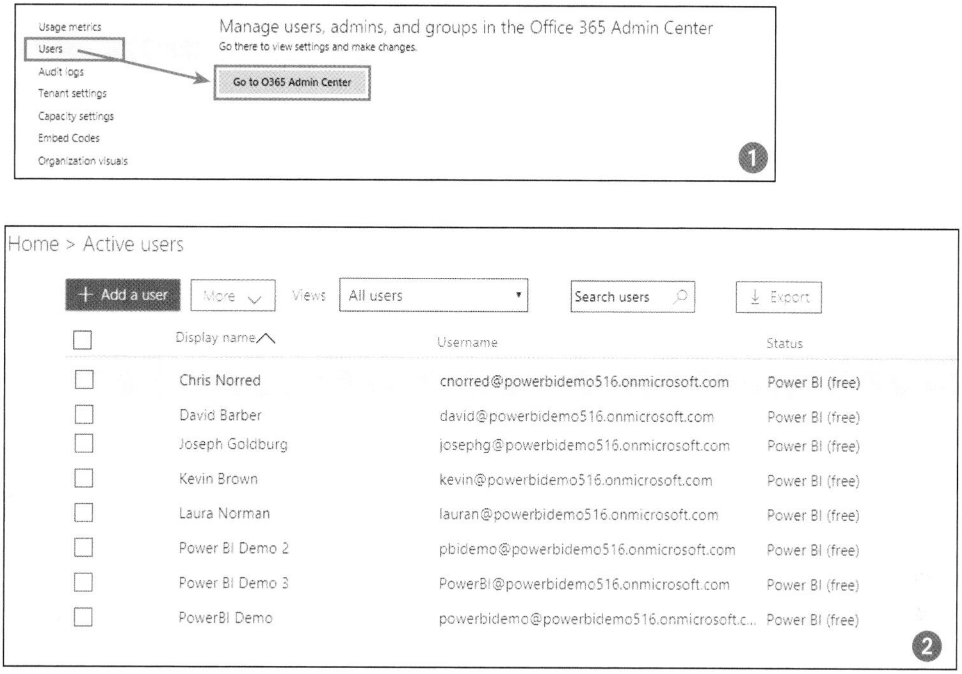

FIGURE 2-9 *Accessing tools for managing users.*

Audit Logs

Power BI enables you to view audit logs for various reports. To do so, click the **Go to O365 Admin Center** button in the Audit Logs page. (See screen 1 in Figure 2-10.) This opens the Office 365 Security and Compliance Center, where you can search for the audit log you want to see. (See screen 2 in Figure 2-10.)

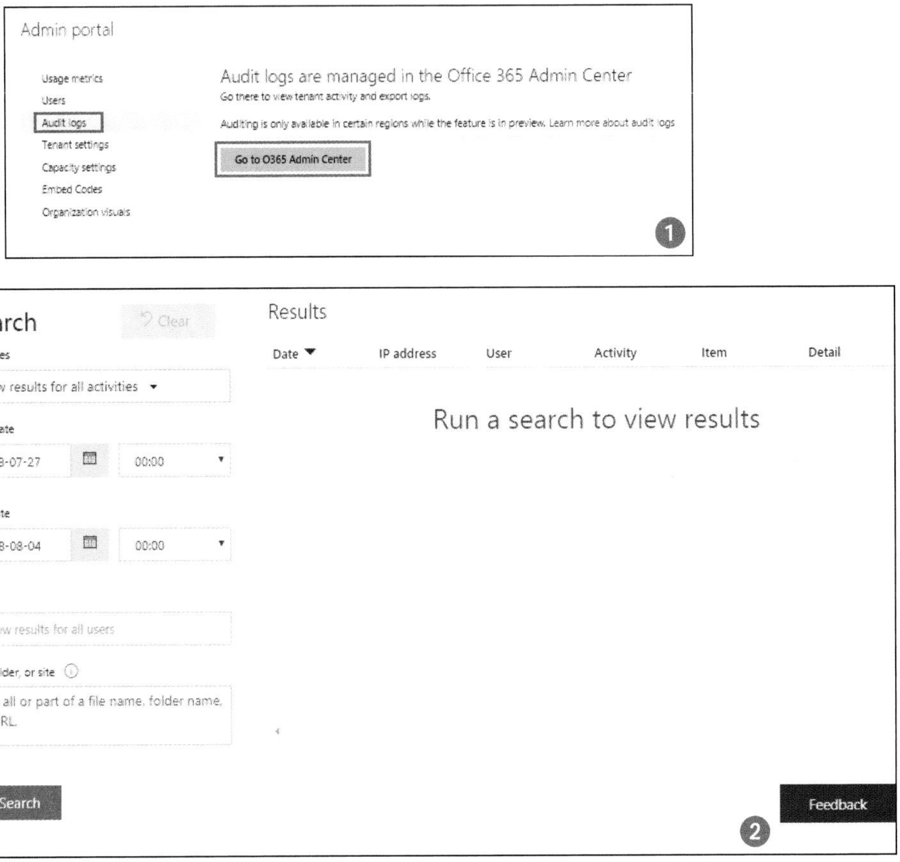

FIGURE 2-10 *Viewing audit logs.*

Tenant Settings

A tenant is the collection of entities within an organization, such as users, domains, subscriptions, and so on. Applying tenant settings enables you to control who in the organization can access what and facilitates the sharing of sensitive data with specific groups. There is also a feature to switch various tenant-level settings on or off based on user needs.

Power BI supports the following tenant settings:

- Export and sharing settings

- Content pack and app settings

- Integration settings

- R visuals settings

- Audit and usage settings

- Dashboard settings

- Developer settings

Export and sharing settings

The Export and Sharing Settings page includes several groups of settings to control how content is exported and shared. These include the following:

- **Share Content with External Users** Settings in this group control whether members of your organization can share content with external users. Your options are as follows. (See screen 1 in Figure 2-11.)

  - **Disabled/Enabled** Click this toggle to disable or enable this feature. Enabling this feature engages the following settings:

    - **Enable for Entire Organization** Select this option button to enable the feature for all the people in an organization.

    - **Specific Security Groups** Select this option button to enable the feature for specific groups in the organization.

    - **Except Specific Security Groups** Select this option button to prevent the setting from being applied to a specific group.

- **Publish to Web** Settings in this group dictate whether members of your organization can publish Power BI dashboards and reports to the web. This group contains the same settings as the Share Content with External Users group. (See screen 2 in Figure 2-11.)

- **Export Data** Settings in this group indicate whether members of your organization can export data from a tile or visualization. Again, this group contains the same settings as the others. (See screen 3 in Figure 2-11.)

- **Export Reports as PowerPoint Presentations** Settings in this group control whether members of your organization can export Power BI reports as PowerPoint presentations. Again, this group contains the same settings as the others. (See screen 4 in Figure 2-11.)

- **Print Dashboards and Reports** Settings in this group control whether members of your organization can print dashboards and reports. (See screen 5 in Figure 2-11.)

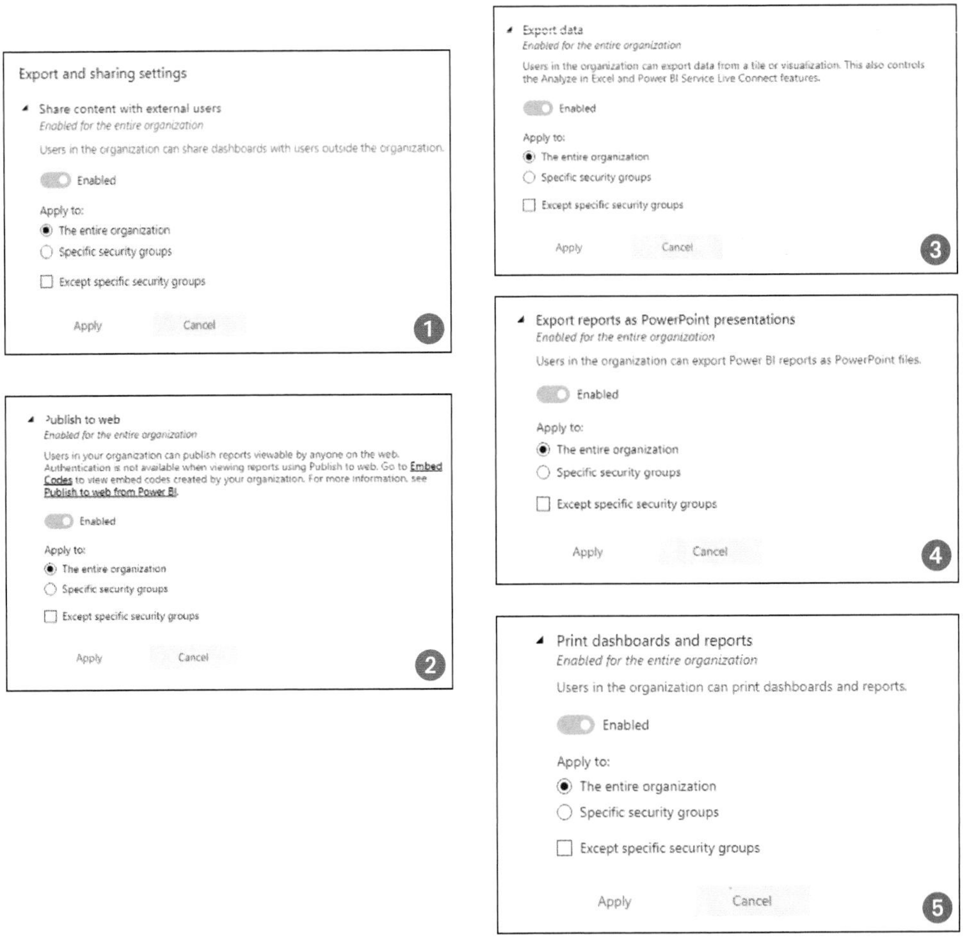

FIGURE 2-11 *Tenant-level settings in the Power BI Admin Portal.*

Content pack and app settings

A content pack combines all the contents that can be updated or published across the web or to various applications, such as datasets, dashboards, reports, Excel workbooks, and so on. As shown in screen 1 of Figure 2-12, there are a few options for handling content packs in Power BI:

- **Publish Content Packs and Apps to the Entire Organization** Enable this feature to allow users to publish content packs to the entire organization.

- **Create Template Organizational Content Packs and Apps** Enable this feature to allow users to create template content packs that use datasets built on one data source in Power BI Desktop.

- **Push Apps to End Users** Enable this feature to allow users to share apps directly with others, without needing to install them from AppSource.

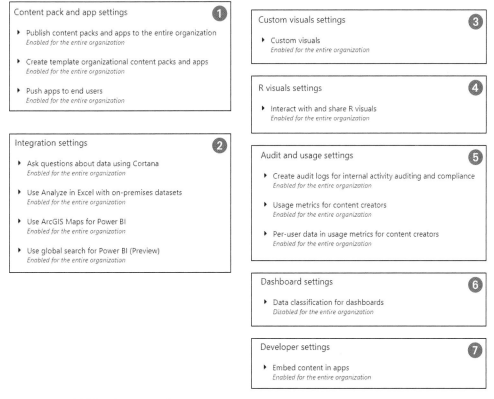

FIGURE 2-12 *Additional tenant settings.*

Integration settings

The Power BI Admin Portal integration settings give users different options to integrate other tools into Power BI, such as Cortana, Excel, ArcGIS, and Azure to search, ask questions, and analyze data in Power BI reports. As shown in screen 2 in Figure 2-12, these options are as follows:

- **Ask Questions About Data Using Cortana** Enable this feature to allow users to use Cortana to ask specific questions about their data.

- **Use Analyze in Excel with On-Premises Datasets** Enable this feature to allow users to use Excel to view and interact with on-premises Power BI datasets.

- **User ArcGIS Maps for Power BI** Enable this setting to allow users to use the ArcGIS Maps for Power BI visualization provided by Esri.

- **Use Global Search for Power BI** Enable this feature to allow users to employ Global Search for Power BI.

> ⚠ **IMPORTANT** These settings apply to the entire organization. They cannot be limited to specific individuals or groups.

Custom visuals settings

This setting (see screen 3 in Figure 2-12) enables you to use custom visuals available for Power BI.

R visual settings

As shown in screen 4 in Figure 2-12, there is only one setting in this group: Interact with and Share R Visuals. You can enable this setting to allow users to interact and share visuals created using R scripts. R scripts, commonly called R visuals, can present advanced data shaping and analytics such as forecasting through the use of R.

> ⚠ **IMPORTANT** This setting applies to the entire organization. It cannot be limited to specific individuals or groups.

2

Audit and usage settings

This option provides details for usage metrics for parameters such as compliance, per user data, report viewing, and internal activity feature. As shown in screen 5 of Figure 2-12, the options are as follows:

- **Create Audit Logs for Internal Activity Auditing and Compliance** Enable this feature to allow users to monitor actions performed by other users in Power BI.

> ⚠ **IMPORTANT** This setting must be enabled for audit log entries to be tracked. The setting applies to the entire organization and cannot be limited to specific individuals or groups.

- **Usage Metrics for Content Creators** Enable this feature to allow users to view usage metrics for dashboards and reports they created.

- **Per-User Data in Usage Metrics for Content Creators** Enable this feature if you want usage metrics for content creators to expose the names and email addresses of users who access their content.

Dashboard settings

As shown in screen 6 in Figure 2-12, there is only one setting in this group: Data Classification for Dashboards. You can enable this setting to allow users to tag dashboards to classify the data they contain.

> ⚠ **IMPORTANT** This setting applies to the entire organization. It cannot be limited to specific individuals or groups.

Developer settings

As shown in screen 7 in Figure 2-12, there is only one setting in this group: Embed Content in Apps. You can enable this setting to allow users to embed Power BI dashboards and reports in various SaaS applications. This setting can be enabled across the organization or limited to specific groups.

> ⚠ **IMPORTANT** If we disable this feature, users cannot use REST APIs to embed Power BI content in applications.

Capacity Settings

Capacity is the heart of Power BI Premium and Power BI Embedded. It refers to the resources reserved for users to perform functions in Power BI, such as publishing dashboards, reports, and datasets.

You manage capacity using the Capacity Settings page in the Power BI Admin Portal. As shown in Figure 2-13, you can adjust capacity for Power BI Premium and Power BI Embedded. The Power BI Premium tab enables you to add capacity. For Power BI Embedded, capacity admins are assigned from the Azure Portal, which you can access from the Power BI Embedded tab.

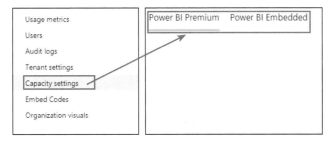

FIGURE 2-13 *Capacity Settings in the Power BI Admin Portal.*

Embed Codes

As an administrator, you can view, add, or delete the embed codes generated for your Power BI tenant. (See Figure 2-14.) (Embed codes are codes for Power BI reports that can be shared across different applications.)

FIGURE 2-14 *Embed codes generated by the Power BI tenant.*

Organization Visuals

The Organization Visuals page in the Power BI Admin Portal enables users to upload custom visualizations for use by other members of the organization in their own dashboards and reports. It also shows all custom visualizations currently available for this type of use.

To add a custom visualization to Power BI, follow these steps:

1. Click the **Organization Visuals** link in the left pane of the Power BI Admin Portal. (See screen 1 in Figure 2-15.)

2. In the Organization Visuals page, click the **Add a Custom Visual** link. (See screen 2 in Figure 2-15.)

3. The Add Custom Visual dialog box opens. (See screen 3 in Figure 2-15.) Click the **Browse** button next to the **Choose a .pbiviz File** box and locate and select the file containing the visualization you want to upload.

> ⚠ **IMPORTANT** Only versioned API custom visuals are supported. Before uploading a custom visual, be sure it meets your organization's security and privacy standards.

4. **Type a descriptive name for the custom visualization in the Name Your Custom Visuals** box.

5. Click the **Upload** link in the **Icon** section to upload the file that contains the icon you want to use to represent your custom visualization in the Power BI Desktop UI.

6. Type a brief description of the custom visualization in the Description box. Then click **Add**.

FIGURE 2-15 *Adding custom visualizations for use across the organization.*

If you need to delete a custom visualization, select it in the list in the Organizational Visuals page, and then click the **Trash Bin** icon.

> ⚠ **IMPORTANT** Deletion is irreversible. After you delete a visualization, it will no longer be rendered in existing reports. Even if you upload the same visualization again, it will not replace the previous one that was deleted. Users will have to import the new visual and use it to replace the old version in their reports.

Power BI data models and report development

Publishing accurate and insightful Power BI reports involves preparing the data model for the Power BI service or Desktop platform, performing basic operations on the data model, and generating Power BI reports.

Prepare a data model using Power BI service

Data modeling involves streamlining content and shaping data to generate more insightful Power BI reports. Fortunately, Power BI makes this task easy. This section shows you how to prepare a data model in Power BI service using a sample Excel file provided by Microsoft called Sales and Marketing Sample.

You can download the file here: *http://go.microsoft.com/fwlink/?LinkId=529785*.

To prepare a data model in Power BI service, follow these steps:

1. Log in to Power BI service.

2. Click the **Get Data** option in the Power BI service portal. (See screen 1 in Figure 2-16.)

3. In the Import or Connect to Data section, under Files, click the **Get** button. (See screen 2 in Figure 2-16.)

4. Select **Local File**. (See screen 3 in Figure 2-16.)

5. Click the **Import** button in the Import Excel Data into Power BI section. (See screen 4 in Figure 2-16.) A progress bar shows the status of the import operation. A notification will appear to indicate when the operation is complete.

FIGURE 2-16 *Preparing a data model in Power BI service.*

Prepare a data model in Power BI Desktop

To prepare a data model in Power BI Desktop, follow these steps:

1. Click the **File** menu, select **Import**, and choose **Excel Workbook Contents**. (See screen 1 of Figure 2-17.)

2. Locate and select the **Sales and Marketing Excel** file to import it into Power BI Desktop.

3. An Import Excel Workbook Contents dialog box opens. Click the **Start** button. (See screen 2 of Figure 2-17.) A progress bar shows the status of the import operation.

4. When the operation is complete, a dialog box opens with a **Migration Completed** message. (See screen 3 in Figure 2-17.) Click the **Close** button. Power BI lists the data model—in this case, the contents of the Excel work-book—in a special Data view. (See screen 4 in Figure 2-17.)

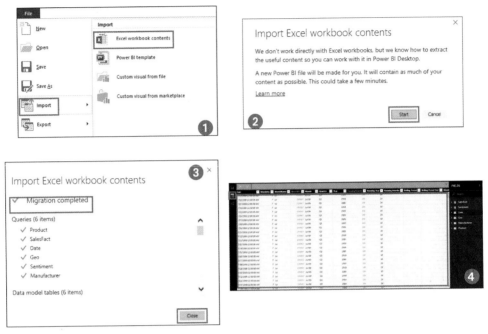

FIGURE 2-17 *Creating a data model in Power BI Desktop.*

Perform basic data-modeling operations

There are lots of types of data-modelling operations. Some of the most commonly used operations are renaming columns and changing the data type, covered here.

Rename a column

You can rename a column in the Power BI Data view in several different ways. (You can access Data view after data has been loaded into the model.)

- Double-click the column name and type a new name
- Right-click the column name, choose **Rename**, and type a new name. (See image 1 in Figure 2-18.)

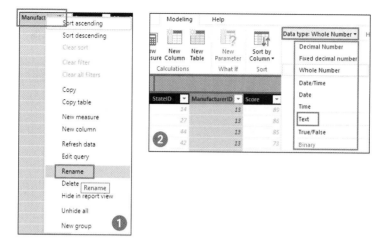

FIGURE 2-18 *Renaming a column and changing the data type in Power BI.*

Change the data type

There are several data types, available from both Data view and Report view:

- Decimal number
- Fixed decimal number
- Whole number
- Date/Time
- Date
- Time
- Text
- True/False
- Binary

These data types are discussed in more detail in upcoming chapters.

To change the data type of a column, follow these steps:

1. In the Power BI Data view, select the column whose data type you want to change—in this case, the **ManufacturerID** column.

2. Click the **Data Type** tab and choose the desired data type from the menu that appears—for example, **Text**. (See image 2 in Figure 2-18.)

Report development in Power BI

The report-development process depends on which version of Power BI you use: Power BI service or Power BI Desktop.

Prepare reports in Power BI service

Before you can prepare a report in Power BI service, it helps to know how to navigate Power BI service. As shown in Figure 2-19, the Power BI service screen contains two navigation tools: the navigation pane (marked with the numeral 1 on the left side of the screen) and the navigation bar (marked with the numeral 2 along the top).

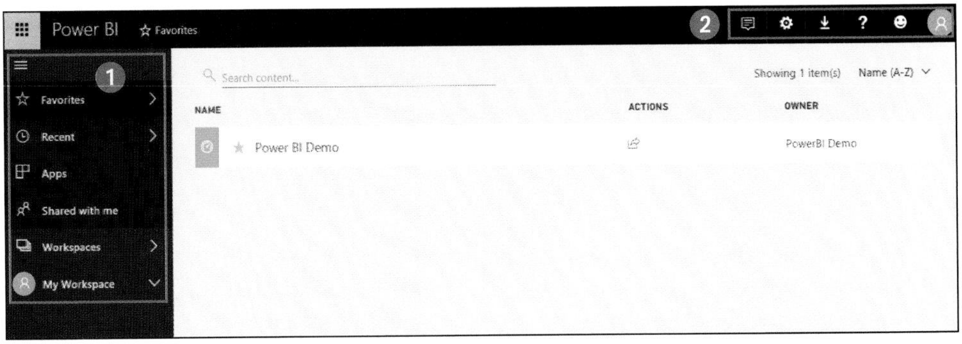

FIGURE 2-19 *Navigational tools in Power BI service.*

The navigation pane contains various options for users to access various reports. These options are as follows:

- **Favorites** Click this option to access reports you've marked as favorites. (You'll learn how to mark a report as a favorite later.)

- **Recent** Click this option to access reports you've opened most recently, in reverse-chronological order.

- **Apps** Click this option to access the entire collection of reports and dashboards.

- **Shared with Me** To access reports that other users have shared with you, click this option.

- **Workspaces** To access workspaces to which you have access, such as a group workspace or a workspace someone else has shared with you, click this option. (You'll learn more about Power BI service workspaces later in this chapter.)

- **My Workspace** Click this to access your own Power BI workspace, from which you can view your dashboards and create and publish your own reports. (Note that the precise name of this option differs depending on what workspaces you have available to you.)

As for the navigation bar, in the top-right corner of the screen, it contains the following icons (from left to right):

- **Notification** Click this icon to view notifications—for example, when one of your reports is updated, when someone shares a report with you, and so on. (If you use the Pro version, you will also receive regular notifications about the number of days remaining on your subscription.)

- **Settings** Click this icon to view statistics on personal storage used, to manage gateways for connecting on-premises reports to Power BI dashboards, create and view content packs, and more.

- **Download** Click this icon to download and save reports available across the Power BI platform.

- **Help and Support** Click this icon to access various help and support resources online, including a help library and user community. (Note that there is a separate help and support section for Power BI developers.)

- **Community Feedback** Click this icon to submit ideas to improve the overall Power BI experience or to report issues.

Power BI Desktop

As shown in Figure 2-20, Power BI Desktop has a more feature-rich main screen than the Online version.

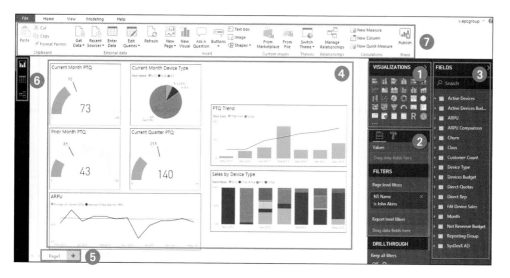

FIGURE 2-20 *Navigating Power BI Desktop.*

This screen contains the following tabs and features:

- **Visualizations pane** This pane allows easy access to several visualizations, including bar charts, line charts, pie charts, statistical graphs, and more to represent your data in reports. (See numeral 1 in Figure 2-20.)

- **Formatting pane** This pane enables you to apply filters to your data to alter the selected visualization, including report-level filters, page-level filters, and drill-through filters. This pane also offers access to tools to change the appearance of reports such as colors, borders, size, and more. (See numeral 2 in Figure 2-20.)

- **Fields pane** This pane includes the active datasets available for generating reports. To add a dataset to your report, simply select its checkbox in the Fields pane. (See numeral 3 in Figure 2-20.)

- **Report pane** This pane displays visualizations selected by the user from various reports. (See numeral 4 in Figure 2-20.)

- **Pages** Some Power BI reports contain multiple pages. To add a page, you click the plus button at the bottom of the screen. You can also use these controls to display a different page. (See numeral 5 in Figure 2-20.)

- **Display tabs** You can click the Report, Data, and Relationship tabs, marked by numeral 6 in Figure 2-20 and shown again in Figure 2-21, to switch among these three views on the main Power BI Desktop screen. Figure 2-20 shows the Report view. The area marked by the numeral 1 in Figure 2-21 shows a snippet of the Data view. (For a better look at this view, refer to image 4 in Figure 2-17.) Finally, the area marked by the numeral 2 in Figure 2-21 shows the Relationship view.

- **Menu bar** The menu bar allows access to menus for editing templates, opening new files, changing page settings, managing report modeling, accessing help, and more. (See numeral 7 in Figure 2-20.)

Report tab
Data tab
Relationship tab

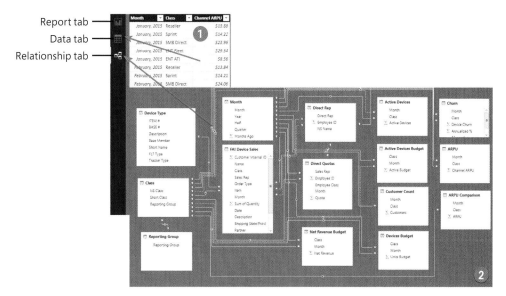

FIGURE 2-21 *Use the Display tabs to switch between Report, Data, and Relationship views.*

Relationship view

The Relationship view shows how different pieces of data relate to each other. Power BI automatically detects the relationships between datasets and displays them on reports and visualizations. Alternatively, users can establish relationships manually.

Power BI service workspace overview

As shown in Figure 2-22, the Power BI service workspace includes four key screens for analyzing data and creating reports. You access these screens by clicking the corresponding links in the top-left corner of the workspace.

- Dashboards
- Reports
- Workbooks
- Datasets

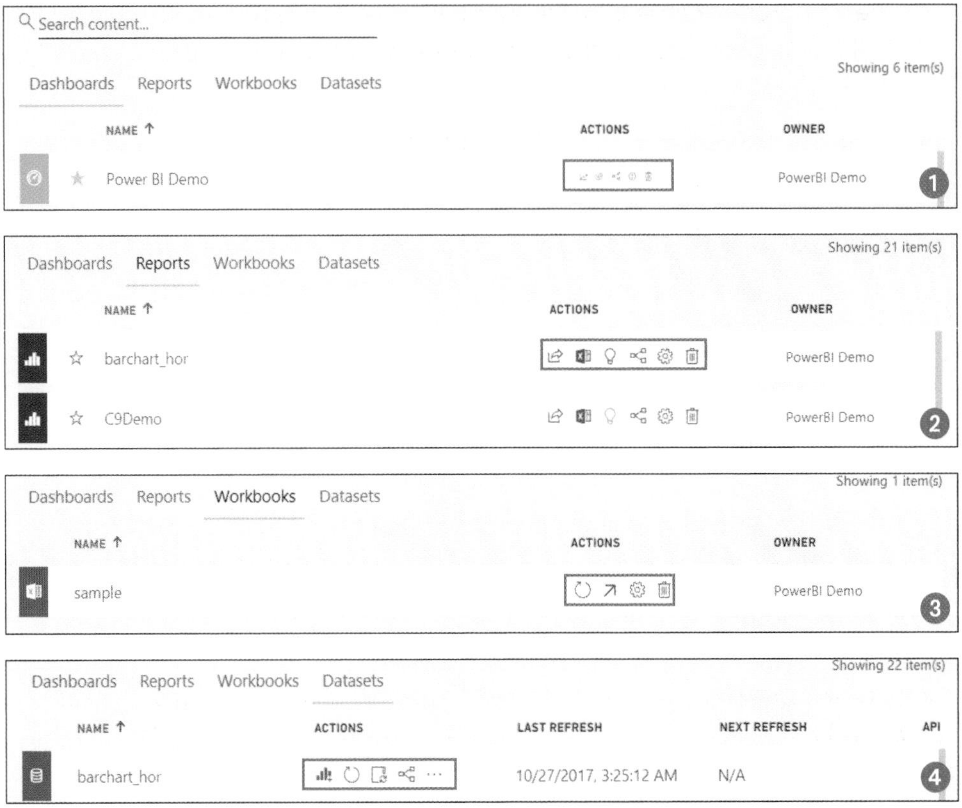

FIGURE 2-22 *Components of the Power BI service workspace.*

Dashboards

The Dashboard screen shows visualizations of data, such as charts and graphs. Users can customize the dashboard by pinning the visualizations they need most often. There are also buttons that allow the user to perform different actions related to the selected dashboard. (See screen 1 in Figure 2-22.)

- **Usage Metrics** Click this button to view usage metrics—including how many people have viewed the dashboard today and the number of unique users for days prior—to gauge user engagement.

- **Share** Click this button to share the dashboard with others.

- **View Related** When you click this button, Power BI checks for related content in the dataset servers. (Note that you can also schedule Power BI to fetch this data automatically.)

- **Settings** Click this to manage Q&A settings and the dashboard tile flow. You can also use this option to change the name of the dashboard.

- **Delete** Click this button to permanently delete the dashboard.

Reports

The Reports screen contains a list of reports created by the user. As with the Dashboard screen, this screen features buttons that allow the user to perform different actions related to the selected report. (See screen 2 in Figure 2-22.) These include Usage Metrics, View Related, Settings, and Delete buttons. The Reports screen also includes the following:

- **Analysis in Excel** Click this button (second from the left) to download the report into Excel. (Note that to use this feature, a one-time update is required for Excel libraries.)

- **Quick Insights** Click this button (third from the left) to view a list of all visualizations available in a report to quickly glean key insights. You can then pin any critical visualizations to the dashboard.

Workbooks

You can upload Excel files into Power BI. When you do they appear in the Workbooks screen. As with the other screens, the Workbooks screen contains buttons you can use to perform different actions on the selected workbook. (See screen 3 in Figure 2-22.)

- **Refresh** Click this button to refresh the data in the selected Excel file.

- **Replace** To replace the selected Excel file with a different one, click this button.

- **Settings** Click this button to access settings that enable you to change the name of the Excel file and see where it is stored on the local server.

- **Delete** Click this button to delete the Excel file.

Datasets

This screen lists the datasets for all reports created by the user. As with the other screens, the Datasets screen contains buttons you can use to perform different actions on the selected dataset. (See screen 4 in Figure 2-22.)

- **Create Report** Click this button to create a new report using the selected dataset.

- **Refresh** Click this button to refresh the dataset.

- **Schedule Refresh** Click this button to schedule a refresh for the dataset.

- **View Related** Click this button to find related datasets.

Edit options in Power BI service

The menu bar in Power BI service (see Figure 2-23) allows access to menus and buttons with several key options. These include the following:

- **File** This menu includes the following commands. (These are quite self-explanatory.)

  - Save As

  - Print

  - Publish to Web

  - Embed in SharePoint Online

  - Export to PowerPoint

  - Download Report

- **View** You can use this menu to access the following view options for Power BI reports:

  - Fit to page

  - Fit to width

  - Actual size

- **Edit Report** Access editing tools to edit your report here.

- **Explore** This provides options for navigating through datasets.

- **Refresh** Click this button to refresh the selected report.

- **Pin Live Page** Click this option to pin the current page in the selected report to your dashboard.

- **View Related** Click this option to view the Related Content pane, which shows you how your Power BI service content—that is, your dashboards, reports, and datasets—are interconnected.

- **Subscribe** Click this button to receive email notifications about changes to the current Power BI report page. (Emails are limited to one per day—assuming the report has been updated.)

- **Generate QR Code** Click this button to create a report-specific QR code that can be accessed from a mobile device.

- **Analyze in Excel** Click this button to open the report in tabular form in Microsoft Excel.

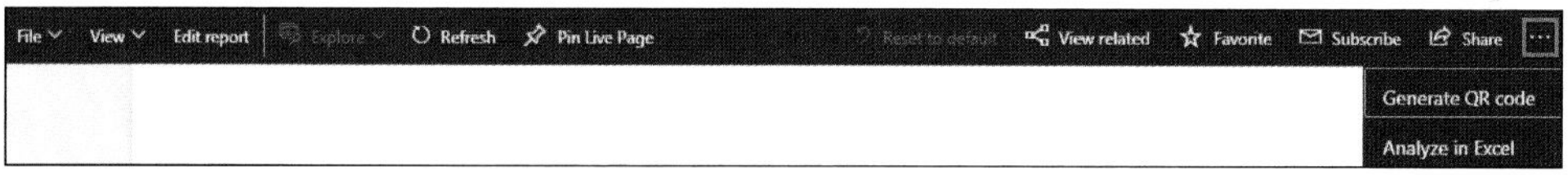

FIGURE 2-23 *The Power BI service menu bar.*

Skills review

In this chapter, you learned about:

- Power BI architecture

- Data processing in Power BI

- How Power BI consumes the OLAP cube for report generation

- The Power BI Admin Portal

- A general overview of data models and report development

Practice tasks

This section provides simple case studies for you to study and solve using information from this chapter. This section also contains a series of practice questions for you to answer.

Case study 1

Consider a large organization that sells shoes on a global scale. They market thousands of shoe styles in specific regions around the world. Regional business units provide the corporate office with real-time reports of daily sales as well as regional marketing reports on a daily basis.

The data used to generate these reports is stored in Azure SQL databases as well as several on-premises non-SQL data sources. This makes it difficult to summarize this information, to collaborate with it, and to obtain specific types of reports used by corporate teams. Employees are left unable to answer analytical questions such as the following:

- How many regions are involved in the business?

- How can we as an organization quickly adapt to the changing needs of our customers?

- How can targeted sales and discounts help specific regions achieve their goals?

- What are the purchasing rates per individual according to region?

- How do targeted marketing campaigns affect sales in specific regions?

Power BI provides the organization with a way to answer these questions by capturing data and conveying it in a more refined way. Users can prepare a single dataset from sourced information and analyze it to glean powerful insights.

Case study 2

Suppose you have already created a Power BI report online, which is available for consumption among multiple users. To gain a better understanding of the various dynamics of report editing, complete the following tasks:

- Generate a SharePoint embedded URL.

- Export a specific report page from Power BI service.

- Generate an embedded URL in Power BI.

- Obtain a QR code for a report for sharing with other users.

Practice questions

1. Outline the ETL process as it relates to Power BI.

2. What phases are involved in Power BI report development?

3. How do you open the Power BI Admin Portal?

4. What process is involved in creating an OLAP cube from raw data?

5. How do you disable the sharing feature in any Power BI report?

6. Name the main features of Power BI Admin Portal.

7. What are embed codes?

8. How do you add a custom visualization to Power BI?

9. What are the key tenant settings available in the Power BI Admin Portal?

Visuals in Power BI

3

This chapter provides an overview of Power BI visuals, or visualizations, available for users to represent their data and for related analysis.

This chapter discusses out-of-the-box (OOTB) visuals from Power BI, and in what scenarios each type of visual works best. It also covers third-party visuals that can be used in Power BI—including how to download and import them into the application.

This chapter also talks about how to drill through data in Power BI and about filters available in Power BI. Filters enable you to choose precisely what data should be depicted by Power BI visuals.

In this chapter:

- Overview of visuals in Power BI
- Power BI out-of-the-box (OOTB) visuals
- Third-party visuals in Power BI
- Drill through visuals in Power BI
- Apply filters in Power BI reports

Overview of visuals in Power BI

Visuals are an integral part of Power BI. Understanding them is crucial to properly implementing them in reports. This section covers the features and benefits of various Power BI visuals.

What are visuals?

A visual, or visualization, is a graphical representation of data in the form of a chart, graph, or map, which allows end users to analyze it in its simplest form. Visualizations enable decision-makers to analyze aspects of the data that are important for organizational growth. With Power BI, visually representing data is easy and straightforward, making it much easier to grasp the available information.

Benefits of using Power BI visuals

Benefits of using Power BI visuals include the following:

- Power BI offers many visuals out of the box, which makes report development very easy. You just need to drag the visual to the report and add the necessary fields.

- You can add filters at the visual level, page level, or report level, to make the report more relevant for users. (For more on filters, see the upcoming section, "Apply filters in Power BI reports.")

- You can use the R-Script Editor in Power BI to create custom visualizations. (Note that to use this feature, you must install R on your local machine.)

- You can share visualizations in reports or on dashboards with others in your organization (assuming you have a Power BI Pro license).

Power BI visuals out of the box

As of this writing, Power BI Desktop offers OOTB visuals, with updated and new visuals released by Microsoft on a regular basis. These OOTB visuals include the following:

- Bar charts
- Column charts
- Line charts
- Area charts
- Line and stacked column charts

- Ribbon charts
- Waterfall charts
- Scatter charts
- Bubble charts
- Pie charts

- Donut charts
- Funnel charts
- Gauge charts
- Cards
- Multi-row card

- KPI visuals
- Tables
- Matrix visuals
- Maps
- ArcGIS maps

3

You'll find these visuals in the Visualizations pane in Power BI. The following sections briefly explore each of these types of visuals.

> ⚠ **IMPORTANT** You'll learn how to add visuals to a report in later chapters.

Bar, column, and ribbon charts

When you have categorical data, then a bar or column chart is an excellent way to display it. Bar charts depict data horizontally, while column charts depict it vertically. Bar and column charts are widely used in organizations. Indeed, you'll generally find that bar and column charts cover 70% of most simple dashboards.

Suppose you are working with a large database of information from a single hospital. The database contains lots of heterogeneous data with details about the hospital's patients, including their age. If, for example, you wanted to build a visual showing the age breakdown of the hospital's patients, a bar or column chart might be a good pick.

Power BI offers the following types of bar and column charts out of the box (see Figure 3-1):

- **Stacked bar charts** This type of chart is useful if you need to know both the values of various subcategories of data as well as the total value. For example, the stacked bar chart in chart 1 in Figure 3-1 shows length of patient stay by program, differentiated by age category, all in a single bar.

- **Clustered bar charts** This type of chart shows a comparison of all categories and subcategories as a part of a whole. For example, the clustered bar chart in chart 2 in Figure 3-1 shows the same data as the chart in screen 1, but with the age group information presented as separate bars (rather than combined into a single bar).

- **100% stacked bar charts** Like a regular stacked bar chart, a 100% stacked bar chart combines various subcategories of data into a single bar. However, it is presented as a percentage. (See chart 3 in Figure 3-1 for an example.)

- **Stacked, clustered, and 100% stacked column charts** These are just like their bar chart counterparts, but turned on their side, so the bars are vertical rather than horizontal. (See charts 4–6 in Figure 3-1.)

- **Ribbon charts** These are similar to stacked column charts but present each category according to rank or value. (See chart 7 in Figure 3-1.)

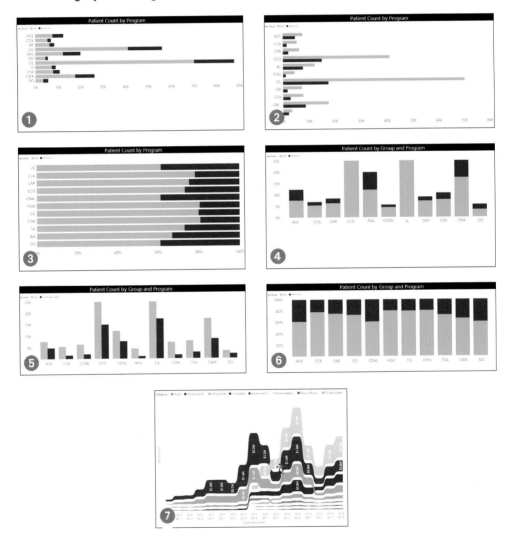

FIGURE 3-1 *Bar, column, and ribbon charts in Power BI.*

Line, area, and combination charts

Line, area, and combination charts are useful for representing data that changes over time, while ribbon charts are simply a variation on column charts. For more on these types of charts, see Figure 3-2, and read on.

- **Line charts** As mentioned, these are useful for time-based data—for example, if you need to analyze sales data for a manufacturing firm, including their unit budget, quota, and quantities, over specific period. (See chart 1 in Figure 3-2.)

- **Area charts** An area chart is a type of line chart. Unlike line charts, however, which simply depict continuous change over a period of time, area charts also reflect volume. (See chart 2 in Figure 3-2.)

- **Stacked area charts** These are similar to area charts but show the data in a stacked format, enabling you to visualize how each category contributes to the total. (See chart 3 in Figure 3-2.)

- **Line and stacked column charts** This type of chart is a combination of a line chart and a stacked column chart. You might use a line and stacked column chart if, for example, you had school data, and you wanted to show how many days students in each grade were present and absent over a specific period. (See chart 4 in Figure 3-2.)

- **Line and clustered column charts** This type of chart is a combination of a line chart and a clustered column chart. You might use a line and clustered column chart in the same scenario as you would a line and stacked column chart, but you want to more clearly see how many days students were marked present versus absent. (See chart 5 in Figure 3-2).

3

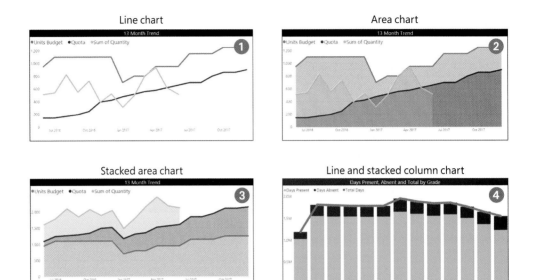

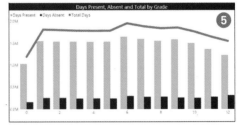

FIGURE 3-2 *Line, area, and combination charts in Power BI.*

Waterfall, treemap, scatter, bubble, pie, donut, funnel, and gauge charts

Power BI offers several more specialized charts for use in reports and dashboards:

- **Waterfall charts** This type of chart shows changes in a value over time. It's useful when you need to maintain a running total. (See chart 1 in Figure 3-3.)

- **Treemaps** A treemap represents data as rectangles in hierarchical form. Treemaps generally show proportions in distinct colors and sizes to enable users to more easily understand large volumes of data. This type of chart is great when data involves multiple subcategories that are difficult to analyze in bar charts. For example, chart 2 in Figure 3-3 shows hospital data that reveals patient count by program and facility. Programs are depicted as color-coded rectangles, with the size of each rectangle reflecting the number of patients in that program.

- **Scatter charts** This type of chart features a horizontal and a vertical axis to represent numerical values, enabling you to show at least two sets of numbers as a series of XY coordinates. An example of a scenario in which a scatter chart would be useful is if you want to show yearly sales data by variance of total sales and by sales value per square foot. (See chart 3 in Figure 3-3.)

- **Bubble charts** This type of chart depicts data in the form of bubbles, with the size of the bubble reflecting the data value. Bubble charts are often used in the same types of scenarios as scatter charts. (See chart 4 in Figure 3-3.)

- **Pie charts** A pie chart is a circular statistical representation of data that is divided into slices to illustrate proportion or percentage. For example, chart 5 in Figure 3-3 shows the spread of patient count by program.

- **Donut charts** These are similar to pie charts, but with circular section cut out in the middle. (See chart 6 in Figure 3-3.)

- **Funnel charts** This type of chart shows linear data with sequential connected stages, with each funnel stage representing a percentage of the whole. It is often used to analyze sales-conversion data across an organization. For example, chart 7 in Figure 3-3 shows a sales-trend analysis for a period of nine months.

- **Gauge charts** A gauge chart depicts data in an arc to show progress toward a goal. The left side of the arc shows the minimum value, while the right side shows the maximum value. (See chart 8 in Figure 3-3.)

3

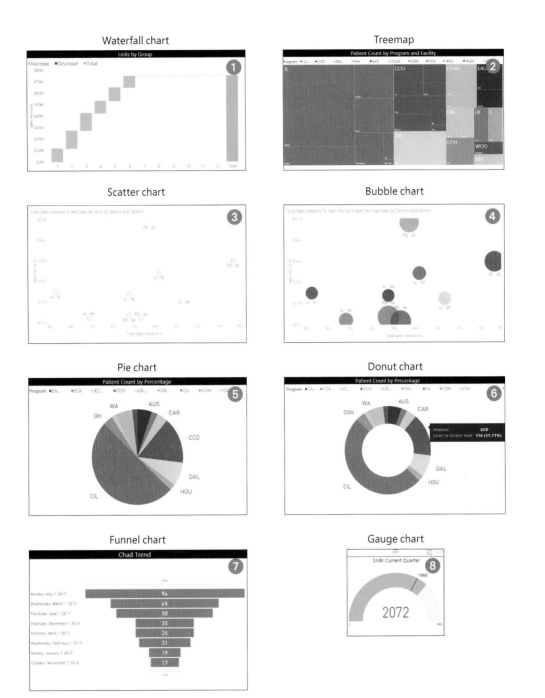

FIGURE 3-3 *More specialized charts available in Power BI.*

Cards, multi-row cards, and KPI visuals

In addition to the charts and graphs already discussed, Power BI offers additional types of visuals, including the following:

- **Cards** These are used to represent a single value of data analyzed according to specific parameters assigned. For example, the card shown in chart 1 in Figure 3-4 features the average length of stay by patients in a hospital.

- **Multi-row cards** These show multiple rows of data in a single card sheet to help users to arrive at a specific conclusion. For example, the multi-row card in chart 2 in Figure 3-4 shows the number of students by class period.

- **KPI visuals** A key performance indicator (KPI) visual tracks the status of progress toward a defined target. It shows whether you are behind (red), on track (yellow), or ahead of the game (green). (You can change this color scheme if you wish.) For example, chart 3 in Figure 3-4 shows attendance information for a school. Because the KPI of 1.52K has not been met, the data appears red.

FIGURE 3-4 *Cards, multi-row cards, and KPI visuals.*

Table and matrix visuals

Tables and matrixes are additional examples of visuals in Power BI. (See Figure 3-5.)

- **Tables** This type of visual is best suited for numbers in tabular format representing certain grades of data grouped together. Tables, which allow for conditional formatting, facilitate easy and efficient group analysis. For example, the table in Figure 3-5 (screen 1) shows attendance data grouped by date.

- **Matrices** Matrix visuals allow for tabular representation of data with drill-down capabilities, enabling you to include additional rows or columns or a particular section. For example, the matrix in Figure 3-5 (screen 2) presents location data such that when users click a division, they are directed to another visual with locations. Drilling down further reveals yet more data.

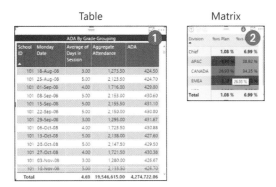

FIGURE 3-5 *Table and matrix visuals.*

Bubble, filled, and ArcGIS maps

Power BI supports the use of the following map visuals:

- **Bubble maps** This visual overlays data in the form of a bubble on a geographical map generated by Bing using location information you provide. The size of the bubble over a specific geographic region reflects the data value. For example, the left map (see screen 1 in Figure 3-6) contains bubbles that represent the number of political parties in Canada and in the United States, with the bubble in Canada appearing smaller than the bubble in the US. To drill down to see the breakdown of parties within the United States, as shown in the map on the right, click the US bubble in the left map. (You will learn more about drilling down for additional information later in this chapter.)

- **Filled maps** This shows data within geospatial areas on a map (again, generated by Bing using location information you provide) rather than as an individual point, with lighter shades indicating lower values and darker shades indicating higher values. (See screen 2 in Figure 3-6.) Filled maps provide an overview of data distribution across a location, such as a country, state, or city, and are a great way to show relationships among data and to check for spatial patterns.

- **ArcGIS maps** Although these maps are provided by a third-party vendor, ESRI, they are offered in Power BI out of the box. They enable you to define specific locations and provide users with rich infographic content. Users can zoom in, zoom out, and select individual or multiple locations. When you add data to the map, it is automatically configured as needed. These maps are extremely beneficial for users who need to visualize data geographically. (See screen 3 in Figure 3-6.)

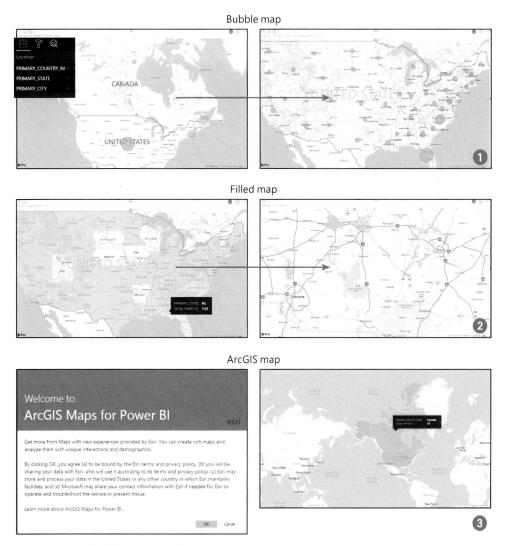

FIGURE 3-6 *Bubble, filled, and ArcGIS maps.*

Third-party visuals in Power BI

Power BI includes several useful visuals. But if none of these visuals meet your needs, you can download and import several third-party visuals into Power BI. There are two ways to obtain these visuals:

- By downloading a third-party visual file from the Microsoft AppSource and importing it into Power BI

- By accessing the Microsoft AppSource directly from Power BI via the Import option

Download and import a third-party visual file into Power BI

To download a third-party visual from the Microsoft AppSource and import it into Power BI, follow these steps:

1. Type *https://appsource.microsoft.com/en-us/marketplace/apps?page= 1&product=power-bi-visuals* in your web browser's address bar.

2. The Microsoft AppSource opens. Under the third-party visual you want to download, click **Get It Now**. (See screen 1 in Figure 3-7.)

3. When prompted, enter your work email address and your Power BI password, and click **Continue** to accept the terms and conditions.

   Power BI Desktop will download a PBVIZ file.

4. In Power BI Desktop, click the **...** link in the Visualizations pane and choose **Import from File**. (See screen 2 in Figure 3-7.)

5. A Caution: Import Custom Visual dialog box opens. (See screen 3 in Figure 3-7.) Click the **Import** button.

6. Locate and select the file you just downloaded and click **Import**.

   After the import operation, you'll see the following message: **The visual was successfully imported into this report**. You can then select the visual from the Visualizations pane.

FIGURE 3-7 *Importing a third-party visual.*

Access the Microsoft AppSource directly to import a third-party visual

To access the Microsoft AppSource from within Power BI to directly import a third-party visual, follow these steps:

1. In Power BI Desktop, click the ... link in the Visualizations pane and choose **Import from Marketplace**. (Refer to screen 2 in Figure 3-7.)

2. The Microsoft AppSource opens and displays a list of third-party visuals. Select a visual and click the **Add** button.

   After the import operation, you'll see the following message: **The visual was successfully imported into this report**. You can then select the visual from the Visualizations pane.

Other ways to import third-party visuals into Power BI

In addition to using the ... menu in the Visualizations pane to access options to import a third-party visual from a file or from the Microsoft AppSource (refer to screen 2 in Figure 3-7), you can also use the File menu (see screen 1 in Figure 3-8) or options in the Home tab (see screen 2 in Figure 3-8).

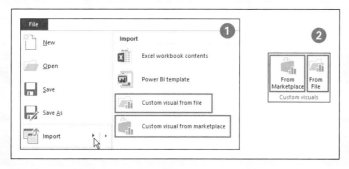

FIGURE 3-8 *Other ways to import third-party visuals into Power BI.*

Drill through Power BI visuals

Power BI visuals allow for the creation of attractive, eye-catching reports. This makes it much easier for users to study the data and helps reduce possible errors.

When considering data in Power BI visuals, it helps to think of it as existing in a hierarchy of sorts. This section discusses what tools you can use to drill through that hierarchy when working with Power BI visuals to gain added insights. (See Figure 3-1.)

- **Drill Down** Each data point in a visualization may contain subsets of information that could provide yet more insight. For example, suppose you have a visual that shows the number of patients enrolled in various hospital programs. If you click the Drill Down option (see numeral 1 in Figure 3-9), you can gain additional information about these patients—for example, their age, their gender, and so on.

More options

A More Options menu (marked by an ellipsis) appears. (See the arrow pointing to screen 6 in Figure 3-9.) It offers you access to additional tools for working with visuals in Power BI. The options are as follows:

- **Export Data** Choose this to convert data in the selected visual into an Excel file in .CSV format.

- **See Data** Select this to see a tabular representation of data in the selected visual.

- **Remove** Choose this to delete the selected visual from the report page.

- **Spotlight** Select this to highlight a specific visual in a Power BI report.

- **Sort** Choose this to sort the data in the selected visual in ascending or descending order.

■ **Expand to Next Level** To drill down all fields at once by one level, click the **Expand to Next Level** button (see numeral 2 in Figure 3-9). This shows all available fields in the next hierarchy. For example, suppose you have a visual that contains country, state and province, and postal code data. Suppose further that the visual contains data about two countries: the US and Canada. If you click **Expand to Next Level**, the visual will change to show all states and provinces in the US and Canada. If you click it again, the visual will change again to show all the postal codes in each state and province.

3

■ **Drill Up** After you click Drill Down or Expand to Next Level, you can click Drill Up (see numeral 3 in Figure 3-9) to go back up one level.

■ **Expand Down** Click this option (see number 4 in Figure 3-9) to expand all levels at once.

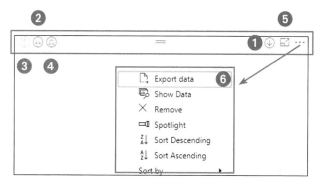

FIGURE 3-9 *Features represented in Power BI visuals.*

> ✅ **TIP** To view a visual in full-screen mode for better visibility and easier navigation, click the Focus Mode button, shown in screen 5 in Figure 3-9.

Apply filters in Power BI reports

Power BI enables you to apply filters to reports to adjust what data they contain depending on your needs. The following types of filters are available:

■ **Visual-level filter** Suppose you have a bar chart, a pie chart, and a table in your report, and you want to filter the data only in the bar chart. In that case, you'd apply a visual-level filter to that chart.

- **Page-level filter** Maybe your report has 10 pages, but you want to apply a filter to just one of those pages. In that case you could apply a page-level filter.

- **Report-level filter** To apply a filter to your entire report, you use a report-level filter.

- **Drill-through filter** This filter enables you to drill through the data in a report much as you would data in a visual. For example, suppose your report contains a table. You could apply the drill-through filter to that table to analyze a piece of data in that table in depth. (See screen 1 in Figure 3-10.) To return to the table, you simply click the Back button (highlighted in screen 2 of Figure 3-10).

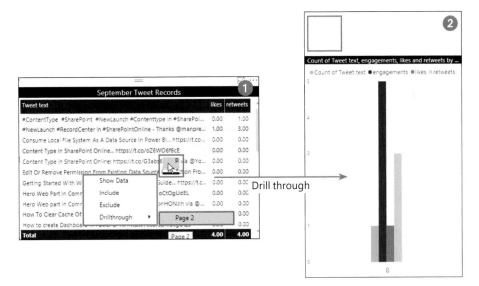

FIGURE 3-10 *Using the drill-through filter on a table in Power BI.*

Slicers

A slicer is a type of visual that enables you to filter data based on different fields or properties. When you select a value in the slicer, the entire report containing the slicer is filtered based on that value. For example, consider a year-by-year analysis of school attendance. You could create a slicer visual that enables you to filter data to show only a specific year. (See image 1 in Figure 3-11.) You could configure the slicer to show the data in list mode (see image 2 in Figure 3-11) or drop-down mode (see image 3 and image 4 in Figure 3-11.) You could also adjust the orientation of the slicer to horizontal mode. (See screens 5 and 6 in Figure 3-11.)

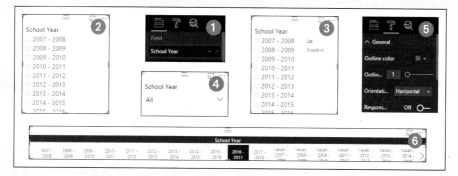

FIGURE 3-11 *Using a slicer to filter data.*

Skills review

In this chapter, you learned about:

- An overview of visuals in Power BI

- Power BI visuals available out of the box

- Obtaining Power BI visuals from third parties

- Drilling through data in Power BI

- Using filters in Power BI

Practice tasks

This section provides a simple case study for you to study and solve using information from this chapter. This section also contains a series of practice questions for you to answer.

Case study

Suppose you work for a company that manufactures hair products and has broad expertise in various channels of the cosmetic industry. You have been given data collected across different dimensions of the business over the preceding five years.

Consider the following scenarios and determine what type of visual would work best in each case.

- **Scenario 1** You want to analyze sales data for various products by region.

  Solution Use a map visual.

- **Scenario 2** You want to view overall sales data for all categories for each month over the past 13 months to identify trends.

  Solution Use a line chart.

- **Scenario 3** You want to compare sales volume data for all products in a region against a sales trend analysis data for that region

  Solution Use an area chart.

- **Scenario 4** You want to compare sales trends for various shampoo brands.

  Solution Use a bar or column chart.

- **Scenario 5** You want to compare sequential data with its running total to assess profitability over time.

  Solution Use a waterfall chart.

Practice questions

1. What are visuals?

2. What type of visual is best for comparing categorical data?

3. What type of visual is best for comparing sequential data?

4. What type of visual might you use to depict volume-based data?

5. What type of visual is best for representing time-based data?

6. Why would you use a pie or donut chart?

7. What type of visual is best-suited for depicting geographical data?

8. Which type of map is provided by ESRI?

9. What type of chart best depicts progress toward a goal?

10. What does KPI stand for?

11. What are the uses and benefits of cards and multi-row cards?

12. Under what circumstance might you use a matrix?

13. Why might you use a treemap?

14. What type of visualization helps filter data?

15. How do you import a third-party visual from within Power BI?

16. What is visual-level filter in Power BI?

17. What is a page-level filter in Power BI?

18. What is a drill-through filter in Power BI?

19. True or false: To filter data for an entire report, you use the report-level filter.

20. What is the difference between a page-level filter and a report-level filter?

Power BI report development

This chapter discusses key elements of report development in Power BI in detail, including strategies and methods for generating Power BI reports. First, you will explore the diverse data sources available within Power BI service and Power BI Desktop. Next, you will use Power BI Desktop to generate an IT spend analysis report. This involves preparing a data model, establishing data relationships, selecting visuals, and formatting the report for standard and mobile viewing. Finally, you will publish the report.

In this chapter:

- Data sources supported by Power BI

- Build a Power BI report in Power BI Desktop

- Publish a Power BI report

Practice files

As you work through this chapter, you'll use three practice files, which you can access from the MSPBIDashboards\ch04 folder on the book's companion website at *https://aka.ms/PowerBIDash/downloads*. The files are as follows:

- **IT Spend Analysis Sample.xlsx** This file contains a dummy data source for IT spend analysis to help you get started with Power BI report development. You'll use this file in the section "Data sources supported by Power BI" next in this chapter.

- **IT Spend Analysis Report 01.pbix** This sample Power BI report consists of IT spend analysis data with no formatting applied. You'll use this file in the section "Prepare the report" later in this chapter.

- **IT Spend Analysis Report 02 - Formatted.pbix** This sample Power BI report is similar to the first sample report, but with formatting applied. You'll see this file in the section "Format the report" later in this chapter.

Data sources supported by Power BI

Power BI enables you to connect with all sorts of data sources. This section reveals which data sources are available in Power BI Desktop.

Data sources in Power BI Desktop

Power BI Desktop supports several data sources. To view and select from the available data sources, open the **File** menu in Power BI Desktop and choose **Get Data**. The Get Data page appears. (See Figure 4-1.)

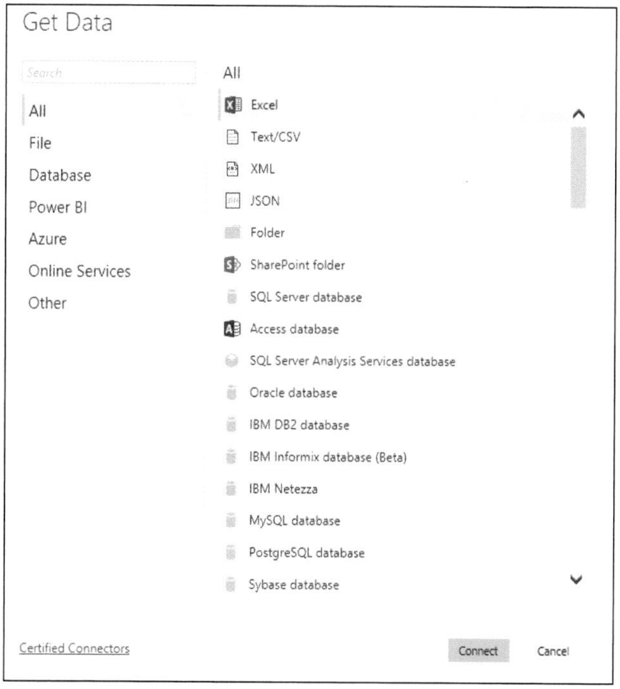

FIGURE 4-1 *The Get Data page lists data sources supported by Power BI Desktop.*

As you can see, Power BI desktop divides these data sources into six categories. Table 4-1 explains which sources fall under which category.

- File
- Database
- Power BI
- Azure
- Online Services
- Other

Table 4-1 *Data sources in Power BI*

Data source categories	Data sources
File	Excel Text/CSV XML file JSON Folders SharePoint folder
Database	SQL Server database Access database SQL Server Analysis Services (SSAS) database Oracle database IBM Db2 database IBM Informix database (beta) IBM Netezza (beta) MySQL database PostgreSQL database Sybase database Teradata database SAP HANA database SAP Business Warehouse Server Amazon Redshift Impala database Google BigQuery (beta) Snowflake database
Azure	Azure SQL Database Azure SQL Data Warehouse Azure Analysis Services database (beta) Azure Blog storage Azure Table storage Azure Cosmos DB (beta) Azure Data Lake Store Azure HDInsight Azure HDInsight Spark (beta) Azure Kusto DB (beta)

Data source categories	Data sources
Online services	Power BI service
	SharePoint Online list
	Microsoft Exchange Online
	Dynamics 365 Online
	Dynamics 365 for Finance and Operations
	Common Data Service
	Microsoft Azure Consumption Insights
	Visual Studio Team Services
	Salesforce objects
	Salesforce reports
	Google Analytics
	Appfigures (beta)
	comScore Digital Analytix (beta)
	Dynamics 365 for Customer Insights (beta)
	Facebook
	GitHub
	MailChimp
	Mixpanel (beta)
	Planview Enterprise (beta)
	Projectplace (beta)
	QuickBooks Online
	Smartsheet
	SparkPost (beta)
	Stripe (beta)
	SweetIQ (beta)
	Troux (beta)
	Twilio (beta)
	tyGraph (beta)
	Webtrends
	Zendesk
Others	Vertica (beta)
	Web
	SharePoint list
	OData Feed
	Active Directory
	Microsoft Exchange
	Hadoop file (HDFS)
	Spark (beta)
	R Script
	ODBC
	OLE DB
	Blank query

4

Data sources in Power BI service

As shown in Figure 4-2, Power BI service organizes its data sources into two main categories. (To access this page, log into Power BI service, and click the Get Data option at the bottom of the page.)

- **Microsoft AppSource** This category contains content packs created and shared by other users within your organization. It also contains online services—in other words, third-party services that offer content packs. (Content packs are pre-made collections of data and reports.)

- **Import or Connect to Data** This category contains files, such as Excel workbooks (XLSX and XLXM) and Power BI Desktop files (PBIX), as well as CSV, XML, and TXT files. It also contains database data stored on the cloud or on-premises. Supported databases include Azure SQL Database, Azure SQL Data Warehouse, Azure HDInsight Spark, SQL Server using DirectQuery, and more.

> ✓ **TIP** Although Power BI service does support a considerable number of data sources, Power BI Desktop supports even more. If you want more data source options, you'll need to switch to Power BI Desktop.

FIGURE 4-2 *Data sources in Power BI service.*

Build a Power BI report in Power BI Desktop

Power BI reports are an excellent way to represent user data. This section describes the procedure for building a Power BI report in Power BI Desktop.

In this section you'll use the IT Spend Analysis Sample file, provided by Microsoft, as the basis for the report. This file contains data that analyzes planned and actual costs in an IT department. This data helps in developing the company's plans for the year and in investigating deviations from that plan. In this example, the company operates on a yearly planning cycle but produces an updated "latest estimate" (LE) on a quarterly basis to help analyze changes in IT spends over the fiscal year.

The basic steps for building a Power BI report are as follows:

1. Select the data source and prepare the data model.

2. Establish relationships.

3. Add visuals.

4. Prepare the report.

5. Optimize the report for mobile view.

After you've done all that, you publish the report. This step is described in the section "Publish the report."

Select the data source and prepare the data model

To prepare the data model, you import the data and load it into Power BI Desktop. In this example, you'll import the IT Spend Analysis Sample Excel file. Follow these steps:

1. Click the **Home** tab in Power BI Desktop.

2. Click **Get Data** and select the **Excel** option.

3. Locate and select the **IT Spend Analysis Sample** file.

4. Power BI Desktop displays the tables in the selected file in the Navigator page. Select the checkmark next to each visual you want to use in the Display Options pane and click the **Load** button.

5. Power BI loads the tables. To view them in list form, you may need to click the **Data View** button. (See Figure 4-3.)

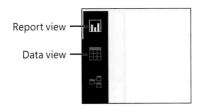

Report view

Data view

FIGURE 4-3 *Click these buttons to switch between Report view and Data view in Power BI Desktop.*

6. In Data view, select the tables you want to include in the data model and click the **Load** button. (See Figure 4-4.)

Navigator

		Scenario		
Display Options ▾		Scenario	Scenario ID	ScenarioDescription
▲ IT Spend Analysis Sample.xlsx [16]		Actual		1 Actual
☐ Table1		LE1		2 Latest Estimate 1
☐ Table2		LE2		3 Latest Estimate 2
☐ Table3		LE3		4 Latest Estimate 3
☐ Table4		Plan		5 Plan
☐ Table5				
☐ Table6				
☐ Table7				
☐ Table8				
☑ Business Area				
☑ Cost Element				
☑ Country Region				
☑ Date				
☑ Department				
☑ Fact				
☑ IT Area				
☑ Scenario				

Load	Edit	Cancel

FIGURE 4-4 *View the tables in Data view.*

Establish relationships

When you load data into Power BI Desktop, it auto-detects relationship between tables. You can also set relationships between tables manually. This section shows you how to enable the auto-detection of relationships, how to create a new relationship manually, and how to edit and delete a relationship. (See Figure 4-5.)

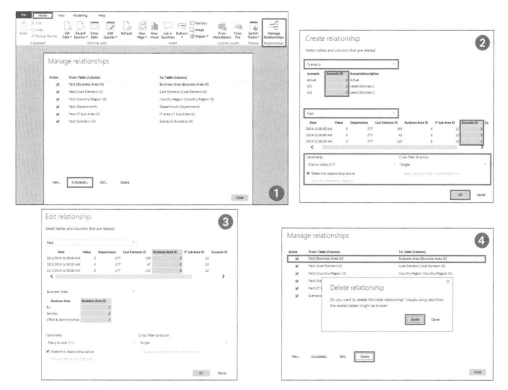

FIGURE 4-5 *Establishing relationships in Power BI Desktop.*

Set up auto-detect

Power BI Desktop automatically detects the relationships between tables when you load them. You can also run an auto-detect operation manually. Here's how:

1. Click the **Home** tab. (See screen 1 of Figure 4-5.)

2. Click **Manage Relationships**. (See screen 1 of Figure 4-5.)

3. In the Manage Relationships page, click the **Autodetect** button. (See screen 1 of Figure 4-5.)

Create a new relationship manually

To create a new relationship manually, follow these steps:

1. In the **Home** tab, click **Manage Relationships**.

2. In the Manage Relationships page, click the **New** button.

   The Create Relationship page opens. (See screen 2 in Figure 4-5.)

3. Open the top drop-down list and select the first table you want to include in the relationship. Then choose the column on which you want to base the relationship.

4. Repeat step 3 for the bottom drop-down list.

5. Click the **OK** button.

Edit a relationship

Maybe once you start building your report you realize you need to edit the relationship between two tables. Here's how:

1. In the **Home** tab, click **Manage Relationships**.

2. In the Manage Relationships page, select the checkbox next to the relationship you want to edit, and click the **Edit** button.

   The Edit Relationship page opens. (See screen 3 in Figure 4-5.) It looks very similar to the Create Relationship page.

3. To set a different table for the relationship, select it from the top or bottom drop-down list. Alternatively, choose a different column on which to base the relationship.

4. Click the **OK** button.

Delete a relationship

To delete a relationship, follow these steps:

1. In the **Home** tab, click **Manage Relationships**.

2. In the Manage Relationships page, select the checkbox next to the relationship you want to delete. (See screen 4 of Figure 4-5.)

3. Click the **Delete** button. (See screen 4 of Figure 4-5.)

4. A Delete Relationship dialog box opens. To confirm the deletion, click the **Delete** button. (See screen 4 of Figure 4-5.)

Relationship view

Power BI Desktop offers a special view for identifying relationships between tables in a report: Relationship view. (See Figure 4-6.) To access this view, simply click the Relationship icon (highlighted in Figure 4-6) on the left side of the report. To edit a relationship, simply double-click the line that connects them in Relationship view, as shown in Figure 4-6.

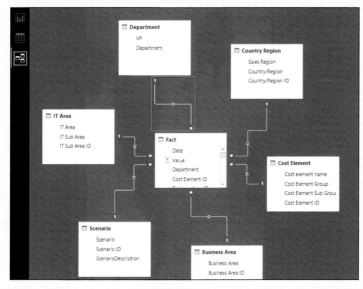

FIGURE 4-6 *Use the Relationship view to quickly identify relationships between tables.*

Add visuals

You've prepared the data model and established relationships. Now you're ready to add visuals. Follow these steps:

1. Open the report to which you want to add visuals in Report view.

2. Click a visual in the Visualizations pane—in this example, the **stacked column chart** visual. (See numeral 1 in Figure 4-7.)

   A blank visual will appear on the report page. This is because no field properties have been set for the visual. At the same time, properties for the selected visual will appear in the Visualizations pane.

3. Select a field you want to include in the visual in the **Fields** pane (in this example, the **IT Area** field) and drag it to one of the visual's properties in the **Visualizations** pane (here, the **Axis** property).

4. Repeat step 3 to add the **IT Sub Area** field to the **Axis** property.

5. Repeat step 3 to add **Actual**, **Value**, **Actual/Plan**, and **Amount** fields to the Value property. (See numerals 2 and 3 in Figure 4-7.)

   See numeral 3 in Figure 4-7 for the resulting stacked column chart.

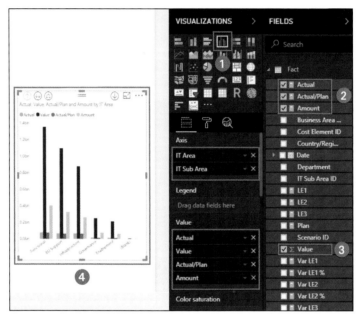

FIGURE 4-7 *Adding a visual to a Power BI report.*

Prepare the report

Let's prepare a Power BI report by adding visuals to convey the sample data in the IT Spend Analysis Sample file as follows. (Refer to the preceding section, "Add visuals," for help adding the visuals noted here.)

1. Add a slicer visual to filter data by the IT Area, IT Sub Area, and Sales Region data. (See screen 1 in Figure 4-8.)

2. Add a gauge chart to represent the percentages of Var Plan, Var LE1, Var LE2, and Var LE3. (See screen 2 in Figure 4-8.)

3. Add a line chart to compare the values of Var LE1% and Var LE2% by cost element group. (See screen 3 in Figure 4-8.)

4. Compare the Actual Sales, Actual/Plan, Amount, and Value information by IT area using a clustered column chart. (See screen 4 in Figure 4-8.)

5. Use a map visual to represent the values of Var Plan% and Var LE3% by country and sales region. (See screen 5 in Figure 4-8.)

6. Add a bar chart to compare the value of Var Plan% by IT area and business area. (See screen 6 in Figure 4-8.)

7. Add a scatter chart to present the Var Plan, Var Plan%, and Actual Sales by business area and period. (See screen 7 in Figure 4-8.)

> ⚠ **IMPORTANT** The scatter chart in Figure 4-8 contains a play option, which shows a progression of the data over time. To add a play option to the chart, select the **Play Axis** property in the **Fields** pane.

> ✓ **TIP** As mentioned, a sample Power BI report IT Spend Analysis Report 01.pbix is provided as a practice file for this chapter. This file contains sample visuals that you can explore to better understand how to prepare a Power BI report.

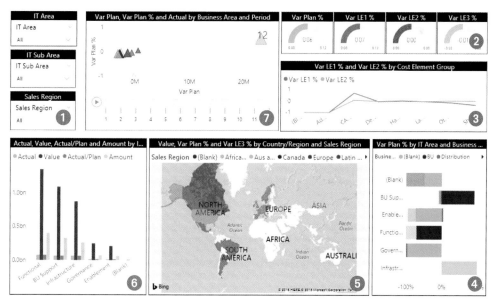

FIGURE 4-8 *Visuals used to prepare a Power BI report.*

Format the report

After you add visuals to a report, you can format them. This section discusses general formatting options for a clustered column chart—in this example, the one created in the preceding section using the data in the IT Spend Analysis Sample file (refer to screen 4 in Figure 4-8). To access these options, follow these steps:

1. Click the visual you want to format in the report to select it.

2. At the bottom of the Visualizations pane, click the **Format** icon (it features a paint roller), as indicated by numeral 1 in Figure 4-9.

3. A list of formatting categories appears. (See numeral 2 of Figure 4-9.) To reveal the options under a particular category, click the down arrow to the left of the category's name.

   Table 4-2 lists the options available under each category.

4. Some categories feature a toggle to enable or disable the settings in that category. To enable or disable a category, click its toggle.

   The clustered column chart marked by numeral 3 in Figure 4-9 shows the effects of applying the changes to the following formatting settings:

   - Legend
   - X-Axis
   - Y-Axis
   - Data Colors
   - Border
   - Title

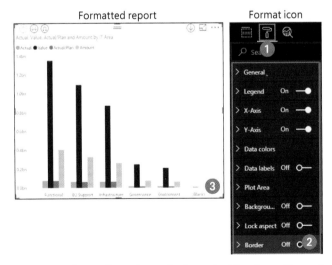

FIGURE 4-9 *Formatting a clustered column chart in a Power BI report.*

Table 4-2 *Format options for visuals in Power BI*

Category	Description	Options
General	The settings in this category enable you to set the size and position of the visual, as well as to enter alt text for the visual. (Alt text briefly describes the visual audibly for people with vision impairments.)	X Position Y Position Width Height Alt Text
Legend	You use the settings in this category to set the position and title of the legend name and to specify the font, font color, and text size.	Position Title Legend Name Color Font Family Text Size
X-Axis	Use these settings to change the format of the X axis.	Color Text Size Font Family Minimum Category Width Maximum Size Inner Padding Concatenate Labels Title
Y-Axis	Use these settings to change the format of the Y axis.	Position Scale Type Start End Color Text Size Font Family Display Units Value Decimal Places Title Gridlines Color Stroke Width Line Style

4

continued

Category	Description	Options
Data Colors	You use the settings in this category to set the color of the bar representing each type of data in the chart. (Note that the options shown here will reflect the data fields contained in the visual.)	Actual Value Actual/Plan Amount
Data Labels	The settings in this category enable you to affix labels to data, and to specify the labels' orientation, position, font, color, text size, and other characteristics.	Color Display Units Value Decimal Places Orientation Position Overflow Text Text Size Font Family Show Background Customize Series
Plot Area	This category contains just one option, which enables you to adjust the transparency of the plot area. (The plot area is the portion of the chart where the data markers are placed.)	Transparency
Title	These settings enable you to display a title for the visual and to specify various characteristics of the text used including its font, color, size, and alignment, as well as a background color.	Title Text Font Color Background Color Alignment Text Size Font Family
Background	The settings in this category enable you to set the background color and transparency. (Background refers to the area behind the chart.)	Background Color Transparency
Lock Aspect	Lock Aspect is a setting rather than a category. You use this setting to lock the visual's aspect ratio when adjusting its size. That way, if you resize the visual, its proportions will remain the same.	
Border	Use the settings in this category to apply a border around the visual and to set its color.	Color

> ⚠️ **IMPORTANT** The formatting properties may vary depending on what type of visual is selected. For example, if you are working with a pie chart, you won't see X-axis options, because pie charts don't have an X-axis.

> ⚠️ **IMPORTANT** Power BI visuals are responsive. They change dynamically to display the maximum amount of data and insight, depending on the screen size. Also, if you change the size of a visual, Power BI prioritizes the Data view for users. In this way it ensures the visual is both informative and beautiful, even as it changes size.

4

Optimize the report for mobile viewing

Power BI Desktop enables you to optimize your report for viewing on a mobile device using the Power BI mobile application, which is available for Android, iOS, and Windows devices.

To optimize the IT Spend Analysis Report 02 - Formatted.pbix sample report for viewing on a mobile device, open the report in Power BI Desktop, and follow these steps:

1. In the Report pane, click the **View** tab (see screen 1 of Figure 4-10) and click the **Phone Layout** button.

   A blank canvas in the shape of a mobile device opens. (See screen 2 in Figure 4-10.)

2. Click a visual in the Visualizations pane (see screen 2 in Figure 4-10) and drag it to the blank canvas.

> ⚠️ **IMPORTANT** The mobile canvas uses a grid layout. As you drag visuals onto the canvas, they will be snapped to the grid. You can also resize visuals based on the grid.

3. Repeat step 3 until all the desired visuals appear on the mobile canvas.

4. Resize and rearrange the visuals as desired.

> ⚠️ **IMPORTANT** You cannot modify the formatting of the visuals—for example, fonts, colors, and so on—for mobile view.

5. To switch back to Desktop view, click the **View** tab and click **Desktop Layout**. (See screen 3 in Figure 4-10.)

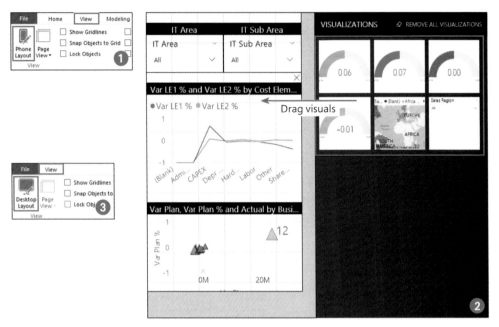

FIGURE 4-10 *Optimizing a Power BI report for mobile view.*

To remove a visual from the mobile canvas, do one of the following:

- While in Phone Layout view, click the **X** button in the top-right corner of the visual in the mobile canvas. (See Figure 4-11.)

- Select the visual in the mobile canvas and press the **Delete** button on the keyboard.

> ⚠ **IMPORTANT** Removing the visual from the mobile canvas only removes it from mobile view. The visual will remain in the original report.

FIGURE 4-11 *Removing a visual from the mobile view.*

Publish your report to Power BI service

As a final step, after you prepare and format your report, you can publish it to Power BI service. When you publish a report to Power BI service, other people can access it from the cloud.

> ⚠️ **IMPORTANT** You can only publish a report to Power BI service if you have a Power BI Pro license. If you don't have this type of license, you are limited to publishing your report in your own workspace (My Workspace).

To publish a report from Power BI Desktop to Power BI service, follow these steps:

1. Open the **File** menu. (See screen 1 of Figure 4-12.)

2. Select **Publish**. (See screen 1 of Figure 4-12.)

3. Choose **Publish to Power BI**. (See screen 1 of Figure 4-12.)

   Alternatively, you can click the **Home** tab (see screen 2 of Figure 4-12) and click the **Publish** button (see screen 2 of Figure 4-12).

4. If prompted, enter your Power BI access credentials.

5. The Publish to Power BI page opens. Select the workspace on which you want to publish the report (in this case, **My Workspace**) and then click the **Select** button. (See screen 3 of Figure 4-12.)

6. A progress dialog box opens. When the operation is complete, you'll see a success message. (See screen 4 of Figure 4-12.)

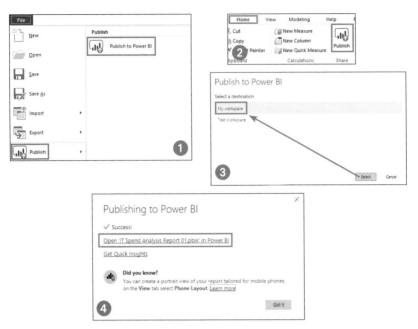

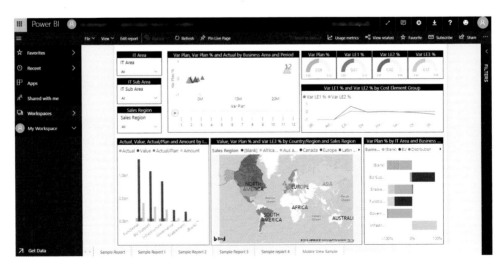

FIGURE 4-12 *Publishing Power BI report.*

After you publish the report, you can log into your Power BI service account to verify that the report appears in the selected workspace. You can also view the report using the Power BI app on your iOS, Android, or Windows mobile device. Figure 4-13 shows the published report in web view, while Figure 4-14 shows it in mobile view. (In mobile view, you may need to scroll down to see the report in full.)

FIGURE 4-13 *The published report in web view.*

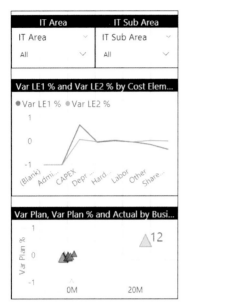 

FIGURE 4-14 *The published report in mobile view.*

⚠️ **IMPORTANT** To view the report on your mobile device, you must first install the Power BI mobile application and log in using your Power BI username and password. After you do, the application will provide you with the option to view the report.

Skills review

In this chapter, you learned about:

- Data sources supported by Power BI

- Preparing the data model for a report

- Establishing relationships between tables

- Adding visuals

- Preparing a report

- Formatting a report

- Optimizing a report for mobile viewing

- Publishing a report

Chapter 4

Practice tasks

This section provides a simple case study for you to study and solve using information from this chapter. This section also contains a series of practice questions for you to answer.

Case study

Suppose you work for a large engineering firm that is well-established worldwide. The firm, which has been in business for 15 years, has units spread across locations that produce sales differentiated by category. The firm—whose expertise relates to manufacturing hardware, servers, VPNs, and software for internal communications—has focused its growth mainly around IT products and launches new products every quarter.

You've been asked to prepare a report for specific users that shows sales data for each quarter on a yearly basis. The report's visuals will convey data fed from various data sources into Power BI. It's important that you develop the report in such a way that it will be easy for your users to understand. The report should also present data in geographical form.

Practice questions

1. How do you import data from an Excel spreadsheet?
2. How do you establish relationships between tables?
3. How do you format the colors used in a bar chart?
4. How do you apply a Play button to a clustered column chart?
5. How do you apply a title to a visual?
6. How do you prepare a report for mobile view?
7. How do you publish a report to Power BI service?
8. How do you view a published Power BI report in the Power BI mobile app?

Use DAX in Power BI

Data Analysis Expressions (DAX) is a collection of functions, operators, and constants for handling basic data calculations to better analyze data and solve business problems. With DAX, you can build or apply functions that use existing data within Power BI. For example, suppose you have a data set in a Power BI report that consists of information about product sales, and you want to add a column that calculates sales growth as a percentage. You could easily achieve this using DAX.

In this chapter, you will learn how to use DAX in Power BI. First, you'll learn about calculated columns and measures. Next, you'll explore important DAX expressions, including the concept of context. Finally, you'll learn about DAX functions.

In this chapter:

- Calculated columns and measures
- DAX expressions syntax and context
- DAX functions

Calculated columns and measures

Before you dive into DAX, there are two terms you need to know:

- **Calculated column** When you use DAX to calculate data from two existing columns, the result of the calculation appears in a new column. This new column is called a calculated column.

- **Measure** A measure dynamically performs calculations on your data as you interact with your Power BI reports—for example, by applying filters and so on—and updates the results in real time. There are two types of measures:

    - **Simple measures** These are simple data calculations. An example of a simple measure is the total sum of sales for an organization.

    - **Complex measures** These are calculations that contain additional filters or combine two or more tables of data.

> ⚠️ **IMPORTANT** Both calculated columns and measures play a vital role in performing calculations for Power BI reports.

When should you use a calculated column, and when should you use a measure? Table 5-1 offers some guidance.

Table 5-1 *Calculated columns versus measures*

Use a calculated column when...	Use a measure when...
The data is stored in memory.	The data is not stored in memory.
You want the data to be calculated when you refresh the report.	You want the data to be calculated on the fly when you apply a filter.
Values are visible in the DAX expression.	Values are not visible in the DAX expression.
You want to perform a row-by-row calculation.	You want to calculate aggregated data.
You want to perform a simple calculation.	You want to perform a complex calculation.

> ⚠️ **IMPORTANT** Calculated columns consume memory, while measures consume CPU space.

Create a calculated column in Power BI

To create a calculated column in Power BI, switch to Data view. Then do one of the following steps:

- In the **Modeling** tab, click the **New Column** button in the **Calculations** group. (See screen 1 in Figure 5-1.)

- Right-click the table name (in this example, **Sales**) and select **New Column** in the menu that appears. (See screen 2 in Figure 5-1.)

After you create the new column, a box appears where you can add the desired calculation in DAX form. (See screen 3 in Figure 5-1.) After you enter the calculation, press **Enter** or click the checkmark to the left of the box.

For example, suppose the table contains the following sales data: unit per price and quantity sold. In that case you could combine these two sets of data in the calculated column to show the total sales amount. (See screen 4 in Figure 5-1.)

> ⚠ **IMPORTANT** In Power BI Desktop, calculated columns are marked with a special column icon in the Field list. (See screen 5 in Figure 5-1.) This is not the case in Power BI service, however.

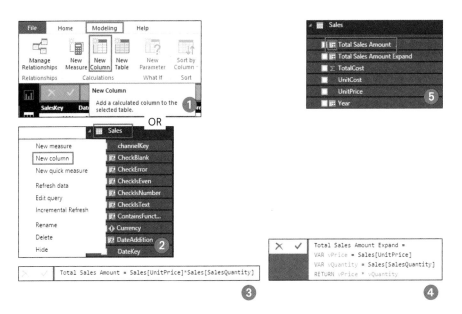

FIGURE 5-1 *Creating a new calculated column in Power BI.*

You can define variables for various functions for use in your calculations. For example, the calculation shown in screen 4 of Figure 5-1 contains the following variables:

- **vPrice** This variable is for the sales value per unit price.

- **vQuantity** This variable is for the quantity of sales.

In the RETURN function, vPrice is multiplied by vQuantity to obtain the total sales amount. (Refer to screen 5 in Figure 5-1.)

Create a measure in Power BI

As with calculated columns, you can create a new measure from within Data view in one of two ways:

- In the **Modeling** tab, click the **New Measure** button in the **Calculations** group. (See screen 1 in Figure 5-2.)

- Right-click the table name and select **New Measure** in the menu that appears. (See screen 2 in Figure 5-2.)

Again, after you create the measure, a box appears where you can add the desired function or expression in DAX form. (See screen 3 in Figure 5-2.) After you do, press **Enter** or click the checkmark to the left of the box.

For example, suppose you have sales data and you want to identify sales trends. To obtain this you could create a new measure (Sales Measure) with the following expression, which combines total sales.

```
Sales Measure = sum(Sales[Total Sales Amount])
```

> ⚠ **IMPORTANT** In Power BI Desktop, measures are marked with a special calculator icon in the Field list. (See screen 4 in Figure 5-2.) This is not the case in Power BI service, however.

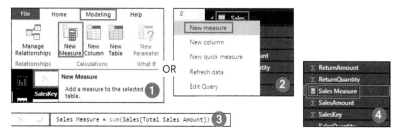

FIGURE 5-2 *Adding a new measure in Power BI.*

Use quick measures

In addition to writing your own measures using DAX, you can select from several pre-defined ones provided by Microsoft. These pre-defined measures, called quick measures, are available online.

> ⚠ **IMPORTANT** You can use quick measures with any visuals in a report.

Quick measures are divided into the following categories:

- Aggregate Within a Category
- Filters
- Time Intelligence
- Total
- Mathematical Operations
- Text

Table 5-2 lists the available measures by category.

Table 5-2 *Quick measures*

Quick measure function	Description
Aggregate Within a Category	
Average per category	This calculates the average of the base value within the category.
Variance per category	This calculates the variance of the base value within the category.
Max per category	This calculates the maximum of the base value within the category.
Min per category	This calculates the minimum of the base value within the category.
Weighted average per category	This calculates a weighted average of the base value for each category. You multiply the value by the weight of each category, sum the total, and then divide by the sum total of the weight.

continued

Quick measure function	Description
Filters	
Filtered value	This calculates a value with a filter applied.
Difference from filtered value	This calculates the difference between a value and its value with a filter applied.
Percentage difference from filtered value	This calculates the percentage difference between a value and its value with a filter applied.
Sales from new categories	This calculates sales from customers making their first purchase. You might also use this measure to find the number of first-time help desk callers, the average age of customers taking out a life insurance premium, and so on.
Time Intelligence	
Year-to-date total	This calculates the total of the base value starting from the beginning of the current year.
Quarter-to-date total	This calculates the total of the base value starting from the beginning of the current quarter.
Month-to-date total	This calculates the total of the base value starting from the beginning of the current month.
Year-over-year change	This calculates the year-over-year change of the base value.
Quarter-over-quarter change	This calculates the quarter-over-quarter change of the base value.
Month-over-month change	This calculates the month-over-month change of the base value.
Rolling average	This calculates the average of the base value over a certain number of periods before and/or after each date.
Totals	
Running total	This calculates the running total of a measure in a specific field.
Total for category (filters applied)	This calculates the total across all the values in a category, applying filters in your report.
Total for category (filters not applied)	This calculates the total across all the values in a category, ignoring filters applied in your report.

Quick measure function	Description
Mathematical Operations	
Addition	This calculates the sum of two values.
Subtraction	This calculates the difference between two values.
Multiplication	This calculates the product of two values.
Division	This calculates the ratio of a value to another one.
Percentage difference	This calculates the percentage difference between two values.
Correlation coefficient	This calculates the correlation coefficient between two values in a category.
Text	
Star rating	This converts a numeric value into a variable star rating.
Concatenated list of values	This creates a comma-separated list of distinct values in a column.

> ⚠ **IMPORTANT** You cannot use quick measures with DirectQuery or live connections. Also, SSAS is not supported.

Suppose a report contains the total sales amount for all product categories, and you want to analyze the total sales for each category individually, calculated year to date. This type of data is dynamic, calling for the use of a quick measure. Here's how to create one:

1. In the **Home** tab, click the **New Quick Measure** button. Alternatively, right-click the table for which you want to create a new quick measure and select New Quick Measure.

   The Quick Measures dialog box opens. (See screen 1 in Figure 5-3.) The left side of the dialog box contains all available quick measure function parameters, while the right side contains available fields within the selected function.

2. Open the **Calculation** drop-down list and choose **Average Per Category**. (See screen 1 in Figure 5-3.)

3. Open the **Base Value** drop-down list and choose **Sum of Sales Amount**. (See screen 1 in Figure 5-3.)

5

4. Open the **Category** drop-down list and choose **Product Key**. (See screen 1 in Figure 5-3.)

5. Click **OK** to apply the quick measure. Double-click the quick measure name to view a formula bar containing the DAX code for the quick measure. (See image 2 in Figure 5-3.)

Quick measures ①

Calculation	Fields
Average per category ▼	🔍 Search
Calculate the average of the base value within the category. Learn more	channelKey
	DateKey
Base value ①	Σ DiscountAmount
Sum of SalesAmount ▼ ×	Σ DiscountQuantity
	▦ Measure 2
Category ①	▦ Month
ProductKey ×	ProductKey
	PromotionKey
	Σ ReturnAmount
	Σ ReturnQuantity
	▦ Sales Measure
	Σ SalesAmount
	Σ SalesKey
	SalesQuantity
	StoreKey
	▦ Total Sales Amount
	▦ Total Sales Amount Expand
	Σ TotalCost
	UnitCost
	UnitPrice
	▦ Year
	▸ ▦ Stores

Don't see the calculation you want? Post an idea.   OK   Cancel

```
SalesAmount average per ProductKey 2 =
AVERAGEX(
    KEEPFILTERS(VALUES('Sales'[ProductKey])),
    CALCULATE(SUM('Sales'[SalesAmount]))
)
```

FIGURE 5-3 *Creating a quick measure in Power BI.*

⚠ **IMPORTANT** You can double-click a quick measure in a report to view the DAX formula associated with it.

DAX expressions syntax and context

As you've learned, you can use DAX expressions to analyze critical data for use in Power BI reports. These expressions use a specific syntax and context.

DAX capabilities

When using DAX expressions to perform complex calculations, keep these points in mind:

- DAX expressions accept tables and columns as a reference. They do not require you to repeatedly enter a function to create separate expressions across the table.

- DAX operations apply to the entire selected column of data.

- It is possible to return a value of an entire table instead of returning a single value.

- DAX supports several time-based functions, including functions for calculating date, time, and year variables from column data.

- You can use DAX expressions to create powerful functions for calculating the length of a dataset.

- You can apply as many as 64 nested functions in one DAX expression.

Syntax of DAX expressions

As mentioned, DAX expressions use a specific syntax. For example, consider the following DAX expression to calculate the total sales from a table of sales data:

```
Total Sales = SUM (Sales[Price])
```

This expression contains the following elements:

- **Total Sales** This is the name of the measure or calculated column.

- **=** This operator marks the start of the function.

- **SUM** This is a DAX function that adds up all the numbers in the Sales[Price] column.

- ■ () The parentheses contain at least one argument.

- ■ **Sales** This refers to the name of the table being analyzed.

- ■ **Price** This is the column in the table to which the SUM function will be applied.

Context of DAX expressions

When performing complex dynamic analysis, you must consider context. Context refers to the data that is available for a calculation to be performed upon. DAX expressions allow for two contexts:

- ■ **Row context** Row context applies when a DAX formula contains a function that applies filters that identify a single row in a table. In other words, the calculation operates only on a specific row. In general, it cannot reference any data that is outside that row without the proper use of certain functions. The row context is calculated at processing time rather than run time. This type of context is useful when generating calculated columns.

- ■ **Filter context** Filter context describes the application of one or more filters in a calculation to determine a specific result or value. Filter context does not replace row context; rather, it extends it. You use the following DAX functions to apply a filter context:

  - • ALL
  - • RELATED
  - • FILTER
  - • CALCULATE

> ⚠ **IMPORTANT** You'll learn more about these functions in the next section.

Figure 5-4 shows an example of a calculation with row context. It shows two tables in Power BI Desktop: **Sales** (image 1 in Figure 5-4) and **Category** (image 2 in Figure 5-4). It also shows a new calculated column.

Note that the row context does not move across the relationship between the two tables. To achieve this, I applied the RELATED DAX expression (refer to image 3 in Figure 5-4):

```
CategoryType = RELATED(Category[Category Type])
```

This converted the row context to the filter context. (This process is called context transition.)

Sales table

Order Number	Category	Price
1	1	50
2	5	87
3	4	45
4	1	48
5	5	95
6	4	14
7	3	26
8	2	75
9	6	14
10	4	62
11	3	123
12	4	156

Category table

	A	B
1	Category	Category Type
2	1	A
3	2	B
4	3	C
5	4	D
6	5	E
7	6	F

```
CategoryType = RELATED(Category[Category Type])
```

Sales table

Order Number	Category	Price	CategoryType
1	1	50	A
2	5	87	E
3	4	45	D
4	1	48	A
5	5	95	E
6	4	14	D
7	3	26	C
8	2	75	B
9	6	14	F
10	4	62	D
11	3	123	C
12	4	156	D

FIGURE 5-4 *Row context in a DAX expression.*

DAX functions

DAX functions calculate the data within a table. There are several types of DAX functions:

- Date and time functions
- Time intelligence functions
- Filter functions
- Information functions
- Logical functions

- Math functions
- Parent and child functions
- Statistical functions
- Text functions
- Other functions

Date and time functions

These functions are used in expressions that relate to dates and times. The functions are as follows:

- **CALENDAR** This function returns a series of dates within a start date and end date you specify. (If the start date is later than the end date, the function returns an error.) It uses the following syntax:

  ```
  CALENDAR(<start_date>, <end_date>)
  ```

  where <start_date> and <end_date> use the DATE function (discussed in the next bullet). For example, the following expression returns every date between January 1, 2005 and December 31, 2015 in table format:

  ```
  Table = CALENDAR (DATE (2005, 1, 1), DATE (2015, 12, 31))
  ```

- **DATE** This function returns a specific date. It uses the following syntax:

  ```
  DATE(<year>, <month>, <day>)
  ```

  For example, the following expression returns a date in year-month-date format:

  ```
  Column = DATE(2017,5,12)
  ```

- **DATEDIFF** This function returns an interval count between two specified dates. (If the start date is later than the end date, the function returns an error.) It uses the following syntax:

  ```
  DATEDIFF(<start_date>, <end_date>, <interval>)
  ```

  This function accepts the following interval values:

  - Second
  - Minute
  - Hour
  - Day
  - Week
  - Month
  - Quarter
  - Year

  For example, the following expression returns the difference between two dates in minutes:

  ```
  Date Difference = DATEDIFF('Table'[Date],'Table'[Column],MINUTE)
  ```

- **NOW** This function returns the current date and time. If you want to display this information in a calculated column, the expression will calculate the value using all the column data. It uses the following syntax:

  ```
  NOW()
  ```

- **TIME** This converts a time value from an hour-minute-second format to one that is standard for calculated columns. This is recommended to improve table readability. It uses the following syntax:

```
TIME(<hour>, <minute>, <second>)
```

The `<hour>` parameter can contain values between 0 and 23, and the `<minute>` and `<second>` parameters can contain values between 0 and 59. As an example, the following DAX expression will return a time value:

```
Time = TIME(14,50,9)
```

- **WEEKDAY** This returns a number between 0 and 6 or between 1 and 7 to indicate a specific day of the week. You specify which number represents which day. Here are some common patterns:

  - **Pattern 1** The number 0 equates to Sunday, in which case 1 equates to Monday, 2 to Tuesday, 3 to Wednesday, and so on.

  - **Pattern 2** The number 1 equates to Sunday, in which case 2 equates to Monday, 3 to Tuesday, 4 to Wednesday, and so on.

  - **Pattern 3** The number 1 equates to Monday, in which case 2 equates to Tuesday, 3 to Wednesday, 4 to Thursday, and so on.

  This function uses the following syntax:

```
WEEKDAY(<date>, <return_type>)
```

  For example, the following DAX expression returns a weekday from a date-time field:

```
WeekDay = WEEKDAY('Table'[Date],2)
```

- **TODAY** This function returns the current date and time. It uses the following syntax:

```
TODAY(<date>)
```

- **YEAR** This function returns the current year. It uses the following syntax:

```
YEAR(<date>)
```

5

Time intelligence functions

These functions use calendar data to perform calculations—for example, to generate data for sales inventories and so on. They include the following:

- **DATEADD** This function starts with a particular date, adds (or subtracts) a specified number of years, quarters, months, or days to that date, and returns the resulting value. It uses the following syntax:

  ```
  DATEADD(<date>, <number_of_intervals>, <interval>)
  ```

  The parameters are as follows:

  - **<date>** This is the initial date value, obtained from a relevant column in a table.

  - **<number_of_intervals>** This indicates how many years, quarters, months, or days to add (or subtract) to the initial date value.

  - **<interval>** This indicates whether the number of intervals refers to years, quarters, months, or days.

  For example, to add a one-month interval to dates listed in a DateKey column in a Calendar table, you would use the following DAX expression:

  ```
  DateAddition = DATEADD('Calendar'[DateKey],1,MONTH)
  ```

- **DATESMTD** This month-to-date function returns a series of dates from the start of the month to the current day in chronological order. It uses the following syntax:

  ```
  DATESMTD(<dates>)
  ```

  where <dates> refers to the column containing the relevant dates.

- **DATESQTD** This quarter-to-date function returns a series of dates from the start of the quarter to the current day in chronological order. It uses the following syntax:

  ```
  DATESQTD(<dates>)
  ```

- **DATESYTD** This year-to-date function returns a series of dates from the start of the year to the current day in chronological order. It uses the following syntax:

  ```
  DATESYTD(<dates> [,<year_end_date>])
  ```

  where <year_end_date> refers to the current date of the year.

- **TOTALMTD** This function calculates a value and presents data used to obtain that value in a month-to-date format. It uses the following syntax:

  ```
  TOTALMTD(<expression>, <dates>[, <filter>])
  ```

For example, suppose you want to calculate total sales and organize them in month-to-date format. In that case you would use the following expression:

```
TotalMTD = TOTALMTD(SUM('Sales'[Sales]), 'Dates'[Dates])
```

- **TOTALQTD** This function is identical to TOTALMTD but organizes the data in a quarter-to-date format. It uses the following syntax:

```
TOTALQTD(<expression>, <dates>[, <filter>])
```

- **TOTALYTD** This function is identical to TOTALMTD and TOTALQTD but organizes the data in a year-to-date format. It uses the following syntax:

```
TOTALYTD(<expression>, <dates>[, <filter>][, <year_end_date>]
```

Filter functions

These functions use commands to filter data and return a subset of an expression. They allow for complex dynamic calculations using tables and relationships. They include the following:

- **FILTER** This function filters data from a table and returns a subset of a table or an expression as required. It uses the following syntax:

```
FILTER(<table>, <filter>)
```

For example, suppose you want to view all sales data for products that cost more than $150. To achieve this, you could apply the FILTER function as follows:

```
FilterSample = COUNTROWS(FILTER('Sales', 'Sales' [Sales] > 150))
```

The result will be a subset of rows whose sales value is greater than 150.

- **RELATED** This function identifies relationships between values in multiple tables. It uses the following syntax:

```
RELATED(<column>)
```

For example, suppose you want to retrieve sales data for the United States from multiple tables. You would use the following expression:

```
RelatedSample = COUNTROWS(FILTER(ALL('Sales'), RELATED('SalesGeography' [Countries])
= "United States"))
```

- **ALL** This function returns all values in a table or column, irrespective of any filters applied. It uses the following syntax:

```
ALL(<table> or <column>)
```

5

As an example of the ALL function, consider counting all the rows of sales data irrespective of any page level filters being applied. The expression used in this condition is:

```
All Sales Order = COUNTROWS(ALL('Sales'))
```

The filters are ignored in such an expression and therefore users can fetch the entire count of data collection from the ALL function.

- **CALCULATE** This is one of the most important DAX functions. This calculates the value of an expression with filters applied. It uses the following syntax:

```
CALCULATE(<expression>, <filter1>, <filter2> ....)
```

For example, to calculate total sales at all locations, you could use the following expression:

```
CalculateSample = CALCULATE(SUM('Sales'[Sales]), ALL('SalesGeography'))
```

Information functions

These functions provide information about the cell or row flagged in a query, and include the following:

- **CONTAINS** This function returns TRUE if the value or string for which you are searching actually appears in the specified column or row or FALSE if it does not. It uses the following syntax:

```
CONTAINS (<table>. <columnName>, <value>[, <columnName>, <value>]....)
```

This expression contains the following parameters:

- **<table>** This is the table you want to search.

- **<columnName>** This is the column you want to search.

- **<value>** This is the value or string for which you are searching.

- **ISBLANK** This function checks whether a cell in a table is blank. If so, it returns TRUE; if not, it returns FALSE. It uses the following syntax:

```
ISBLANK(<value>)
```

- **ISERROR** This function checks whether a value or string contains an error. If so, it returns TRUE; if not, it returns FALSE. It uses the following syntax:

```
ISERROR (<value>)
```

- **ISTEXT** This function checks whether a value is text. If so, it returns TRUE; if not, it returns FALSE. It uses the following syntax:

    ```
    ISTEXT (<value>)
    ```

- **ISNUMBER** This function checks whether a value is a number. If so, it returns TRUE; if not, it returns FALSE. It uses the following syntax:

    ```
    ISNUMBER (<number>)
    ```

- **ISEVEN** This function checks whether a numerical value is even. If so, it returns TRUE; if not, it returns FALSE, indicating the number is odd. It uses the following syntax:

    ```
    ISEVEN (<number>)
    ```

5

Logical functions

Logical functions enable you to introduce decision-making capabilities into your DAX expressions. These functions include the following:

- **IF** This function checks the condition of a statement. If the condition is TRUE, the function executes one argument. If it is FALSE, the function executes a different argument (or no argument at all). It uses the following syntax:

    ```
    IF(<logical_test>, <value_if_true>, <value_if_false>)
    ```

    This expression has the following parameters:

    - **<logical_test>** This is the condition you want to check.

    - **<value_if_true>** This is the argument executed if the condition is TRUE.

    - **<value_if_false>** This is the argument executed if the condition is FALSE.

    For example, suppose you want to identify large orders (greater than 100 units). To achieve this, you could use the following expression:

    ```
    CheckLargeOrder = IF(Sales[Sales]>100,"Large Order","Small Order")
    ```

- **AND** This function checks multiple conditions. If all the conditions are TRUE, it returns TRUE. Otherwise, it returns FALSE. It uses the following syntax:

    ```
    AND(<logic1>, <logic2>)
    ```

    Where <logic 1> and <logic 2> are conditions to be checked.

For example, suppose you want to identify all large orders (greater than 100 units) in a specific country (whose country ID is 4). To achieve this, you could use the following expression:

```
CheckLargewithAND = IF(AND(Sales[Sales]>100,Sales[CountryID]=4),"Correct","In Correct")
```

- **OR** This function checks multiple conditions. If any one condition is TRUE, the function returns TRUE. Otherwise, it returns FALSE. It uses the following syntax:

```
OR(<logic1>, <logic2>)
```

For example, suppose you want to identify all large orders (greater than 100 units) or orders in a specific country (whose country ID is 4). In that case, you would use the following expression:

```
CheckLargewithOR = IF(OR(Sales[Sales]>100,Sales[CountryID]=4),"Correct","In Correct")
```

- **SWITCH** This function enables you to switch one value for another. It uses the following syntax:

```
SWITCH(<expression>, <value>, <result>[, <value>, <result>]…[, <else>])
```

For example, suppose you want to swap out month names with month numbers. The following expression achieves this:

```
MonthName = SWITCH(Dates[Month], 1, "January", 2, "February", 3, "March", 4,
"April", 5, "May", 6, "June", 7, "July", 8, "August", 9, "September", 10,
"October", 11, "November", 12, "December", "Unknown month number" )
```

Math functions

Math functions enable you to perform mathematical calculations on your data. These functions include the following:

- **SUM** This function adds all values in a given column. It uses the following syntax:

```
SUM(<column>)
```

Here the column contains all the values for which the sum operation has to be performed. The value returned is a decimal number.

- **SUMX** This function is similar to the SUM function, but it applies conditions to the rows and columns in an entire table and performs its calculation on a row-by-row basis. It uses the following syntax:

```
SUMX(<table>, <expression>)
```

This expression has the following parameters:

- **<table>** This is the table whose values you want to calculate.

- **<expression>** This contains the conditions to be applied to the table before the SUMX calculation occurs.

For example, suppose you want to calculate total sales for products over $500. You could use the following expression:

```
Total Unit Cost = SUMX([Sales], Sales[UnitPrice]>500)
```

- **FACT** This function returns the factorial of a specified number. It uses the following syntax:

```
FACT(<number>)
```

- **GCD** This function returns the greatest common divisor (with no remainder) for two or more integers. It uses the following syntax:

```
GCD(number1, [number2], ….)
```

For example, the following expression returns the greatest common divisor (4) for the numerals 4 and 12:

```
GCDValue = GCD(4, 12)
```

If any values found are non-numeric in nature, GCD returns a #VALUE! error. If any values are less than zero, GCD returns a #NUM! error.

- **LCM** The function returns the least common multiple for two or more integers. It uses the following syntax:

```
LCM(number1, [number2], …)
```

For example, the following expression returns the least common multiple (15) for the numerals 5 and 15:

```
LCM= LCM(5, 15)
```

- **POWER** This function returns the value of a number raised to a specific power in decimal form. It uses the following syntax:

```
POWER(<number>, <power>)
```

For example, the following expression returns 25, which is the value of 5 raised by a power of 2.

```
Power = POWER(5,2)
```

■ **ROUND** This function returns the value of a number rounded to the nearest decimal. It uses the following syntax:

```
ROUND(<number>, <num_digit>)
```

For example, the following expression returns a value of 555.7, which is 555.66 rounded to the nearest decimal:

```
RoundValue = ROUND(555.66, 1)
```

Parent and child functions

You can use various DAX functions to manage the parent/child hierarchy. With these functions, you can obtain a row's entire lineage of parents, the number of levels to the top parent, the parent *n* levels above the current row, the descendant *n* levels from the top of the current row hierarchy, and the parent in the current row hierarchy. These functions include the following:

■ **PATH** This function enables you to identify all parents of the selected child value. It uses the following syntax:

```
PATH(<ID_columnName>, <parent_columnName>)
```

This expression has the following parameters:

- **<ID_columnName>** This is the column that contains the child values whose parents you want to identify.

- **<parent_columnName>** This is the column that contains parent values.

The following expression applies the PATH function to search a Name column and a Parent column and combine information from these columns into a delimited string (see column 1 in Figure 5-5):

```
Path Function = PATH(Data[Name],Data[Parent])
```

■ **PATHITEM** The PATH function returns a delimited string with parent nodes. To return a specific item retrieved by the PATH function, based on the item's position in the results (from left to right or top to bottom), you use the PATHITEM function. It uses the following syntax:

```
PATHITEM(<path>, <position>[, <type>])
```

This expression has the following parameters:

- **<path>** This is the PATH expression on whose results you want to base the PATHITEM expression.

- **<position>** This is the position of the specific item you want to identify in the results.

- **<type>** This is an enumeration that defines the data type of the result. By default, its value is Text. You can also set the enumeration value to INTEGER.

For example, the following expression returns the second item in the results of a PATH expression (see column 2 in Figure 5-5).

```
Path Item = PATHITEM(PATH(Data[Name], Data[Parent]),2)
```

■ **PATHLENGTH** This function returns the number of parents between two specified items. It uses the following syntax:

```
PATHLENGTH(<path>)
```

where <path> is the PATH expression that returns a specific parent/child relationship. For example, column 3 in Figure 5-5 shows the results of the following PATHLENGTH expression:

```
Path Length = PATHLENGTH(Data[Path Function])
```

■ **PATHITEMREVERSE** This function is the reverse of PATHITEM. It returns a specific item in the PATH results from right to left or bottom to top. It uses the following syntax:

```
PATHITEMREVERSE(<path>, <position>[, <type>])
```

The parameters are the same as with the PATHITEM function. Column 4 in Figure 5-5 shows the results of the following PATHITEMREVERSE expression:

```
Path Item Reverse = PATHITEMREVERSE (Data[Path Function],1)
```

Original table

Node Number	Name	Parent	Sales	Parent Node ID	Path Function	Path Item	Path Lenght	Path Item Reverse
1	Emiliy				Emiliy		1	Emiliy
2	Saraha				Saraha		1	Saraha
3	Jessica	Saraha	32	2	Saraha|Jessica	Jessica	2	Jessica
4	Harry	Saraha	16	2	Saraha|Harry	Harry	2	Harry
5	Michael	Saraha	8	2	Saraha|Michael	Michael	2	Michael
6	Kayla	Emiliy		1	Emiliy|Kayla	Kayla	2	Kayla
7	Brad	Emiliy	4	1	Emiliy|Brad	Brad	2	Brad
8	Chris	Kayla	2	6	Emiliy|Kayla...	Kayla		Chris
9	Nick	Kayla	1	6	Emiliy|Kayla|Nick	Kayla	3	Nick

FIGURE 5-5 *Parent and child functions in Power BI.*

Statistical functions

These functions deal with aggregations, sums, and averages of numbers in a column. These include the following:

- **AVERAGE** This function calculates the average of all numbers in a column. It uses the following syntax:

  ```
  AVERAGE(<column>)
  ```

- **COUNT** This function counts the total number of cells that contain numbers within a given column. It uses the following syntax:

  ```
  COUNT(<column>)
  ```

- **MAX** This function returns the largest number from a column or between two scalar expressions. It uses the following syntax:

  ```
  MAX(<column>)
  ```

  ```
  MAX(<expression1>, <expression2>)
  ```

- **MIN** This function returns the smallest number from a column or between two scalar expressions. It uses the following syntax:

  ```
  MIN(<column>)
  ```

  ```
  MIN(<expression1>, <expression2>)
  ```

Text functions

Text functions enable you to conduct operations on text in tables and columns. These functions include the following:

- **CONCATENATE** This function combines two strings of text, numbers, or Boolean values into a single string. It uses the following syntax:

  ```
  CONCATENATE(<Text1>, <Text2>)
  ```

  For example, suppose you want to combine two text strings—"Hello" and "World"—into a new single string. You could use the following expression:

  ```
  CONCATENATE("Hello", "World")
  ```

- **REPLACE** This function replaces any part of a text string with a new text string. It uses the following syntax:

  ```
  REPLACE (<old_text>, <start_num>, <num_chars>, <new_text>)
  ```

  This expression has the following parameters:

  - **<old_text>** This is the text string you want to alter.

- **<start_num>** Suppose your text string has 20 characters, and you want to start replacing the text that starts 10 characters in. In that case, `10` would be the <start_num>.

- **<num_chars>** This indicates the number of characters you want replaced.

- **<new_text>** This is the text string you want to use to replace the old text.

For example, the following expression would return `"HelloPower BI"`:

```
Replace Demo = REPLACE("Hello world", 6, 7, "Power BI")
```

- **TRIM** This function removes any spaces in a text string except for single spaces between words. It uses the following syntax:

```
TRIM(<text>)
```

- **UPPER** This function converts all letters in a text string to uppercase letters. It uses the following syntax:

```
UPPER (<text>)
```

Other functions

This section covers two functions that do not fit into any other category:

- **EXCEPT** This function returns values that appear in one table but not in another one. (Note that both tables must contain the same number of columns.) It uses the following syntax:

```
EXCEPT(<table_expression1>, <table_expression2>)
```

For example, suppose you ran the following expression on the tables in Figure 5-6. It would return the value `Alabama` because it appears in the first table but not the second one.

```
EXCEPT(State1, State2)
```

State1	State2
Alabama	California
California	Delaware
Colorado	Colorado

FIGURE 5-6 *Use of the Except function in Power BI.*

- **UNION** This function returns a new table composed of selected columns in an existing table. It uses the following syntax:

```
UNION(<table_expression1>, <table_expression2> [, <table_expression>] …)
```

Skills review

In this chapter, you learned about:

- Calculated columns and measures
- DAX expressions syntax and content
- DAX functions

Practice tasks

This section provides a simple case study for you to study and solve using information from this chapter. This section also contains a series of practice questions for you to answer.

Case study

Suppose you work as a stock trader on the New York Stock Exchange (NYSE). You buy shares on the market at one price and sell them at another for either a profit or a loss.

To use DAX to analyze your business, you want to collect the following four key data points:

- The number of shares bought
- The price you paid for each share
- The number of shares sold
- The amount you sold each share for

Using this data, create calculated column or measures to generate the following information:

- Your total investment for the entire fiscal year
- Your total sales for the entire fiscal year
- Profits and losses from individual stocks
- Total profits and losses for the entire fiscal year
- Total profits and losses for month-to-date (MTD), quarter-to-date (QTD), and year-to-date (YTD)

Practice questions

1. What are DAX expressions?
2. What is a calculated column?
3. What is a measure?
4. What is the difference between a calculated column and a measure?
5. What is the best method to prepare a column for row-wise data?

6. How do you combine two columns in a table?

7. Suppose you have a table that contains total sales for several years. How could you explore the calculated data for a specific year?

8. What are the two types of contexts?

9. How would you define row context?

10. How would you define filter context?

11. What type of functions are associated with concatenation?

Develop Power BI reports from Excel

In this chapter, you'll learn how to develop a Power BI report that relies on a Microsoft Excel workbook as its data source. The report will analyze sales for a retail chain.

This chapter is the first of a series of chapters designed to show you how to import data from various sources and step through the creation of various types of reports. Note, however, that the types of reports discussed in the context of one data source, such as Excel, could be used with other data sources, too—for example, a SharePoint Online list. The idea here is to guide you as you explore the myriad uses of Power BI and to reinforce your learning when it comes to creating Power BI reports.

In this chapter:

- Import data from an Excel workbook into Power BI
- Add a measure and a calculated column
- Add Power BI visuals to the report
- Arrange the visuals
- Prepare the report for mobile view
- Publish and view the report
- Prepare a dashboard from the report

Practice files

As you work through this chapter, you'll use two practice files, which you can access from the MSPBIDashboards\ch06 folder on the book's companion website at *https://aka.ms/PowerBIDash/downloads*. The files are as follows:

- **Retail Analysis Sample.xlsx** This file contains a dummy data source for a retail analysis sample to help step you through the process of importing an Excel workbook into Power BI. You'll use this file in the section "Import data from an Excel workbook into Power BI" next in this chapter.

- **Retail Analysis Sample Report.pbix** This file is a sample Power BI report that reflects the final version of the report you'll create in this chapter.

Import data from an Excel workbook into Power BI

To import the data from the Retail Analysis Sample.xlsx Excel workbook into Power BI Desktop, follow these steps:

1. Click the **Home** tab in Power BI Desktop. (See screen 1 of Figure 6-1.)

2. Click **Get Data** (see screen 1 of Figure 6-1) and select the **File** option.

3. Click **Excel Workbook** and choose **Connect**. (See screen 2 of Figure 6-1.)

4. Locate and select the **Retail Analysis Sample.xlsx** workbook.

   You'll see all available sheets in the selected workbook and a preview of the selected table. (See screen 3 in Figure 6-1.)

5. Select the tables (Store table, etc.) you want to include in your report and click **Load**.

6. To switch to Data view, click the **Data View** button on the left side of the screen. (See screen 4 in Figure 6-1.)

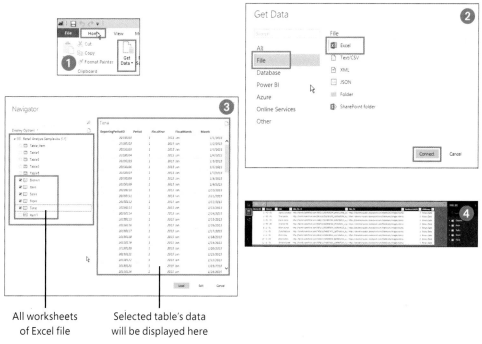

All worksheets   Selected table's data
of Excel file   will be displayed here

FIGURE 6-1 *Importing data from an Excel workbook.*

Add a measure and a calculated column

Suppose you want this report to include a measure that performs various calculations based on the sales data and a calculated column that derives some other fields based on the columns or data you already have.

To add the measure, follow these steps:

1. With the Store table you imported from Excel selected, click the **Modeling** tab, and click **New Measure**. Alternatively, right-click the Store table and choose **New Measure** from the menu that appears.

   A new measure opens in the formula bar.

2. Rename the new measure **Total Stores**.

3. Type the DAX expression you want to apply—in this case, **COUNTA**.

4. Click the column placeholder and select the column to which the measure should apply—in this case, **Store([StoreNumberName])**. (See Figure 6-2.) Then add a closing parenthesis.

5. Press **Enter** or click the **checkmark** in the formula bar to complete the formula.

FIGURE 6-2 *Creating a measure for the report.*

Now follow steps 1–5 to create the measures listed in Table 6-1. You'll use these measures later in the chapter.

Table 6-1 *Measures used in the Power BI report in this chapter*

Measure name	Formula
TotalSales	TotalSales = [Regular_Sales_Dollars]+[Markdown_Sales_Dollars]
Total Units This Year	Total Units This Year = CALCULATE([TotalUnits], Sales[ScenarioID]=1)
Regular_Sales_Dollars	Regular_Sales_Dollars = SUM([Sum_Regular_Sales_Dollars])
Markdown_Sales_Dollars	Markdown_Sales_Dollars = SUM([Sum_Markdown_Sales_Dollars])
Avg $/Unit TY	Avg $/Unit TY = IF([Total Units This Year]<>0, [TotalSalesTY]/[Total Units This Year], BLANK())
TotalSalesTY	TotalSalesTY = CALCULATE([TotalSales], Sales[ScenarioID]=1)
TotalUnits	TotalUnits = [Regular_Sales_Units]+[Markdown_Sales_Units]
Regular_Sales_Units	Regular_Sales_Units = SUM([Sum_Regular_Sales_Units])
Markdown_Sales_Units	Markdown_Sales_Units = SUM([Sum_Markdown_Sales_Units])
Total Sales Variance	Total Sales Variance = [Total Sales Var]
Total Sales Var	Total Sales Var = [TotalSalesTY]-[TotalSalesLY]
TotalSalesTY	TotalSalesTY = CALCULATE([TotalSales], Sales[ScenarioID]=1)
TotalSalesLY	TotalSalesLY = CALCULATE([TotalSales], Sales[ScenarioID]=2)
This Year Sales	This Year Sales = [TotalSalesTY]
TotalSalesTY	TotalSalesTY = CALCULATE([TotalSales], Sales[ScenarioID]=1)

To create the calculated column, follow these steps:

1. With the **Store** table selected, click the **Modeling** tab, and click **New Column**.

   Alternatively, right-click the **Store** table and choose **New Column** from the menu that appears.

   The formula bar appears.

2. Rename the new calculated column **Open Month**.

3. Type the DAX expression you want to apply—in this case, **FORMAT**.

4. Select the **[OpenDate]** parameter.

5. As shown in Figure 6-3, type the following format parameter:

   "MMM"

   Then add a closing parenthesis.

6. Press **Enter** or click the **checkmark** in the formula bar to complete the formula.

```
Open Month = FORMAT([OpenDate],"MMM")
```

FIGURE 6-3 *Creating a calculated column for the report.*

Add Power BI visuals to the report

Visuals enable you to enhance your Power BI report. In this section you'll add the following visuals to your report:

- **Attribute slicer** You'll use an attribute slicer to show the total sales value by category.

- **Multi-row card** A multi-row card will contain store details by category.

- **Waterfall chart** A waterfall chart will show total unit price by month and category.

- **Bubble chart** You'll use a bubble chart to convey the total sales variance, the average price per unit this year, and the current year sales by category.

- **Line chart** A line chart will show the current year sales by district manager and category.

> ⚠ **IMPORTANT** For a refresher on adding Power BI visuals to a report, refer to the section "Add visuals" in Chapter 4.

> ⚠ **IMPORTANT** You can use the settings in the Format section of the Visualizations pane to format your visuals—for example, by applying a border, changing the border color, changing the title color, and so on. To access these settings, click the button that features a paint roller icon.

Attribute slicer (total sales by category)

To show total sales by category, add an attribute slicer to the report. An attribute slicer is a third-party custom visual, which you can download free from the Microsoft Office store at the following link:

https://appsource.microsoft.com/en-us/product/power-bi-visuals/ WA104380794?tab=Overview

After you download and install the attribute slicer, you can access it like any other visual in the Visualizations pane in Power BI.

An attribute slicer enables you to filter data based on different categories. In this case, you'll add an attribute slicer that filters data by category and total sales. To create this visual, follow these steps:

1. Expand the **attribute slicer** settings in the Visualizations pane.

2. Select the **Category** field in the Fields pane to the right of the Visualizations pane and drag it to the **Items** entry in the attribute slicer settings.

3. Drag the **TotalSales** field to the **With Values** entry.

   In this example, TotalSales refers to the TotalSales measure you created earlier. (Refer to Table 6-1.) To review, this measure has the following syntax:

   ```
   TotalSales = [Regular_Sales_Dollars]+[Markdown_Sales_Dollars]
   ```

   Figure 6-4 shows the settings for the attribute slicer (image 1) and the corresponding visual (image 2).

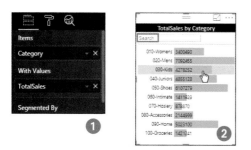

FIGURE 6-4 *Add an attribute slicer to your Power BI report.*

Multi-row card (store details by category)

To display store details by category, you'll add a multi-row card. Follow these steps:

1. Expand the **multi-row card** settings in the Visualizations pane.

2. Select the **Chain** field in the Fields pane to the right of the Visualizations pane and drag it to the **Fields** entry in the multi-row card settings.

3. Drag the **Name** field below the **Chain** field.

4. Drag the **Category** field below the **Name** field.

5. Drag the **Avg $/Unit TY** field below the **Category** field. Figure 6-5 shows the results.

FIGURE 6-5 *Add a multi-row card to your Power BI report.*

Waterfall chart (total unit price by month and category)

A waterfall chart enables you to show time-based data with running calculations—such as total unit price by month and category, as in this report. To construct this chart, follow these steps:

1. Expand the **waterfall chart** settings in the Visualizations pane.

2. Select the **Month** field in the Fields pane to the right of the Visualizations pane and drag it to the **Category** entry in the waterfall chart settings.

   When you add a Month field to the Category entry, it expands to show a date hierarchy, with Year, Quarter, Month, and Day options.

3. Select **Month** from the date hierarchy.

4. To include a categorical breakdown in the visual, drag the **Category** field to the **Breakdown** entry.

5. Drag the **Total Units This Year** field to the **Y Axis** entry.

   In this example, Total Units This Year refers to the Total Units This Year measure you created earlier. (Refer to Table 6-1.) To review, this measure has the following syntax:

   ```
   Total Units This Year = CALCULATE([TotalUnits], Sales[ScenarioID]=1)
   ```

   Figure 6-6 shows the resulting visual. Notice that if you hover your mouse cursor over the various visual elements, a tooltip appears.

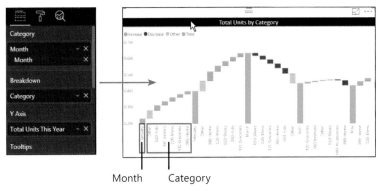

FIGURE 6-6 *Build a waterfall chart for your Power BI report.*

Bubble chart (total sales variance, average price per unit this year, and current year sales by category)

A bubble chart illustrates the volume of data for various categories—in this case, total sales variance, average price per unit this year, and current year sales by category. To create this chart, follow these steps:

1. Expand the **bubble chart** settings in the Visualizations pane.

2. Select the **Category** field in the Fields pane to the right of the Visualizations pane and drag it to the **Details** entry in the bubble chart settings.

3. Drag the **Category** field to the **Legend** entry.

4. Drag the **Total Sales Variance** field to the **X Axis** entry.

5. Drag the **Avg $/Unit TY** field to the **Y Axis** entry.

6. Drag the **This Year Sales** field to the **Size** entry.

   Figure 6-7 shows the resulting visual. Again, hovering your mouse cursor over the various visual elements reveals a tooltip.

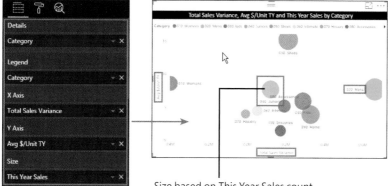

Size based on This Year Sales count

FIGURE 6-7 *Add a bubble chart to your Power BI report.*

Line chart (current year sales by district manager and category)

The best way to show current year sales by district manager and category is to use a line chart. Follow these steps:

1. Expand the **line chart** settings in the Visualizations pane.

2. Select the **DM** field in the Fields pane to the right of the Visualizations pane and drag it to the **Axis** entry in the line chart settings.

3. Drag the **Category** field to the **Legend** entry.

4. Drag the **This Years Sales** field to the **Values** entry.

   Figure 6-8 shows the resulting visual, complete with tooltip support.

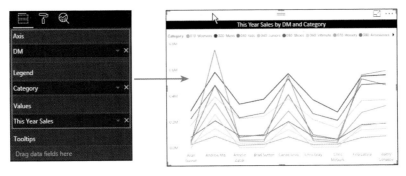

FIGURE 6-8 *Create a line chart for your Power BI report.*

Arrange the visuals

After you add all the necessary visualizations to your report, you can move and resize them as needed.

To move a visual, click anywhere inside the visual and drag it to the desired location. To resize a visual, click inside the visual. Then click any of the frame handles—these appear on the visual's border—or corner handles and drag inward or outward to make the visual small or larger, respectively. Figure 6-9 shows the final report.

 IMPORTANT If you want to maintain the visual's current aspect ratio, use the corner handles to resize it.

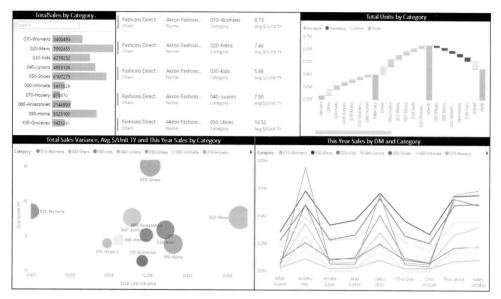

FIGURE 6-9 *Your Power BI report, complete with visuals.*

Prepare the report for mobile view

If you want to make your report available for viewing through the Power BI app on an iOS, Android, or Windows mobile device, you'll want to prepare your report accordingly. You learned how to do this Chapter 4. To review, the steps are as follows:

1. In the Report pane, in Desktop view, click the **View** tab and click the **Phone Layout** button.

   A blank canvas in the shape of a mobile device opens.

2. Click a visual in the Visualizations pane and drag it to the blank canvas.

3. Repeat step 2 until all the desired visuals appear on the mobile canvas.

4. Resize and rearrange the visuals as desired.

5. To switch back to Desktop view, click the **View** tab and click **Desktop Layout**.

Figure 6-10 shows the report you built in this chapter optimized for mobile view.

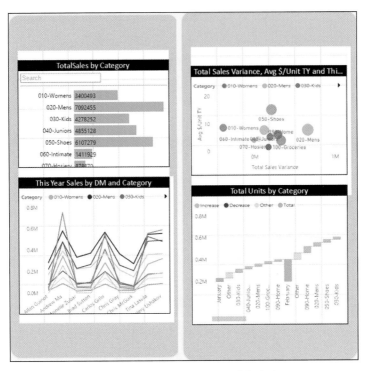

FIGURE 6-10 *Prepare the report for display on a mobile device.*

Publish and view the report

As a final step, you must publish your report for public consumption. This was discussed in detail in Chapter 4. To review, here are the steps you need to take:

1. Open the **File** menu, select **Publish**, and choose **Publish to Power BI**.

2. The Publish to Power BI page opens. Select the workspace on which you want to publish the report. Then click the **Select** button.

   A progress dialog box opens. When the operation is complete, you'll see a success message.

After you publish the report, you can log into your Power BI service account to verify that the report appears in the selected workspace. You can also view the report using the Power BI app on your iOS, Android, or Windows mobile device.

Prepare a dashboard from the report

As shown in Chapter 1, you can combine visuals from Power BI reports into a custom dynamic dashboard. (See Figure 6-11.) To review, to add a visual in a report to a dashboard, follow these steps:

1. Open the report that contains the visual you want to add to a dashboard.

2. Hover your mouse pointer over the visual you want to add to the dashboard and click the **Pin Visual** button that appears in the visual's upper-right corner.

   The Pin to Dashboard dialog box opens.

3. To create a new dashboard for the visual, select the **New Dashboard** option button and type a name for the new dashboard. Alternatively, select the **Existing Dashboard** option button and choose the desired dashboard.

4. Click the **Pin button** to add the visual to the dashboard.

FIGURE 6-11 *A dashboard containing visuals from various reports in Power BI.*

Skills review

In this chapter, you learned about:

- Importing data from an Excel workbook into Power BI

- Adding a measure and a calculated column

- Adding Power BI visuals to a report

- Arranging the visuals

- Preparing the report for mobile view

- Publishing and viewing the report

- Preparing a dashboard from the report

Practice tasks

This section provides a simple case study for you to study and solve using information from this chapter. This section also contains a series of practice questions for you to answer.

Case study

Suppose you work for a leading motion picture company that distributes the following products across various channels using various methods:

- Movies

- Short stories/Films

- Regional language movies

- Songs

- Advertisements

You want to assemble a report from an existing Excel data source to unearth the following data points:

- Most watched movie of all time

- Top 20 favorite songs categorized by region

- Best rated movies categorized by region

- Top 15 songs categorized weekly

- Most watched advertisement among users

Because the company is a subsidiary of a bigger organization that is listed on the New York Stock Exchange (NYSE), you could consider generating this report on a monthly or even weekly basis to better understand the perspective of potential stock buyers.

Practice questions

1. How do you import an Excel worksheet into Power BI?

2. How do you build a measure to obtain total sales data in the current quarter?

3. How do you build a calculated column to obtain month data from the date-time field?

4. How do you obtain a third-party visual from the Microsoft Office store?

5. What are the steps to prepare a Power BI report for mobile devices?

6. How do you choose the best visual to represent Power BI data?

7. What visuals can be used for slicer functionality?

8. How do you publish a report in Power BI?

9. How do you create a dashboard in Power BI?

Develop Power BI reports from SharePoint Online

7

In this chapter, you'll learn how to develop Power BI reports that rely on SharePoint Online as their data source. SharePoint is generally used for document-management and collaboration purposes.

In this chapter, you'll create two reports: one from a SharePoint Online list, and one from a SharePoint Online folder. As its name suggests, a SharePoint Online list stores information in list form. In contrast, a SharePoint Online folder stores information in a document library.

You'll also learn how to embed a Power BI report in SharePoint Online, and how to refresh the data source for a Power BI report.

In this chapter:

- Build a Power BI report based on data from a SharePoint Online list

- Build a Power BI report based on data from a SharePoint Online folder

- Refresh the data source in Power BI service

- Embed Power BI reports in SharePoint Online

Practice files

As you work through this chapter, you'll use four practice files, which you can access from the MSPBIDashboards\ch07 on the book's companion website at *https://aka.ms/PowerBIDash/downloads*. The files are as follows:

- **Expense Budgets.stp and Expense.stp** These files contain dummy data for an expense budget and an expense list, respectively. You'll use these files in the section "Import data from a SharePoint Online list into Power BI" later in this chapter.

- **SharePoint Online.pbix** This file consists of a sample Power BI expense report that matches the report you create in the first half of this chapter. It contains various visuals that can be arranged as desired. You can use this file in the section "Arrange the visuals and finalize the report" later in this chapter.

- **SharePoint Folder.pbix** This file consists of a sample Power BI report with various visuals for use in embedding in a SharePoint Online folder. You'll use this file in the section "Prepare a Power BI report for a SharePoint Online folder" later in this chapter.

Build a Power BI report based on data from a SharePoint Online list

This section steps you through the creation of a report based on two SharePoint Online lists: Expense Budget.stp and Expense.stp. These are included among the aforementioned practice files. You'll want to load these files into your SharePoint Online environment before you continue with this section.

Import data from a SharePoint Online list into Power BI

To start, you load the SharePoint Online lists into Power BI. After that you must establish the relationship between the lists; this ensures the data in the lists will flow smoothly into the Power BI report. Follow these steps:

1. Click the **Home** tab in Power BI Desktop.

2. Click **Get Data**.

3. Choose **Online Services** and select **SharePoint Online List**. (See screen 1 in Figure 7-1.)

4. Enter the **URL** for the SharePoint Online site that contains the lists from which you want to generate a Power BI report.

5. To sign in to the SharePoint Online site, click the **Microsoft Account** authentication option, click **Sign In**, and enter your username and password. (See screen 2 in Figure 7-1.)

6. Click **Connect**.

7. Select the lists you want to import (in this example, **Expense Budgets** and **Expense**) and click **Load**. (See screen 3 in Figure 7-1.)

8. Power BI loads the lists, including all their internal and external columns. If either file contains a column you don't want to include in your report, right-click that column and choose **Delete**. (See screen 4 in Figure 7-1.)

    There is one column that is common to both lists: Budget Key. If for some reason Power BI fails to detect this relationship automatically, you can establish it manually, as discussed in Chapter 4. The following steps review this process.

9. In the **Home** tab in Power BI Desktop, click **Manage Relationships**.

10. In the Manage Relationships page, click the **New button**.

11. In the Create Relationship page, open the top drop-down list and select the first list you want to include in the relationship. Then choose the column on which you want to base the relationship.

12. Repeat step 11 for the bottom drop-down list.

13. Click **OK**.

    Power BI creates a relationship between the two lists. (See screen 5 in Figure 7-1.)

FIGURE 7-1 *Loading a SharePoint list from SharePoint Online.*

Add Power BI visuals to the report

Visuals enable you to enhance your Power BI report. In this section you'll add the following visuals to your report:

- **Slicer** You'll use a slicer to filter by budget period and expense category.

- **Waterfall chart** A waterfall chart will show the total expenses by date.

- **Area chart** An area chart will show the total expenses by budget period and expense category.

- **Ribbon chart** You'll use a ribbon chart to show the budget used by expense category and budget period.

- **Funnel chart** To show the budget by expense category, you'll use a funnel chart.

- **Matrix** A matrix will contain the budget period, expense categories, total expenses, budget, and budget used.

> ⚠ **IMPORTANT** For a refresher on adding Power BI visuals to a report, refer to the section "Add visuals" in Chapter 4.

> ⚠ **IMPORTANT** You can use the settings in the Format section of the Visualizations pane to format your visuals—for example, by applying a border, changing the border color, changing the title color, and so on. To access these settings, click the button that features a paint roller icon.

7

Slicer (budget period and expense category)

A slicer enables you to filter data based on different categories. In this case, you'll add a slicer that filters data by budget period and expense category. To create this visual, follow these steps:

1. Expand the **slicer** settings in the Visualizations pane.

2. Select the **Budget Period** field in the Fields pane and drag it to the **Field** entry in the slicer settings. (See screen 1 in Figure 7-2.)

3. Drag the **Expense Category** field from the Fields pane to the **Field** entry in the slicer settings. (See screen 2 of Figure 7-2.)

    Let's change the orientation of the slicer.

4. Click the **paint roller** icon in the Visualizations pane, click the **Orientation** drop-down list, and select **Horizontal**. (See screen 2 of Figure 7-2.)

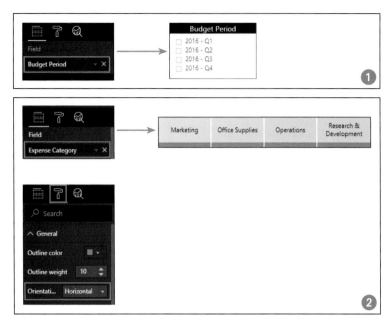

FIGURE 7-2 *Add a slicer to your Power BI report.*

Waterfall chart (total expenses by date)

A waterfall chart enables you to show time-based data with running calculations—such as total expenses by date, as in this report. To construct this chart, follow these steps:

1. Expand the **waterfall chart** settings in the Visualizations pane.

2. Select the **Date** field in the Fields pane and drag it to the **Category** entry in the waterfall chart settings.

3. Drag the **Total Expenses** field to the **Y Axis** entry.

   Figure 7-3 shows the resulting visual.

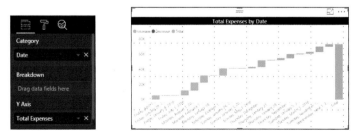

FIGURE 7-3 *Build a waterfall chart for your Power BI report.*

Area chart (total expenses by budget period and expense category)

An area chart shows changes in values over time, including volumes. To create an area chart that shows changes in total expenses by budget period and expense category, follow these steps:

1. Expand the **area chart** settings in the Visualizations pane.

2. Select the **Budget Period** field in the Fields pane and drag it to the **Axis** entry in the area chart settings.

3. Drag the **Expense Category** field below the **Legend** field.

4. Drag the **Total Expenses** field below the **Values** field.

   Figure 7-4 shows the resulting visual.

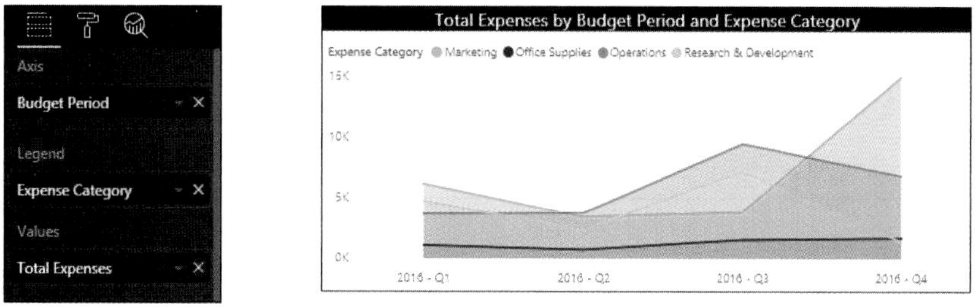

FIGURE 7-4 *Add an area chart to your Power BI report.*

Ribbon chart (budget used by expense category and budget period)

To show budget used by expense category and budget period, you can use a ribbon chart. Follow these steps:

1. Expand the **ribbon chart** settings in the Visualizations pane.

2. Select the **Expense Category** field in the Fields pane and drag it to the **Axis** entry in the ribbon chart settings.

3. Drag the **Budget Period** field below the **Legend** field.

4. Drag the **Budget Used** field below the **Value** field.

   Figure 7-5 shows the resulting visual.

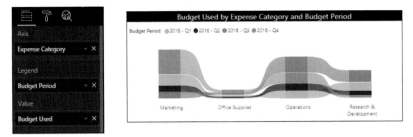

FIGURE 7-5 *Add a ribbon chart to your Power BI report.*

Funnel chart (budget by expense category)

Add a funnel chart to the report to show the budget by expense category. Follow these steps:

1. Expand the **funnel chart** settings in the Visualizations pane.

2. Select the **Expense Category** field in the Fields pane and drag it to the **Group** entry in the funnel chart settings.

3. Drag the **Budget** field below the **Values** field.

   Figure 7-6 shows the resulting visual.

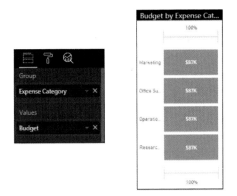

FIGURE 7-6 *Use a funnel chart to illustrate budget by expense category.*

Matrix (budget period, expense categories, total expenses, budget, and budget used)

To convey information such as the budget period, expense categories, total expenses, budget, and budget used, add a matrix to the report. Follow these steps:

1. Expand the **matrix** settings in the Visualizations pane.

2. Select the **Budget Period and Expense Category** fields in the Fields pane and drag them to the **Rows** entry in the matrix settings.

3. Select the **Total Expenses**, **Budget**, and **Budget Used** fields in the Fields pane and drag them to the **Values** entry in the matrix settings.

   Figure 7-7 shows the resulting visual.

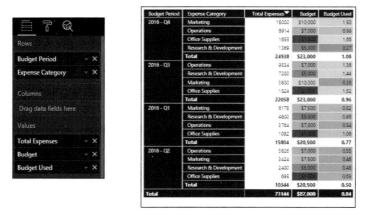

FIGURE 7-7 *Add a matrix to convey the budget period, expense categories, total expenses budget, and budget used.*

Arrange the visuals

After you add all the necessary visualizations to your report, you can arrange them as desired. For help, refer to Chapter 4. Figure 7-8 shows the final report.

> ⚠️ **IMPORTANT** In case you didn't actually build the report, I provided a final version of it for your use: SharePoint Online Final.pbix. As mentioned, you can access this file from the MSPBIDashboards\ch07 folder on the book's companion website.

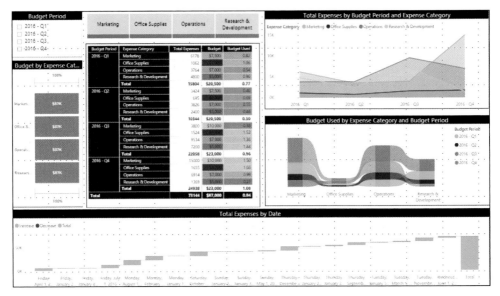

FIGURE 7-8 *Your Power BI report, complete with visuals.*

Prepare the report for mobile view

You can also prepare your report for display on a mobile device, as shown in Figure 7-9. For more details, refer to Chapter 4.

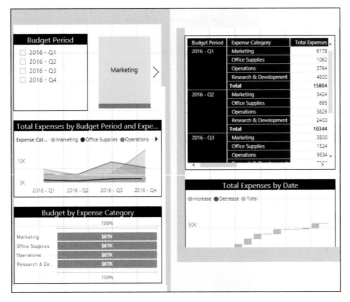

FIGURE 7-9 *Prepare the report for display on a mobile device.*

Publish and view the report

As a final step, you must publish your report for public consumption. This was discussed in detail in Chapter 4. To review, here are the steps you need to take:

1. Open the **File** menu, select **Publish**, and choose **Publish to Power BI**.

2. The Publish to Power BI page opens. Select the workspace on which you want to publish the report. Then click the **Select** button.

   A progress dialog box opens. When the operation is complete, you'll see a success message.

After you publish the report, you can log into your Power BI service account to verify that the report appears in the selected workspace. You can also view the report using the Power BI app on your iOS, Android, or Windows mobile device.

Prepare a dashboard from the report

As discussed in Chapter 1, you can combine visuals from Power BI reports into a custom dynamic dashboard. (See Figure 7-10 for an example of a dashboard.) To review, follow these steps to add a visual in a report to a dashboard:

1. Open the report that contains the visual you want to add to a dashboard.

2. Hover your mouse pointer over the visual you want to add to the dashboard and click the **Pin Visual** button that appears in the visual's upper-right corner.

   The Pin to Dashboard dialog box opens.

3. To create a new dashboard for the visual, select the **New Dashboard** option button and type a name for the new dashboard. Alternatively, select the **Existing Dashboard** option button and choose the desired dashboard.

4. Click the **Pin button** to add the visual to the dashboard.

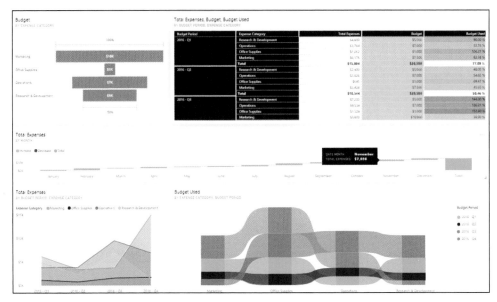

FIGURE 7-10 *Preparing a dashboard from different Power BI reports.*

Build a Power BI report based on data from a SharePoint Online folder

In addition to creating reports based on data from a SharePoint Online list, you can create them from data from a SharePoint Online folder, such as a document library. In this example, data in a document library called **Informative Documents** is used to create the report.

Import data from a SharePoint Online folder into Power BI

To start, you must load data from the SharePoint Online folder into Power BI. Follow these steps:

1. Click the **Home** tab in Power BI Desktop.

2. Click **Get Data**.

3. Choose **Online Services** and select **SharePoint Folder**.

4. Enter the **URL** for the SharePoint Online site that contains the folder from which you want to generate a Power BI report.

5. To sign in to the SharePoint Online site, click the **Microsoft Account** authentication option, click **Sign In**, and enter your username and password.

6. Click **Connect**.

7. You'll see all available files in the SharePoint folder. To load them into Power BI, click **Load**.

In this report, you want to use only the data in the Informative Documents document library as your source data. To achieve this, you'll use the Edit Query option in Power BI. Follow these steps:

1. Switch to Data view in Power BI Desktop.

2. Select **Edit Query** to open the Edit Query window.

   This window contains a Queries pane (see numeral 1 in Figure 7-11), a preview of loaded data (see numeral 2 in Figure 7-11), and a Query Settings pane (see numeral 3 in Figure 7-11).

3. Select the query you want to edit in the Queries pane.

4. Click the **Advanced Editor** option in the Query section of the Ribbon. (See numeral 4 in Figure 7-11.)

   An Edit Query window opens, where you can edit the selected query. (See numeral 5 in Figure 7-11.)

5. Change the Source line of the query to read as follows:

```
Source = SharePoint.Contents("https://{your-tenant-name}.sharepoint.com/sites/demo/
powerbidemo/", [ApiVersion = 15]),
```

   where {your-tenant-name} is the name of your SharePoint tenant.

6. Click **Done**. (See numeral 6 in Figure 7-11.)

7

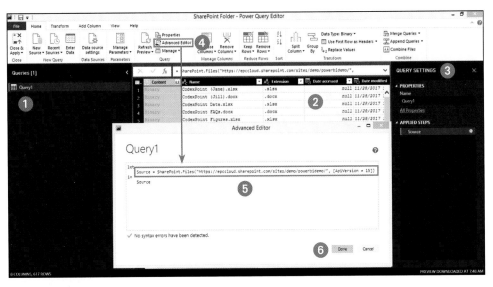

FIGURE 7-11 *Using the Advanced Editor to edit a query.*

Now it's time to generate a report using the Information Documents document library. Follow these steps:

1. In Data view, locate the **Informative Documents** entry in the **Name** column (see numeral 1 in Figure 7-12) and click its corresponding **Table** entry in the **Content** column (see numeral 2 in Figure 7-12).

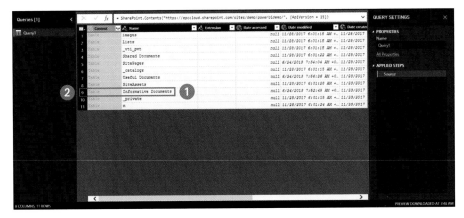

FIGURE 7-12 *Select the Table entry next to Informative Documents.*

Power BI displays data from the Informative Documents library in table form. (See numeral 1 in Figure 7-13.)

> ⚠️ **IMPORTANT** Notice that the Query Settings pane now contains a Navigation entry in the **Applied Steps** section. (See numeral 2 in Figure 7-13.) This refers to an automated step performed by the Power BI query editor.

FIGURE 7-13 *The data from the Informative Documents library in table form.*

2. Click the **Close and Apply** button in the Ribbon to apply the changes to the data model.

Add Power BI visuals to the report

As with the report you created earlier in this chapter, you can add visuals to this report. These might include the following:

- **Slicer** You'll use a slicer to filter by file extension.

- **Multi-row card** A multi-row card will show file count by extension.

- **Pie chart** A pie chart will also show file count by extension.

- **Slicer for date filter** You'll add two slicers for date filters—one to sort files by the date created and one to sort files by the date modified.

- **Table** A table will contain a list of files, their folder path, their extension, the date created, and the date modified.

> ⚠️ **IMPORTANT** Again, for a refresher on adding Power BI visuals to a report, refer to the section "Add visuals" in Chapter 4.

Slicer (file extension)

To add a slicer that filters data by file extension, follow these steps:

1. Expand the **slicer** settings in the Visualizations pane.

2. Select the **Extension** field in the Fields pane and drag it to the **Field** entry in the slicer settings. Figure 7-14 shows the result.

FIGURE 7-14 *Add a slicer to your Power BI report.*

Multi-row card (file count by extension)

To display the file count by extension, you'll add a multi-row card. Follow these steps:

1. Expand the **multi-row card** settings in the Visualizations pane.

2. Select the **Extension** field in the Fields pane and drag it to the **Fields** entry in the multi-row card settings.

3. Drag the **Count of File Name** field below the **Extension** field. Figure 7-15 shows the result.

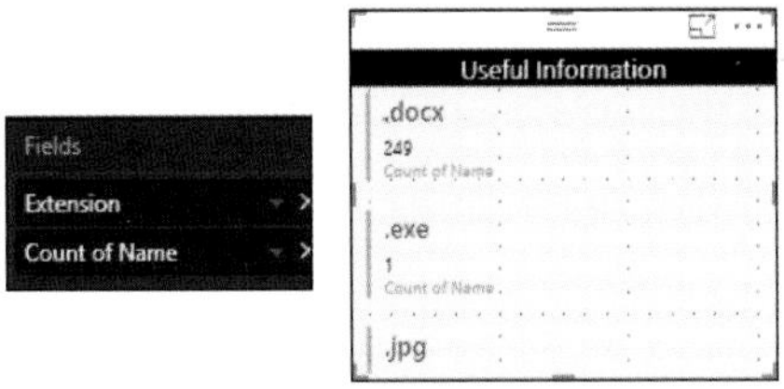

FIGURE 7-15 *Add a multi-row card to your Power BI report.*

Pie chart (file count by extension)

To show the file count by extension in pie-chart form, follow these steps:

1. Expand the **pie chart** settings in the Visualizations pane.

2. Select the **Extension** field in the Fields pane and drag it to the **Legend** entry in the pie chart settings.

3. Select the **Count of Name** field in the Fields pane and drag it to the **Values** entry in the pie chart settings. Figure 7-16 shows the result.

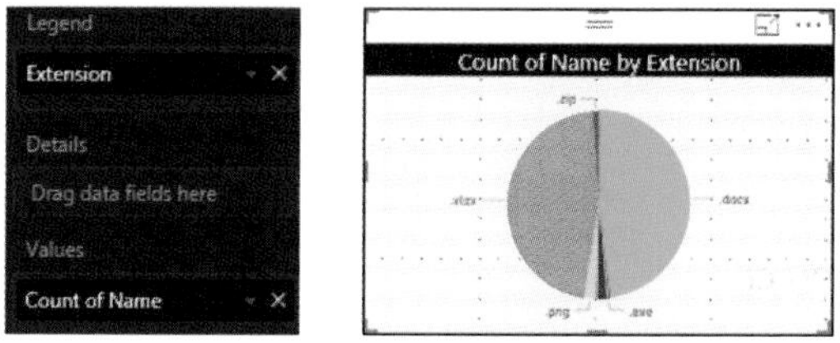

FIGURE 7-16 *Add a pie chart to your Power BI report.*

Slicer for date filter (date created, date modified)

Here, you'll add two slicer for date filters—one to sort by date created and one to sort by date modified. Follow these steps:

1. Expand the **slicer for date** settings in the Visualizations pane.

2. Select the **Date Created** field in the Fields pane and drag it to the **Field** entry in the slicer for date settings.

3. Repeat steps 1 and 2 for the **Date Modified** field. Figure 7-17 shows the result.

FIGURE 7-17 *Add a slicer to your Power BI report.*

Table (name, folder path, extension, date created, date modified)

To create a table that includes file names, folder paths, file extensions, date created, and date modified, follow these steps:

1. Expand the **table** settings in the Visualizations pane.

2. Select the **Name**, **Folder Path**, **Extension**, **Date Created**, and **Date Modified** fields in the Fields pane and drag them to the **Values** entry in the table settings. Figure 7-18 shows the result.

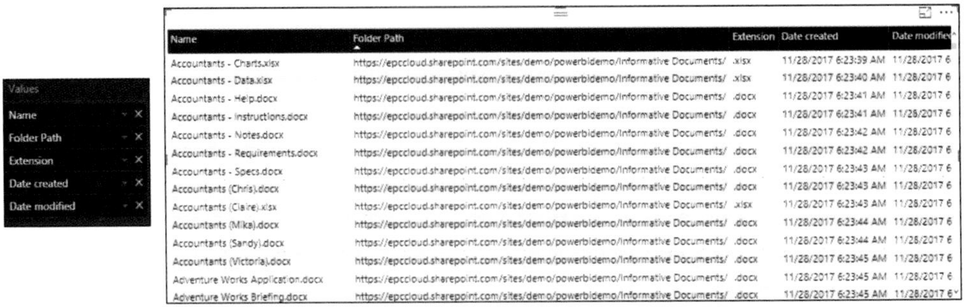

Name	Folder Path	Extension	Date created	Date modified
Accountants - Charts.xlsx	https://epccloud.sharepoint.com/sites/demo/powerbidemo/Informative Documents/	.xlsx	11/28/2017 6:23:39 AM	11/28/2017 6
Accountants - Data.xlsx	https://epccloud.sharepoint.com/sites/demo/powerbidemo/Informative Documents/	.xlsx	11/28/2017 6:23:40 AM	11/28/2017 6
Accountants - Help.docx	https://epccloud.sharepoint.com/sites/demo/powerbidemo/Informative Documents/	.docx	11/28/2017 6:23:41 AM	11/28/2017 6
Accountants - Instructions.docx	https://epccloud.sharepoint.com/sites/demo/powerbidemo/Informative Documents/	.docx	11/28/2017 6:23:41 AM	11/28/2017 6
Accountants - Notes.docx	https://epccloud.sharepoint.com/sites/demo/powerbidemo/Informative Documents/	.docx	11/28/2017 6:23:42 AM	11/28/2017 6
Accountants - Requirements.docx	https://epccloud.sharepoint.com/sites/demo/powerbidemo/Informative Documents/	.docx	11/28/2017 6:23:42 AM	11/28/2017 6
Accountants - Specs.docx	https://epccloud.sharepoint.com/sites/demo/powerbidemo/Informative Documents/	.docx	11/28/2017 6:23:43 AM	11/28/2017 6
Accountants (Chris).docx	https://epccloud.sharepoint.com/sites/demo/powerbidemo/Informative Documents/	.docx	11/28/2017 6:23:43 AM	11/28/2017 6
Accountants (Claire).xlsx	https://epccloud.sharepoint.com/sites/demo/powerbidemo/Informative Documents/	.xlsx	11/28/2017 6:23:43 AM	11/28/2017 6
Accountants (Mika).docx	https://epccloud.sharepoint.com/sites/demo/powerbidemo/Informative Documents/	.docx	11/28/2017 6:23:44 AM	11/28/2017 6
Accountants (Sandy).docx	https://epccloud.sharepoint.com/sites/demo/powerbidemo/Informative Documents/	.docx	11/28/2017 6:23:44 AM	11/28/2017 6
Accountants (Victoria).docx	https://epccloud.sharepoint.com/sites/demo/powerbidemo/Informative Documents/	.docx	11/28/2017 6:23:45 AM	11/28/2017 6
Adventure Works Application.docx	https://epccloud.sharepoint.com/sites/demo/powerbidemo/Informative Documents/	.docx	11/28/2017 6:23:45 AM	11/28/2017 6
Adventure Works Briefing.docx	https://epccloud.sharepoint.com/sites/demo/powerbidemo/Informative Documents/	.docx	11/28/2017 6:23:45 AM	11/28/2017 6

FIGURE 7-18 *Add a table to your Power BI report.*

Arrange the visuals

After you add all the necessary visualizations to your report, you can arrange them as desired. (See Figure 7-19.)

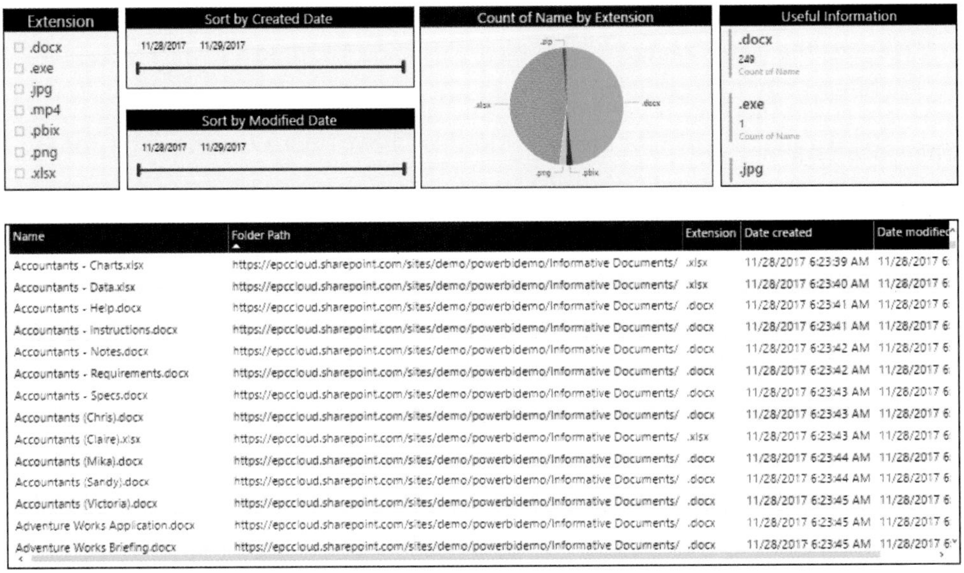

Name	Folder Path	Extension	Date created	Date modified
Accountants - Charts.xlsx	https://epccloud.sharepoint.com/sites/demo/powerbidemo/Informative Documents/	.xlsx	11/28/2017 6:23:39 AM	11/28/2017 6:
Accountants - Data.xlsx	https://epccloud.sharepoint.com/sites/demo/powerbidemo/Informative Documents/	.xlsx	11/28/2017 6:23:40 AM	11/28/2017 6:
Accountants - Help.docx	https://epccloud.sharepoint.com/sites/demo/powerbidemo/Informative Documents/	.docx	11/28/2017 6:23:41 AM	11/28/2017 6:
Accountants - Instructions.docx	https://epccloud.sharepoint.com/sites/demo/powerbidemo/Informative Documents/	.docx	11/28/2017 6:23:41 AM	11/28/2017 6:
Accountants - Notes.docx	https://epccloud.sharepoint.com/sites/demo/powerbidemo/Informative Documents/	.docx	11/28/2017 6:23:42 AM	11/28/2017 6:
Accountants - Requirements.docx	https://epccloud.sharepoint.com/sites/demo/powerbidemo/Informative Documents/	.docx	11/28/2017 6:23:42 AM	11/28/2017 6:
Accountants - Specs.docx	https://epccloud.sharepoint.com/sites/demo/powerbidemo/Informative Documents/	.docx	11/28/2017 6:23:43 AM	11/28/2017 6:
Accountants (Chris).docx	https://epccloud.sharepoint.com/sites/demo/powerbidemo/Informative Documents/	.docx	11/28/2017 6:23:43 AM	11/28/2017 6:
Accountants (Claire).xlsx	https://epccloud.sharepoint.com/sites/demo/powerbidemo/Informative Documents/	.xlsx	11/28/2017 6:23:43 AM	11/28/2017 6:
Accountants (Mika).docx	https://epccloud.sharepoint.com/sites/demo/powerbidemo/Informative Documents/	.docx	11/28/2017 6:23:44 AM	11/28/2017 6:
Accountants (Sandy).docx	https://epccloud.sharepoint.com/sites/demo/powerbidemo/Informative Documents/	.docx	11/28/2017 6:23:44 AM	11/28/2017 6:
Accountants (Victoria).docx	https://epccloud.sharepoint.com/sites/demo/powerbidemo/Informative Documents/	.docx	11/28/2017 6:23:45 AM	11/28/2017 6:
Adventure Works Application.docx	https://epccloud.sharepoint.com/sites/demo/powerbidemo/Informative Documents/	.docx	11/28/2017 6:23:45 AM	11/28/2017 6:
Adventure Works Briefing.docx	https://epccloud.sharepoint.com/sites/demo/powerbidemo/Informative Documents/	.docx	11/28/2017 6:23:45 AM	11/28/2017 6:

FIGURE 7-19 *Your Power BI report, complete with visuals.*

> **IMPORTANT** In case you didn't actually build the report, I provided a final version of it for your use: SharePoint Folder Final.pbix. As mentioned, you can access this file from the MSPBIDashboards\ch07 folder on the book's companion website.

Prepare the report for mobile view

To prepare your report for mobile display, see Chapter 4.

Publish and view the report

As a final step, you must publish your report for public consumption. This was discussed earlier in this chapter in the discussion about creating a report from a SharePoint Online list, as well as in Chapter 4.

Prepare a dashboard from the report

You can combine visuals from Power BI reports into a custom dynamic dashboard. This was discussed earlier in this chapter in the discussion about creating a report from a SharePoint Online list, as well as in Chapter 1.

7

Refresh report data in a Power BI report

You can configure your report to refresh automatically to show the most up-to-date data. Here's how:

1. Open Power BI service.

2. Open the workspace that contains the report you want to refresh automatically (in this example, **Temp Workspace**).

3. In the **Datasets** section, hover your mouse pointer over the report you want to refresh (in this example, **Power BI Report1**) and click the ellipsis that appears. (See Figure 7-20.)

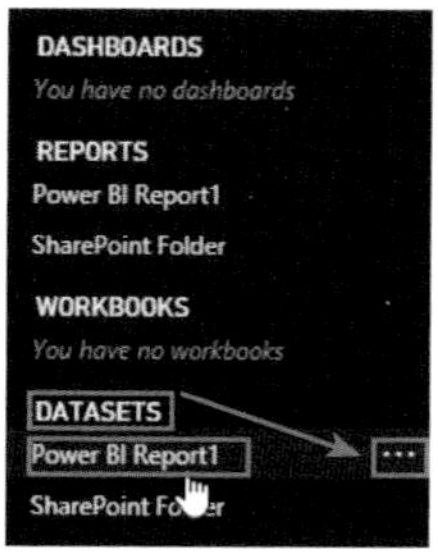

FIGURE 7-20 *Hover your mouse pointer over the report you want to refresh and click the ellipsis that appears.*

A window for the Power BI Report 1 report opens.

4. Click **Schedule Refresh**. (See Figure 7-21.)

FIGURE 7-21 *Click Schedule Refresh in the Power BI Report 1 window.*

5. In the window that opens, expand the **Gateway Connection** section.

Power BI displays a message indicating that you don't need a gateway for this dataset because all of its data sources are in the cloud, but you could use a gateway for enhanced control over how you connect. (See Figure 7-22.)

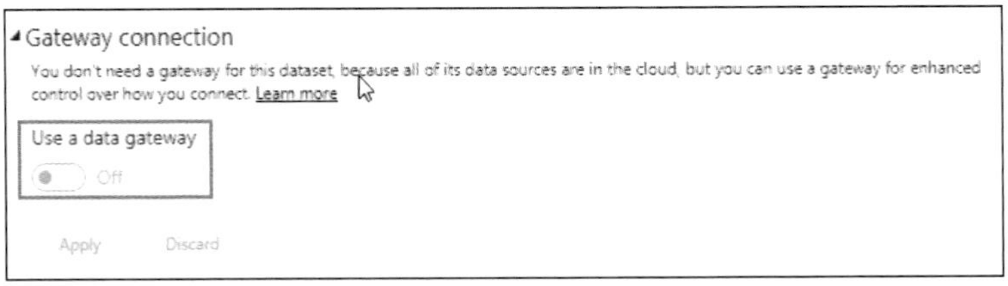

FIGURE 7-22 *Select whether to use a data gateway under Gateway Connection.*

6. Expand the **Data Source** section and click the **Edit Credential** option.

A window opens in which you can sign in to the SharePoint Online site.

7. Open the **Authentication Method** drop-down list and choose **OAuth2**.

8. Click the **Sign In** button and enter your username and password.

After you have successfully logged in, you'll return to the Schedule Refresh page, where you'll see a message that reads **Data Source Updated**.

9. Under **Scheduled Refresh**, toggle the **Keep Your Data Up to Date** setting to **On**.

10. Open the **Refresh Frequency** drop-down list and select how often you want to refresh the data.

11. Open the **Time Zone** drop-down list and indicate your time zone.

12. Click **Apply**. (See Figure 7-23.)

▲ Scheduled refresh

Keep your data up to date

⬤ On

Refresh frequency

| Daily ▼ |

Time zone

| (UTC) Coordinated Universal Time ▼ |

Time

Add another time

☑ Send refresh failure notification email to me

Apply   Discard

7

FIGURE 7-23 *The Scheduled Refresh settings.*

To find out when the last refresh occurred, follow these steps:

1. Click **Data source**.

2. Click the **Refresh History** link to see detailed information about recent schedule refresh operations. (See Figure 7-24.)

FIGURE 7-24 *Checking refresh history for a dataset in Power BI.*

Embed Power BI reports in SharePoint Online

You can embed reports you create in Power BI in a SharePoint Online page—*if* you have a Power BI Pro license. Here's how:

1. In Power BI service, open the Power BI report you want to embed.

2. Open the **File** menu and choose **Embed in SharePoint Online**. (See Figure 7-25.)

> ⚠️ **IMPORTANT** If your Power BI portal does not show this option, contact your administrator to enable it.

FIGURE 7-25 *Embed a Power BI report in SharePoint Online.*

Power BI displays a URL. You'll use this URL to embed the report in SharePoint Online.

3. Copy the **URL**.

4. Open the SharePoint Online page in which you want to embed the report.

5. Click the + button and select **Power BI** from the menu that appears. (See Figure 7-26.)

> ⚠️ **IMPORTANT** The Power BI option is accessible only in modern SharePoint pages. Classical SharePoint pages do not have this option.

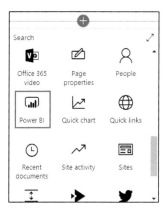

FIGURE 7-26 *The SharePoint page with the Power BI menu option selected.*

6. Click **Add Report**.

7. A Power BI window opens. (See Figure 7-27.) In the **Power BI Report Link** field, paste the URL you copied in step 3.

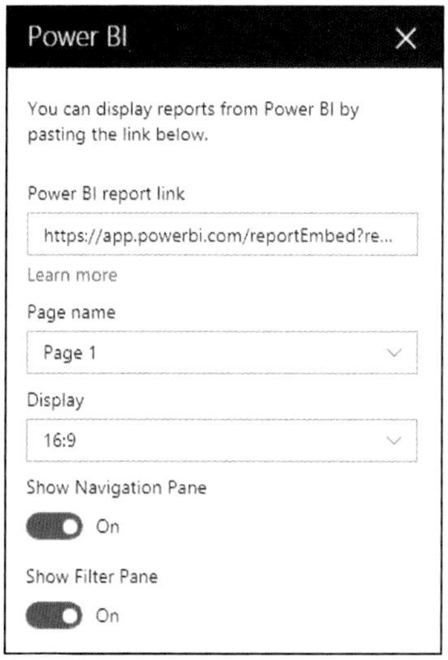

FIGURE 7-27 *The Power BI window in SharePoint Online.*

8. Open the **Page Name** drop-down list and choose which page of the report the user should see first.

9. Open the **Display** drop-down list and choose a display setting. This setting will dictate how the report fits within the SharePoint Online page.

10. To show the report's navigation pane, toggle the **Navigation Pane** setting to **On**. To hide the pane, toggle the setting to **Off**.

11. To show the report's filter pane, toggle the **Filter Pane** setting to **On**. To hide the pane, toggle the setting to **Off**.

The Power BI report appears on the SharePoint Online page. (See Figure 7-28.)

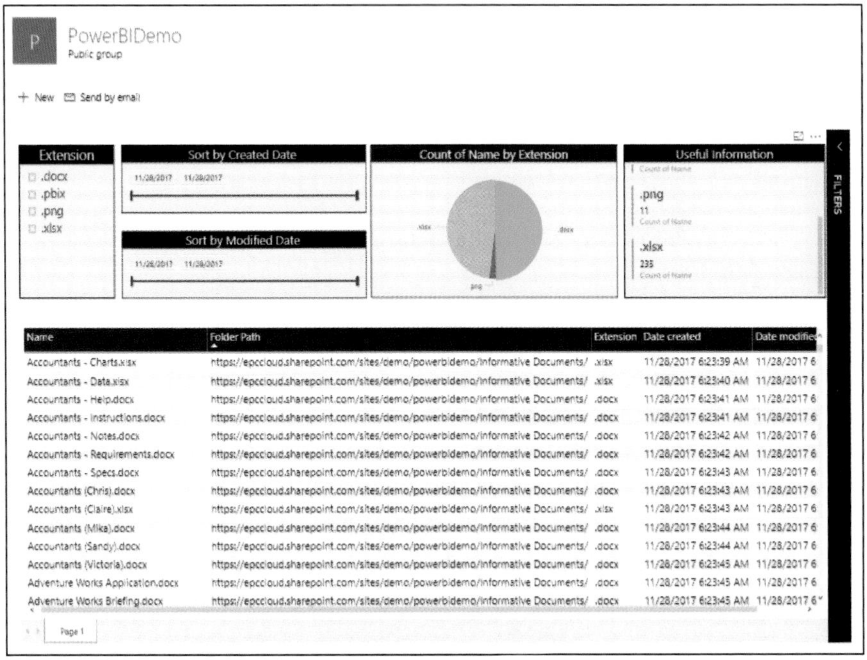

FIGURE 7-28 *The Power BI report embedded in SharePoint Online.*

Power BI service provides the functionality to refresh data at specific intervals of time. This helps to update the data sources and refresh Power BI reports accordingly.

Skills review

In this chapter, you learned about:

- Building a Power BI report based on data from a SharePoint Online list
- Building a Power BI report based on data from a SharePoint Online folder
- Refreshing the data source in Power BI service
- Embedding Power BI reports in SharePoint Online

Practice tasks

This section provides a simple case study for you to study and solve using information from this chapter. This section also contains a series of practice questions for you to answer.

Case study

Suppose you work for a hospital whose SharePoint Online intranet portal consists of anonymous patient data for clinical trials. The data is segregated according to disease category. Therefore, different wards have distinct categories of data to represent patient problems.

You want to build a report that analyzes the following:

- Patient data that is stored in different lists

- Patient historical data that has been cleansed for HIPAA and PHI compliance contained in a different document library

To build this report, you'll need the following data:

- The number of high-priority patients admitted in the hospital

- The highest number of patients admitted chronologically according to disease for the year 2017

- A general comparison showing the number of patients admitted last year versus the number of patients admitted in the current year

- Patient data segregated by age

- Most common diseases among children

- Most common diseases among adults

- Most commonly administered vaccines for admitted patients

Practice questions

1. What is the general process of importing a SharePoint Online list?

2. How do you sign in to SharePoint Online when you connect via Power BI?

3. How do you establish a connection with a SharePoint Online document library?

4. How do you create a Power BI report from data in a SharePoint Online folder?

5. Suppose you import two SharePoint Online lists with one common column. How do you establish a relationship between these common columns?

6. How do you set up Power BI to automatically refresh report data?

7. How do you embed a Power BI report in SharePoint Online?

Develop Power BI reports from SharePoint On-Premises

In this chapter, you'll learn how to develop a Power BI report that relies on data from SharePoint On-Premises as its source. (Unlike SharePoint Online, which stores data on the cloud at Microsoft-managed data centers, SharePoint On-Premises is stored in a data center managed by your IT department.) You'll also learn how to set up and configure a data gateway to enable Power BI users to access SharePoint On-Premises data more easily.

In this chapter:

- Import data from a SharePoint On-Premises list into Power BI
- Create a Power BI report
- Set up a data gateway
- Configure Power BI to use the data gateway and set up data refresh functionality

Practice files

As you work through this chapter, you'll use three practice files, which you can access from the MSPBIDashboards\ch08 on the book's companion website at *https://aka.ms/PowerBIDash/downloads*. The files are as follows:

- **Expense Budget.stp and Expense.stp** You used these files in Chapter 7. They contain dummy data for an expense budget and an expense list, respectively. You'll use them in the section "Import data from a SharePoint On-Premises list into Power BI" next in this chapter.

- **Expense - SharePoint On Premises.pbix** This file is a sample Power BI report prepared from a SharePoint On-Premises list that contains various visuals. Note that it's the same as the report you created in Chapter 7. You'll use this file in the section "Prepare a Power BI report from a SharePoint On-Premises list" later in this chapter. You can access this file from the MSPBIDashboards\ch08 folder on the book's companion website.

Import data from a SharePoint On-Premises list into Power BI

In this section, you'll learn how to load data from SharePoint On-Premises into Power BI. For the sake of simplicity, the lists used here are the same as the lists you imported in Chapter 7: Expense Budget.stp and Expense.stp. You'll want to load these files into your SharePoint On-Premises environment before you continue with this section. (See Figure 8-1.)

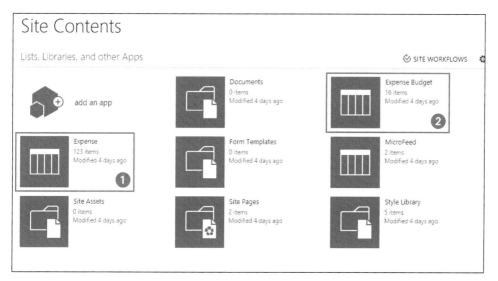

FIGURE 8-1 *You'll import these lists from SharePoint On-Premises into Power BI.*

To load data from SharePoint On-Premises lists to Power BI, follow these steps:

1. Click the **Home** tab in Power BI Desktop.

2. Click **Get Data**.

3. Choose **Other** and select **SharePoint List**. (See screen 1 in Figure 8-2.)

4. Enter the **URL** for the SharePoint On-Premises site that contains the lists from which you want to generate a Power BI report. (See screen 2 in Figure 8-2.)

5. When prompted to select an authentication method, choose **Windows** and, if SharePoint On-Premises is installed on the local machine, select the **Use My Current Credentials** option button. (See screen 3 in Figure 8-2.)

   Alternatively, if SharePoint On-Premises is installed on another machine, select the **Use Alternate Credentials** option button, and enter the desired username and password in the appropriate boxes.

6. Click **Connect**.

7. Select the files you want to import (in this example, **Expense Budget** and **Expense**) and click **Load**. (See screen 4 in Figure 8-2.)

FIGURE 8-2 *Importing data from SharePoint On-Premises into Power BI.*

Power BI loads the files, including all their internal and external columns.

8. If either file contains a column you don't want to include in your report, right-click that column and choose **Delete**.

Create a Power BI report

You prepare a Power BI report from a SharePoint On-Premises list the same way you do a report from a SharePoint Online list. Rather than rehash those steps here, we'll just use the same report you created in Chapter 7. (See Figure 8-3.)

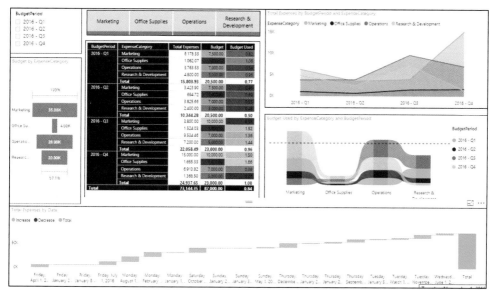

FIGURE 8-3 *You can use the same Power BI report you created in Chapter 7 here.*

8

> ⚠️ **IMPORTANT** In case you didn't actually create the report in Chapter 7, I provided a final version of it for your use here: Expense - SharePoint On Premises.pbix. As mentioned, you can access this file from the MSPBIDashboards\ch08 folder on the book's companion website.

Set up a data gateway

You use a data gateway to establish a secure connection between SharePoint On-Premises and Power BI. Through this secure connection, Power BI reports generated from SharePoint On-Premises data remain up to date. In essence, the gateway acts as a bridge between SharePoint On-Premises and Power BI (as well as other Microsoft tools such as PowerApps, Logic Apps, and Microsoft Flow).

To use a data gateway, you must install it on your computer. This machine must meet the following minimum requirements:

- .NET 4.6 Framework

- 64-bit version of Windows 7 or Windows Server 2008 R2 or later (64-bit version of Windows 2012 R2 or later recommended).

In addition, Microsoft recommends that your computer have at least 8 GB memory and an 8-core CPU.

Before you install the data gateway, keep these points in mind:

- You must publish your report to Power BI service before setting up the data gateway.

- You need not have Analysis Services to use the data gateway. You can use the gateway to connect to an Analysis Services data source.

- You cannot install a data gateway on a domain controller.

- You should not install a data gateway on a laptop or PC that could fall asleep, be turned off, or be disconnected from the Internet.

- To apply Windows Authentication, the machine on which you install the data gateway must be a member of the same AD as the data source.

Install the data gateway

Follow these steps to install a data gateway:

1. Type *http://go.microsoft.com/fwlink/?LinkID=820925* in your web browser's address bar to launch the data gateway installer.

2. Right-click the installer and click **Open**. Then click **Next** to start the installation.

   The installer prompts you to select the type of data gateway you want to install. You have two choices (see Figure 8-4):

   - **On-Premises Data Gateway (Recommended)** This type of gateway can be shared and reused by multiple users; can be used by Power BI, PowerApps, Logic Apps, and Microsoft Flow; and supports scheduled refreshes and live queries. (Throughout the rest of this book I frequently refer to this type of gateway as a shared gateway.)

   - **On-Premises Data Gateway (Personal Mode)** This type of gateway can be used only by a specific user, can be used only in Power BI, and supports only scheduled refreshes.

FIGURE 8-4 *Choose whether you want to set up a shared or personal data gateway.*

> ⚠️ **IMPORTANT** You can install only one shared data gateway and one personal data gateway on your system. However, you can install multiple data gateways on different systems. You can then manage these gateways from within Power BI using a single gateway management interface. You'll learn more about this in the section "Configure Power BI to use the data gateway" later in this chapter.

3. In this case, select the **On-Premises Data Gateway (Recommended)** option button and click **Next**.

> ⚠️ **IMPORTANT** In this chapter, you install a shared data gateway, which can be accessed by other users. You'll learn how to install a personal data gateway in Chapter 9.

A pop-up window informs you that it's best to install the gateway on a computer that is always on and warns you that the gateway will perform more slowly on a wireless network.

4. Click **Next** to close the pop-up window.

5. Enter the installation path and accept the terms and conditions. Then click **Next**.

6. Enter the email address associated with your Power BI Pro account and click **Sign In**.

   The installer prompts you to register the gateway. (See Figure 8-5.)

7. Type a name for the data gateway. This can be any name you like. In this example, type **SharePoint On Premise Gateway** in the **Name** box.

8. Type a recovery key in the **Recovery Key** box. Then retype it in the **Confirm Recovery Key** box.

   The recovery key must be at least eight characters long. You'll use it to recover the data gateway if it fails.

9. Click **Configure**.

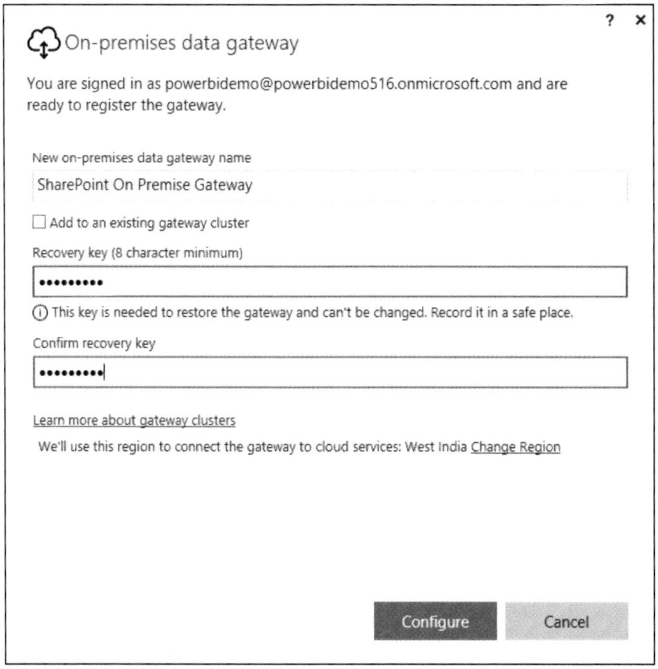

FIGURE 8-5 *Register the data gateway.*

The installer displays a message indicating that the data gateway is online and ready for use. (See Figure 8-6.)

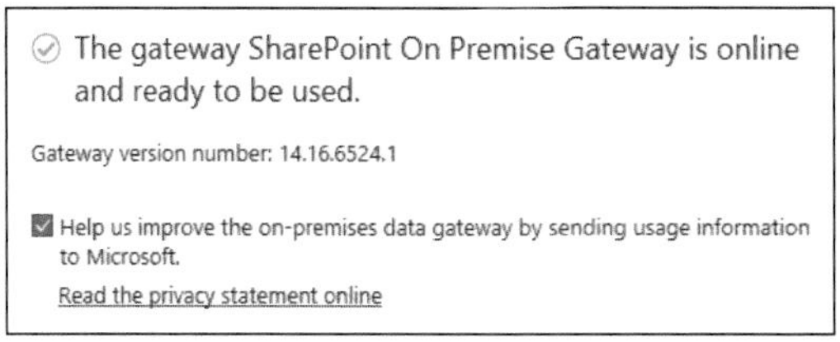

FIGURE 8-6 *The data gateway is online and ready for use.*

Explore the data gateway

Before you set up Power BI to connect with the data gateway, let's take a moment to explore it. To open the data gateway, follow these steps:

1. Click the **Start** button on your Windows desktop.

2. Type **gateway** in the Start menu's search box.

3. Click the entry for the data gateway in the list that appears.

The data gateway interface includes the following screens:

- **Status** As shown in Figure 8-7, this screen indicates the status of the data gateway, including its readiness for use with Logic Apps, PowerApps, Microsoft Flow, and Power BI.

FIGURE 8-7 *The data gateway's Status screen.*

- **Service Settings** As shown in Figure 8-8, this screen contains two sections:

  - **Restart the Gateway** To implement changes made to the gateway configuration files, you must restart the gateway. To do so, click the **Restart Now** link under Restart the Gateway.

- **Gateway Service Account** To change the service account associated with the data gateway (which is **NT SERVICE\PBIEgwService** by default), click the **Change Account** link under Gateway Service Account.

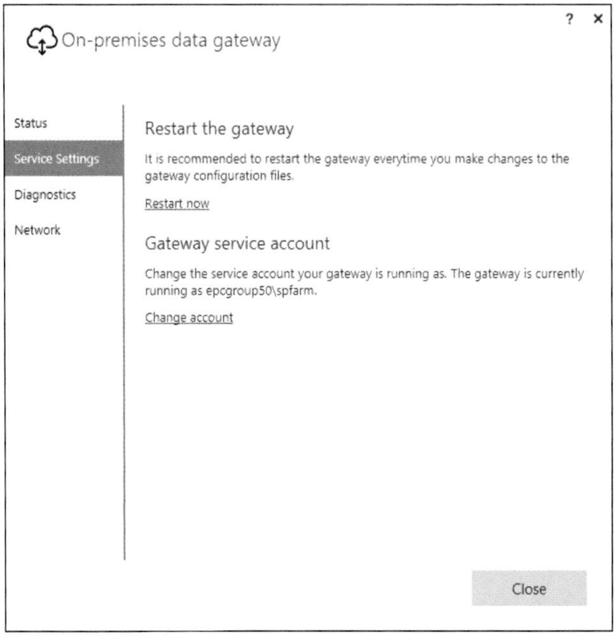

FIGURE 8-8 *The data gateway's Service Settings screen.*

- **Diagnostics** As shown in Figure 8-9, this screen contains two options:

  - **Additional Logging** Toggle this option on to better assess the performance of the data gateway. To learn more about this setting, click the **Learn More** link under Additional Logging.

  - **Gateway Logs** Click the **Export Logs** link under Gateway Logs to export all the data gateway's configuration and service logs to a single ZIP file.

- **Network** As shown in Figure 8-10, this screen contains two options that relate to the data gateway network connection:

  - **Network Status** This shows the status of the network connection. To check whether the gateway reaches outside the network, click the **Check Now** link under Network Status.

  - **HTTPS Mode** Toggle this option on to force the gateway to communicate using HTTPS instead of TCP. For more information on these options, click the **Learn More** link under HTTPS Mode.

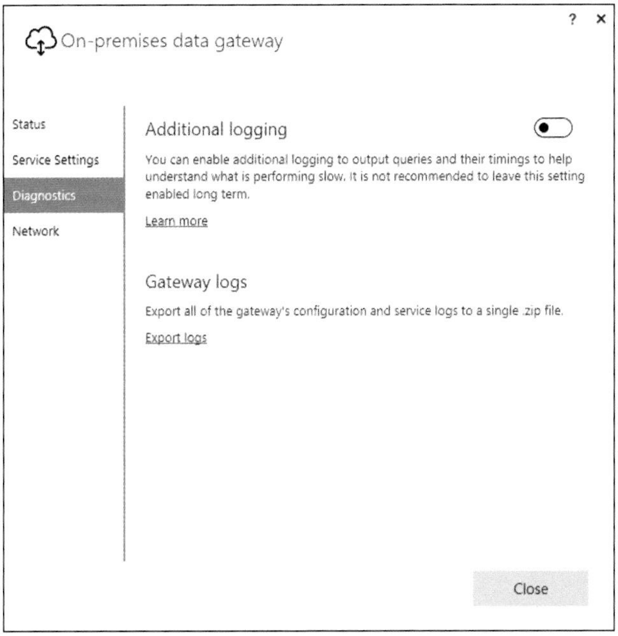

FIGURE 8-9 *The data gateway's Diagnostics screen.*

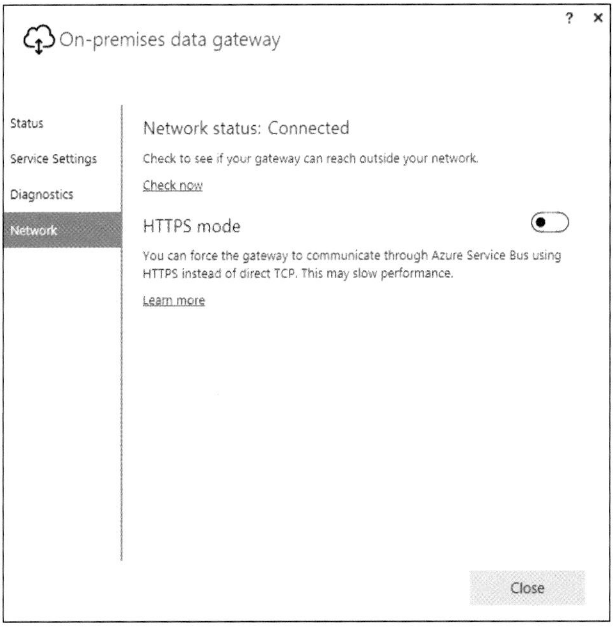

FIGURE 8-10 *The data gateway's Network screen.*

Configure Power BI to use the data gateway and set up refresh functionality

After you set up your data gateway, you need to configure Power BI to use it. Follow these steps:

> ⚠️ **IMPORTANT** This section shows you how to configure Power BI to use a shared data gateway, which, again, can be used by other users. To learn how to configure Power BI to use a personal data gateway, see Chapter 9.

1. Log in to Power BI service.

2. Under **Datasets**, hover your mouse pointer over the Expense report you created using data from SharePoint On-Premises, click the ellipsis that appears, and click **Schedule Refresh**. (See Figure 8-11.)

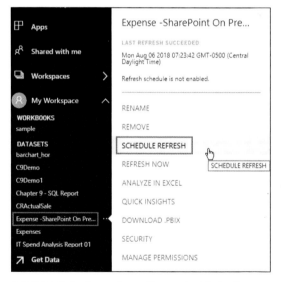

FIGURE 8-11 *Setting up Power BI to work with the data gateway.*

3. In the Settings window that opens for the report, expand the **Gateway Connection** section, and click the **Manage Gateways** link. (See Figure 8-12.)

FIGURE 8-12 *Click the Manage Gateways link under Gateway Connection.*

The Gateway Cluster Settings window opens. (See Figure 8-13.)

4. Click the **Add Data Sources to Use the Gateway** link.

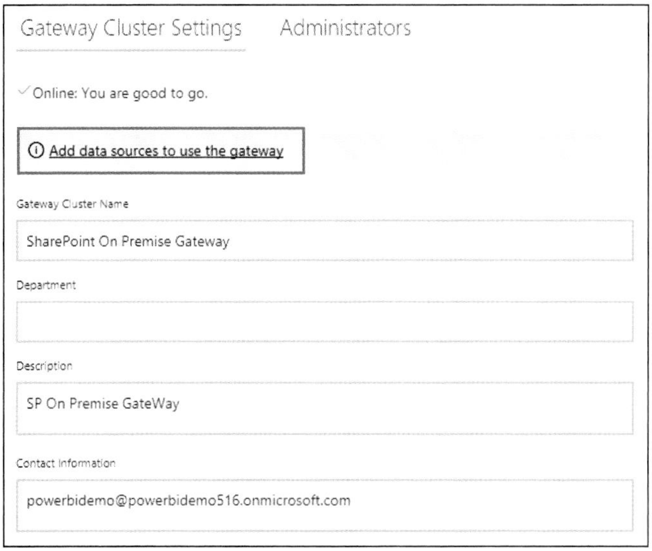

FIGURE 8-13 *Click the Add Data Sources to Use the Gateway link in the Gateway Cluster Settings window.*

The Data Source Settings window opens. (See Figure 8-14.)

5. Type a name for the data source in the **Data Source Name** box.

6. Open the **Data Source Type** drop-down list and choose SharePoint.

7. Enter the **URL** for the SharePoint site in the **SharePoint Site URL** box.

8. Open the **Authentication Method** drop-down list and choose **Windows**.

9. Type your **SharePoint On-Premises** username in the **Username** box.

10. Type your password in the **Password** box.

11. Click **Add**.

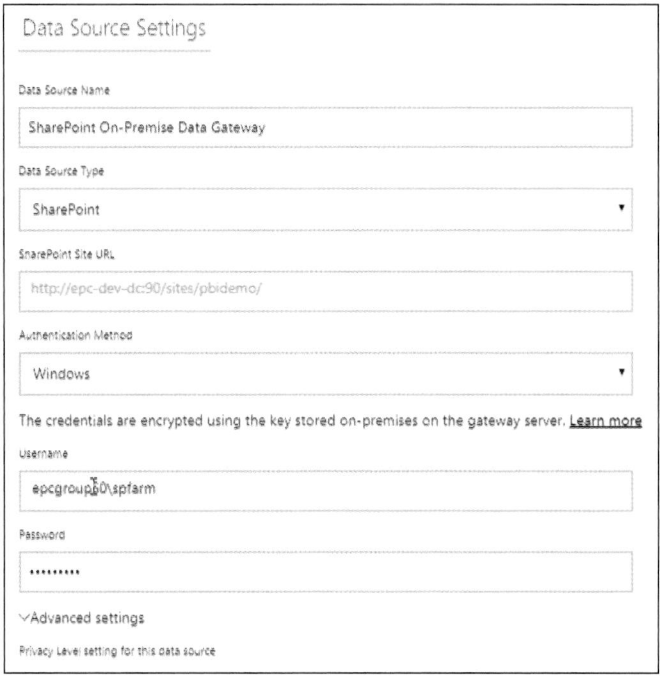

FIGURE 8-14 *Enter the requested information in the Data Source Settings window to configure the data gateway connection.*

The Data Source Settings window should indicate that the connection to the data gateway was successful. (See screen 1 in Figure 8-15.) Your next step is to specify which users may use the data gateway.

12. Click the Users tab. (Refer to screen 2 in Figure 8-15.)

13. To allow someone permission to use the data gateway, type that person's email address in the People Who Can Publish Reports That Use This Data Source box and click Add.

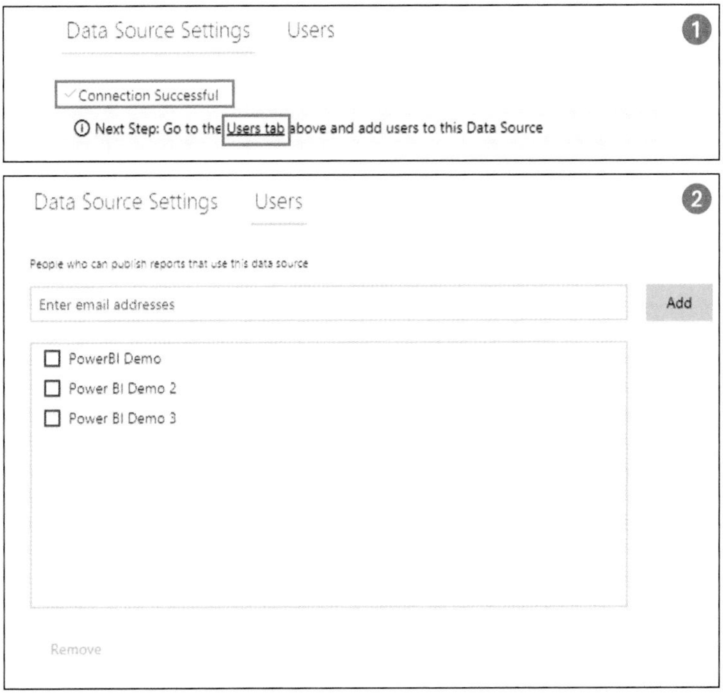

Data Source Settings   Users   ①

✓ Connection Successful

ⓘ Next Step: Go to the Users tab above and add users to this Data Source

---

Data Source Settings   Users   ②

People who can publish reports that use this data source

Enter email addresses   Add

☐ PowerBI Demo
☐ Power BI Demo 2
☐ Power BI Demo 3

Remove

FIGURE 8-15 *The connection was successful.*

14. In the Settings window for the report, under Gateway Connection, select the **Use a Data Gateway** option button, select the gateway you want to use, and click **Apply**. (See Figure 8-16.)

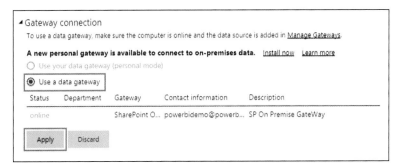

FIGURE 8-16 *Select the Use a Data Gateway option button and click Apply.*

You'll see a Connection Updated message.

15. Expand the **Data Source Credentials** section in the Settings window to see the status of the connection. (See Figure 8-17.)

FIGURE 8-17 *The Data Source Credentials section.*

As a final step, you need to set up the report to refresh automatically through the data gateway.

16. Expand the **Scheduled Refresh** section in the Settings window.

17. Toggle the **Keep Your Data Up to Date** setting to **On**.

18. Open the **Refresh Frequency** drop-down list and select how often you want to refresh the data.

19. Open the **Time Zone** drop-down list and indicate your time zone.

20. Click **Apply**.

Skills review

In this chapter, you learned about:

- Importing data from a SharePoint On-Premises list into Power BI
- Creating a Power BI report from SharePoint On-Premises data
- Setting up a data gateway
- Configuring Power BI to use the data gateway and setting up data refresh functionality

Practice tasks

This section provides a simple case study for you to study and solve using information from this chapter. This section also contains a series of practice questions for you to answer.

Case study

Suppose you work for an organization known for its surround-sound technology. This organization is the leader across several different categories, including the following:

- Broadcast and pro audio products
- Home theater products
- Products to enhance the cinematic experience
- Products to enhance audio and video conferencing
- Products for mobile technology
- Audio-visual receivers
- Products for game development

You want to build a report from data stored in SharePoint On-Premises lists to analyze the following:

- The highest-selling category for your brand for the year 2017
- A comparison of different categories of products sold on a quarter-by-quarter basis
- Top-selling products by region
- Brand popularity by customer age group

Practice questions

1. How do you import a SharePoint On-Premises list into Power BI?

2. How do you refresh data in a Power BI report whose data source is a SharePoint On-Premises list?

3. What is a data gateway?

4. How do you set up a data gateway in SharePoint On-Premises?

5. What are the two types of data gateways?

6. What service is used by default to configure a data gateway in Power BI?

7. How do you set up scheduled refreshes in Power BI service?

Develop Power BI reports from SQL

In this chapter, you'll learn how to develop a Power BI report that relies on data from a SQL Server database as its source. You'll also learn how to set up and configure a data gateway to enable Power BI users to access SQL Server database data through a live database connection and schedule refresh operations, as well as how to configure Row-Level Security (RLS) to restrict access to the report to authorized users only.

In this chapter:

- Import data from a SQL Server database into Power BI
- Create a Power BI report
- Set up a data gateway
- Configure Row-Level Security (RLS)

Practice files

As you work through this chapter, you'll use two practice files, which you can access from the MSPBIDashboards\ch09 on the book's companion website at *https://aka.ms/PowerBIDash/downloads*. The files are as follows:

- **SQLSERVER Sample Report for HR.pbix** This file is a sample Power BI report that consists of HR data including employee names, department, job title, login count, total employees, and associated shifts. You'll use this report in the "Create a Power BI report" section later in this chapter.

- **Sample Report with RLS.pbix** This file is a sample Power BI report containing a list of all employees in an organization filtered by department. You'll use this file in the section "Configure Row-Level Security (RLS) in Power BI" later in this chapter.

Import data from a SQL Server database into Power BI

There are two ways to import data from a SQL Server database into Power BI:

- **Import mode** When you use import mode to import data, that data is cached from the database into Power BI. To ensure you are working with the latest data, you will need to refresh it on a regular basis.

- **DirectQuery mode** DirectQuery does not explicitly import data into Power BI. Rather, it maintains a connection between Power BI and the SQL Server database. When you build a report in Power BI using this data, it will update in real time.

Table 9-1 shows other key differences between these two import modes.

Table 9-1 *Import mode versus DirectQuery mode*

Import mode	DirectQuery mode
Import operations involving large sets of data occur more quickly.	Import operations involving large sets of data occur more slowly.
Large datasets require significant time to refresh upon update.	Current data is used at all times.
Data can be refreshed only eight times per day for Power BI Free and Pro users.	Current data is used at all times.
Data may sometimes become "stale."	Current data is used at all times.
Operations involving the use of DAX expressions are calculated more quickly.	Operations involving the use of DAX expressions are calculated more slowly.
You can connect to multiple databases from the same Power BI server.	You cannot connect to multiple databases from the same Power BI server.
Data in tables can be from different databases.	Data in tables must be from the same database.
Time Intelligence functions are supported.	Time Intelligence functions are not supported.
Errors are generally easy to solve.	Errors are sometimes difficult to solve.
You can use the Query Editor with data imported using import mode.	You cannot use the Query Editor with DirectQuery mode.

9

> ⚠ **IMPORTANT** For more information about the benefits and drawbacks of using DirectQuery, see *https://docs.microsoft.com/en-us/power-bi/desktop-use-directquery.*

> ⚠ **IMPORTANT** In this section you'll learn how to import data from a SQL Server database, called AdventureWorks2014, using both methods. Note, however, that the steps here are simply for your edification. In reality, you'll access this database from the following site:
>
> *https://github.com/Microsoft/sql-server-samples/releases/tag/adventureworks*
>
> After you open this site, simply click the AdventureWorks2014.bak link in the list.

Import data using import mode

To import data from a SQL Server database into Power BI using import mode, follow these steps:

1. Click the **Home** tab in Power BI Desktop.

2. Click **Get Data**.

3. Choose **Database** and select **SQL Server Database**.

4. Click **Connect**.

   The SQL Server Database window opens. (See the left image in Figure 9-1.)

5. Type the name of the SQL Server from which you want to import data in the **Server Name** box.

6. Type the name of the database from which you want to import data in the **Database Name** box (in this case, **AdventureWorks2014**).

7. Under **Data Connectivity Mode**, select the **Import** option.

8. Click **OK**.

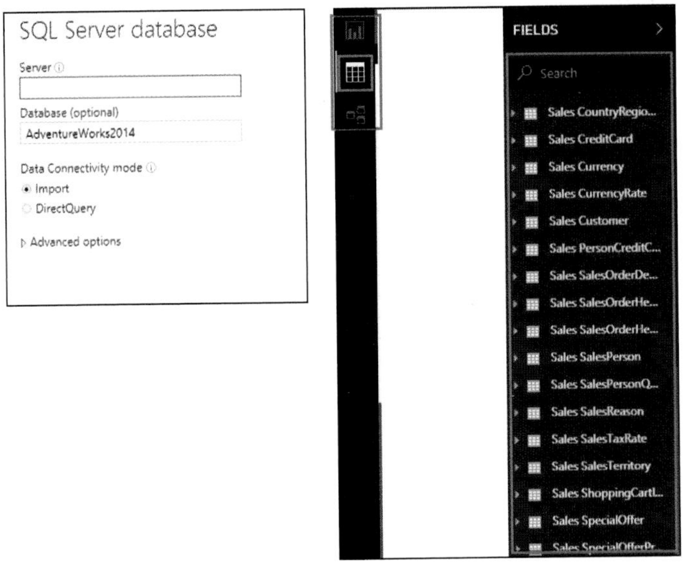

FIGURE 9-1 *Importing data from a SQL Server database using import mode.*

9. When prompted to select the authentication method, choose **Database**. (This is in contrast to Chapter 8, where you chose Windows. Here, I want to familiarize you with this other authentication method.)

10. In the **Username** box, type the username for the SQL Server database.

11. In the **Password** box, type the corresponding password.

12. Click **Connect**.

    You'll see a list of all the tables available in the Azure SQL database on the left, with a preview of the selected table on the right.

13. Select the tables you want to import and click **Load**.

    Power BI Desktop imports the tables and builds a data model from them. (Refer to the right image in Figure 9-1.)

Connect with data using DirectQuery mode

Here's how you connect with data in a SQL Server database from Power BI using DirectQuery mode:

1. Repeat steps 1–6 from the previous section.

2. Under **Data Connectivity Mode**, select the **DirectQuery** option.

3. Click **OK**.

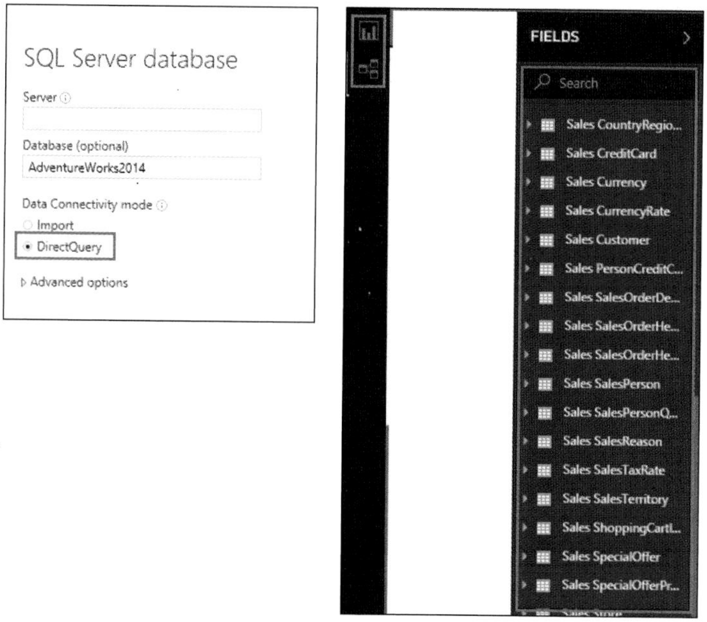

FIGURE 9-2 *Importing data from a SQL Server database using DirectQuery mode.*

4. When prompted to select the authentication method, choose **Database**.

5. In the **Username** box, type the username for the SQL Server database.

6. In the **Password** box, type the corresponding password.

7. Click **Connect**.

   You'll see a list of all the tables available in the SQL Server database, with a preview of each table available.

8. Select the tables you want to connect to and click **Load**.

   Power BI Desktop connects to the tables, but unlike with import mode, it does not build a data model from it. This is because Power BI Desktop is connected directly to the data source. (Refer to the right image in Figure 9-2.)

Import data using an inline query

You can also import data from a SQL Server database into Power BI using an inline SQL query. Inline SQL queries can be used for both import mode and DirectQuery mode imports. These steps show you how to use an inline query to conduct an import mode operation:

1. Repeat steps 1-7 from the section "Import data using import mode."

2. Expand the **Advanced Options** section in the SQL Server Database window and type the following inline query:

```
Select sp.[SalesQuota]
      ,sp.[Bonus]
      ,sp.[CommissionPct]
      ,sp.[SalesYTD]
      ,sp.[SalesLastYear]
      ,st.[Name]
          FROM [Sales].[SalesPerson] as sp inner join[Sales].[SalesTerritory] as st
          on
          sp.[TerritoryID]=st.[TerritoryID]
```

3. Optionally, select the **Include Relationship Columns** and **Navigate Using Full Hierarchy** checkboxes.

4. Click **OK**.

5. When prompted to select the authentication method, choose **Database**.

6. In the **User Name** box, type the username for the Oracle database.

7. In the **Password** box, type the corresponding password.

8. Click **Connect**.

9. Preview the columns of data you specified for import and click **Load**.

Create a Power BI report

In this section you'll create a Power BI report based on data imported via import mode from the AdventureWorks2014.bak SQL Server database. This database contains sample tables with lots of meaningful data that you can consume to prepare a sample Power BI report. Because earlier chapters, including Chapter 6, have discussed the ins and outs of creating reports—such as adding visuals, arranging visuals, preparing a report for mobile view, publishing and viewing the report, and preparing a dashboard from the report—I won't repeat that information here. Instead, I'll simply indicate which visuals to add, and show you the results in report, mobile, and dashboard form.

Let's start with the visuals. Add the following items to your report:

- **Slicer** You'll use a slicer to filter data based on department, job title, and shift.

- **Pie chart** A pie chart will show the employee count by gender.

- **Clustered column chart** A clustered column chart will show the employee count by gender and marital status.

- **Multi-row card** You'll use a multi-row card to show information about each shift.

- **Stacked bar chart** To show the employee count by job title and gender, you'll use a stacked bar chart.

- **Table** A table will contain informational data, like employee first name, employee last name, employee phone number, number of sick leave hours used, and number of vacation hours used.

- **Gauge chart** A gauge will show the total number of employees in the organization.

After you add the visuals, you can arrange them as desired. (See Figure 9-3.)

9

> **IMPORTANT** In case you didn't actually build the report, I provided a final version of it for your use: SQLSERVER - Sample Report for HR.pbix. As mentioned, you can access this file from the book's companion website.

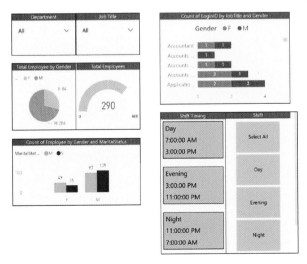

FIGURE 9-3 *Your Power BI report, complete with visuals.*

As you saw in previous chapters, you can also prepare the report for display on a mobile device. (See Figure 9-4.) (For more details, refer to Chapter 4.)

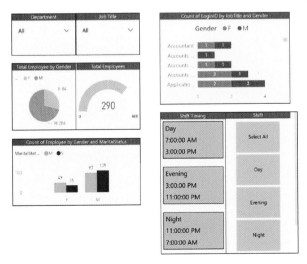

FIGURE 9-4 *Prepare the report for display on a mobile device.*

Figure 9-5 shows a dashboard generated from visuals from various reports, including the one you created in this chapter. (For more details, refer to Chapter 1.)

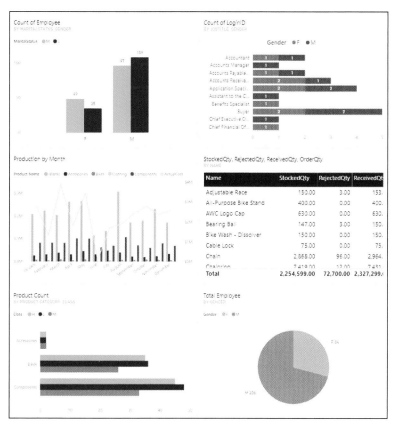

FIGURE 9-5 *Preparing a dashboard from different Power BI reports.*

Set up a data gateway

You use a data gateway to establish a secure connection between the SQL Server database and Power BI. Through this secure connection, you can keep your Power BI reports up to date. In essence, the gateway acts as a bridge between the SQL Server database and Power BI (as well as other Microsoft tools such as PowerApps, Logic Apps, and Microsoft Flow). Using this bridge, Power BI updates reports based on data on the SQL Server database.

Chapter 8 discussed installing and configuring a data gateway for SharePoint On-Premises. It outlined the system requirements for a data gateway and explained what types of data gateways are available: shared and personal. It also stepped you through the procedure for setting up a shared data gateway. Rather than repeating all that information here, this section focuses on installing and configuring a personal data gateway.

> ⚠ **IMPORTANT** Before you set up the data gateway, you must publish your report to Power BI service.

Install a personal data gateway

To install a personal data gateway, follow these steps:

1. Type *http://go.microsoft.com/fwlink/?LinkID=820925* in your web browser's address bar to launch the data gateway installer.

2. Right-click the installer and click **Open**. Then click **Next** to start the installation.

3. Select the **On-Premises Data Gateway (Personal Mode)** option button and click **Next**. (See screen 1 in Figure 9-6.)

   A pop-up window informs you that it's best to install the gateway on a computer that is always on and warns you that the gateway will perform more slowly on a wireless network.

4. Click **Next** to close the window. (See screen 2 in Figure 9-6.)

5. Enter the installation path and accept the terms and conditions. Then click **Next**.

6. Enter the email address associated with your Power BI Pro account and click **Sign In**.

   The installer displays a message indicating that the data gateway is online and ready for use. (See screen 3 in Figure 9-6.)

FIGURE 9-6 *Installing a personal data gateway.*

Configure Power BI to use a personal data gateway

After you set up your personal data gateway, you need to configure Power BI to use it to refresh your report. The following steps demonstrate how to configure Power BI to use a personal data gateway. (To configure Power BI to use a shared data gateway, refer to Chapter 8.)

1. Log in to Power BI service.

2. Under **Datasets**, hover your mouse pointer over the report you created using data from the SQL Server database, click the ellipsis that appears, and click **Schedule Refresh**. (See Figure 9-7.)

3. In the report Settings window that opens, expand the **Gateway Connection** section, click the **Use Your Data Gateway (Personal Mode)** option button, and click **Apply**. Power BI connects to the data gateway.

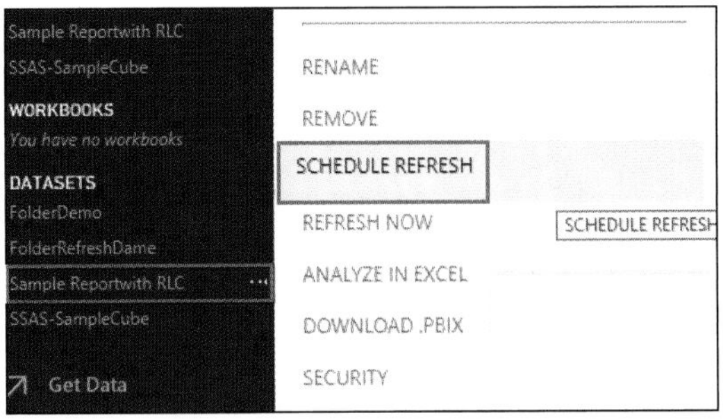

FIGURE 9-7 *Configure the data gateway for use with Power BI.*

Next, configure the report to refresh automatically on a schedule you set through the data gateway.

4. Expand the **Scheduled Refresh** section in the Settings window.

5. Toggle the **Keep Your Data Up to Date** setting to **On**.

6. Open the **Refresh Frequency** drop-down list and select how often you want to refresh the data.

7. Open the **Time Zone** drop-down list and indicate your time zone.

8. Click **Apply**.

Configure Row-Level Security (RLS) in Power BI

Now that you've gotten some practice using Power BI, let's configure Row Level Security (RLS) in a Power BI report. RLS enables you to restrict who can and cannot access certain data in Power BI by applying user-specific roles.

> ⚠ **IMPORTANT** RLS works with all Power BI reports—not just those that use data from a SQL Server database as their data source.

If you publish a report in Power BI, all users will be able to access the tables and fields that underpin that report by default. RLS can help prevent this. Consider the employee data you used to build a report earlier in this chapter. Suppose you wanted to limit users to viewing data from their own department. For example, you wanted people in the engineering department to view employee data from that department, but not, say, from the facilities and maintenance department. To achieve this, you can apply user-specific roles to restrict members of one department from accessing information about members of another department.

In this section you'll use the Sample Report with RLS.pbix file to learn how to apply RLS to limit which users can view the data based on their department. (See Figure 9-8.) As mentioned, you can access this file from the book's companion website in the following folder: MSPBIDashboards\ch09.

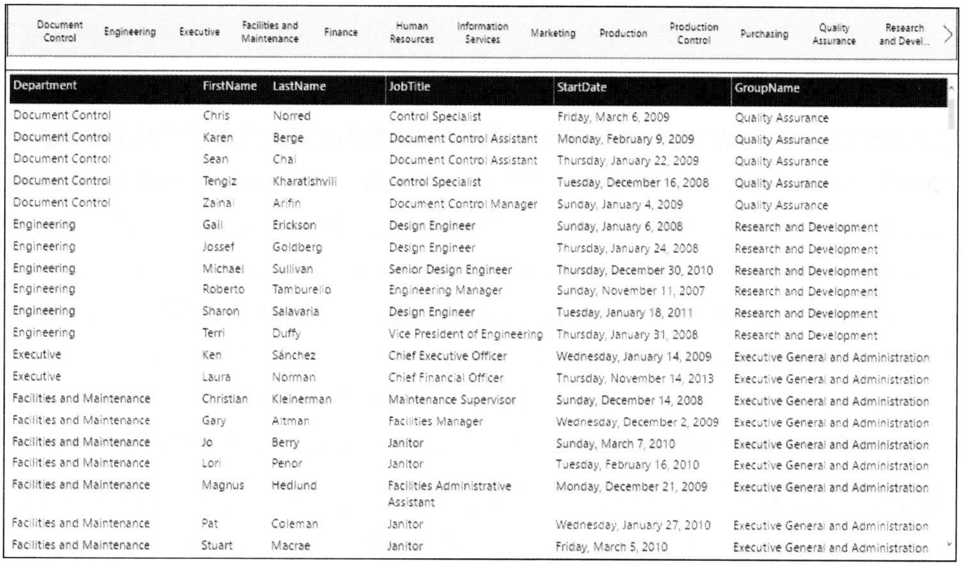

Department	FirstName	LastName	JobTitle	StartDate	GroupName
Document Control	Chris	Norred	Control Specialist	Friday, March 6, 2009	Quality Assurance
Document Control	Karen	Berge	Document Control Assistant	Monday, February 9, 2009	Quality Assurance
Document Control	Sean	Chai	Document Control Assistant	Thursday, January 22, 2009	Quality Assurance
Document Control	Tengiz	Kharatishvili	Control Specialist	Tuesday, December 16, 2008	Quality Assurance
Document Control	Zainal	Arifin	Document Control Manager	Sunday, January 4, 2009	Quality Assurance
Engineering	Gail	Erickson	Design Engineer	Sunday, January 6, 2008	Research and Development
Engineering	Jossef	Goldberg	Design Engineer	Thursday, January 24, 2008	Research and Development
Engineering	Michael	Sullivan	Senior Design Engineer	Thursday, December 30, 2010	Research and Development
Engineering	Roberto	Tamburello	Engineering Manager	Sunday, November 11, 2007	Research and Development
Engineering	Sharon	Salavaria	Design Engineer	Tuesday, January 18, 2011	Research and Development
Engineering	Terri	Duffy	Vice President of Engineering	Thursday, January 31, 2008	Research and Development
Executive	Ken	Sánchez	Chief Executive Officer	Wednesday, January 14, 2009	Executive General and Administration
Executive	Laura	Norman	Chief Financial Officer	Thursday, November 14, 2013	Executive General and Administration
Facilities and Maintenance	Christian	Kleinerman	Maintenance Supervisor	Sunday, December 14, 2008	Executive General and Administration
Facilities and Maintenance	Gary	Altman	Facilities Manager	Wednesday, December 2, 2009	Executive General and Administration
Facilities and Maintenance	Jo	Berry	Janitor	Sunday, March 7, 2010	Executive General and Administration
Facilities and Maintenance	Lori	Penor	Janitor	Tuesday, February 16, 2010	Executive General and Administration
Facilities and Maintenance	Magnus	Hedlund	Facilities Administrative Assistant	Monday, December 21, 2009	Executive General and Administration
Facilities and Maintenance	Pat	Coleman	Janitor	Wednesday, January 27, 2010	Executive General and Administration
Facilities and Maintenance	Stuart	Macrae	Janitor	Friday, March 5, 2010	Executive General and Administration

FIGURE 9-8 *In this section you'll apply RLS to this Power BI report.*

Your first step (after opening the report) is to create and validate the roles you want to apply to the table—in this example, the engineer role. Follow these steps:

1. Click the **Modeling** tab in Power BI Desktop. Then, in the Security group, click **Manage Roles**. (See Figure 9-9.)

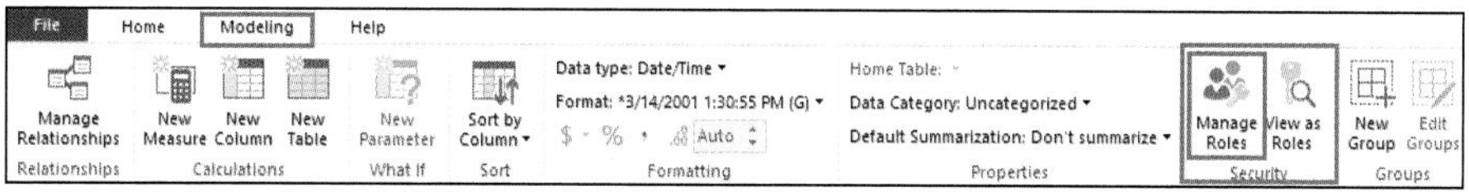

FIGURE 9-9 *Click Manage Roles in the Modeling tab.*

2. A dialog box opens. Click the **Create** button in the Manage Roles section.

3. Type a name for the role in the box that appears—in this case, **Engineering**. Then click **Create** or press **Enter**.

   Power BI creates the role and shows all available tables to which it can apply.

4. Select the table to which you want to apply the role and type the following DAX expression:

   ```
   [Department] = "Engineering"
   ```

   Power BI creates the new role. (See screen 1 in Figure 9-10.)

5. Repeat steps 1–4 to create an Executive role. (See screen 2 in Figure 9-10.) Then repeat them two more times to create a Marketing role and a Finance role.

6. To validate the role, click the **Modeling** tab. Then, in the Security group, click the **View as Roles** button. (Refer to Figure 9-9.)

7. The View as Roles dialog box opens listing all the roles you created. Select the **Engineer** checkbox.

   Power BI filters the table contents to show employee data only for members of the engineering department. (See screen 3 in Figure 9-10.)

8. Click **Stop Viewing** to return to the previous view.

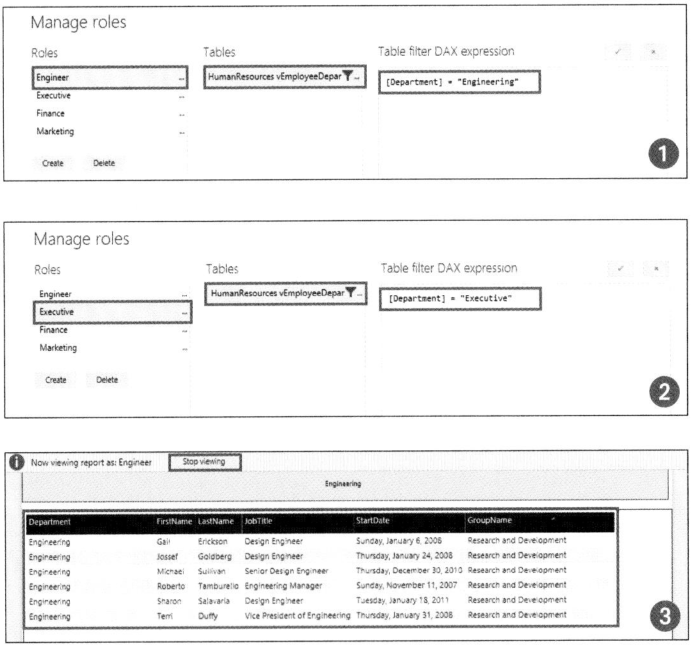

FIGURE 9-10 *Creating user roles in Power BI service.*

To apply a rule to a specific user, follow these steps:

1. Under **Datasets**, click the appropriate report and then click **Security** in the window that appears. (See Figure 9-11.)

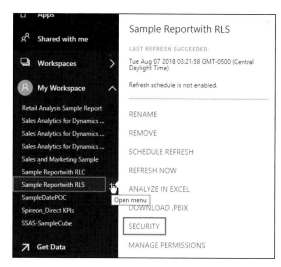

FIGURE 9-11 *Assign a role to a user.*

The Row-Level Security window opens. The left side of the window lists the roles you created, with the number of people assigned that role in parentheses. (See the top image in Figure 9-12.)

2. To assign the Engineer role to a user, click the **Engineer** entry in the list on the left.

3. In the **People or Groups Who Belong to This Role** box on the right side of the window, type the email address of a user to whom you want to apply the Engineering role. (I typed **Joseph Goldburg**.) Then click **Add**.

The user's name appears below the box where you typed their email address, and the count in parentheses next to the Engineering entry on the left increases by 1. (See the bottom image in Figure 9-12.)

4. Click **Save**.

Row-Level Security

Engineer (0)   Members (0)
Executive (0)
Finance (0)   People or groups who belong to this role
Marketing (0)   Enter email addresses

                                Add

Engineer (1)   Members (1)
Executive (0)   ...
Finance (0)   People or groups who belong to this role
Marketing (0)   Enter email addresses

                                Add

                                Joseph Goldburg   ×

FIGURE 9-12 *Apply a role to a user.*

5. Log in to Power BI service using the credentials of the user to whom you applied the role (Joseph).

    You'll see data for employees in the engineering department—but no one else. (See Figure 9-13.)

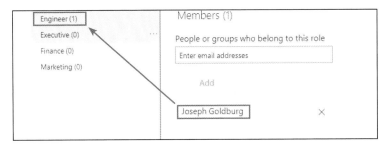

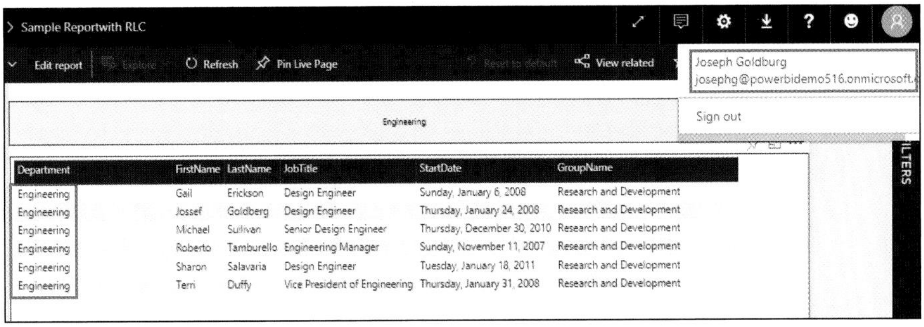

FIGURE 9-13 *Log in to Power BI with the user's account.*

Limitations of RLS in Power BI

RLS is an effective way to secure your data in Power BI. It does, however, have a few limitations:

- You must define roles and rules in Power BI Desktop. You cannot do this in Power BI service. You can, however, apply roles to users in Power BI service.

- To use RLS, the dataset you must restrict must first be loaded into Power BI Desktop. For example, if you want to apply RLS to a report based on data in an Excel file, the Excel file must be loaded into Power BI Desktop.

- RLS is well-supported on ETL and DirectQuery platforms. If you can handle live connections for analysis services, you can implement the on-premises model. For example, if you load an SSAS tabular model with a live connection into Power BI, you can implement RLS in the on-premises model.

- RLS is not supported for Q&A and Cortana.

9

Skills review

In this chapter, you learned about:

- Importing data from a SQL Server database via import mode and DirectQuery mode

- Authenticating SQL Server using Database authentication

- Creating a Power BI report

- Setting up a data gateway

- Applying RLS to a Power BI report

- Defining user roles in Power BI and assigning users to specific roles

Practice tasks

This section provides a simple case study for you to study and solve using information from this chapter. This section also contains a series of practice questions for you to answer.

Case study

Suppose you work for a hospitality group with regional offices all over the world that has been in business for 15 years. Company data (including historical details and current growth) is spread across several different tables on SQL Server databases, including the following:

- Customer satisfaction index
- Overall sales by category
- Associated hotels chains and their profit calculations
- Associated resorts and their profit calculations
- Associated caterers and their profit calculations
- Associated restaurants and their profit calculations
- Special delegates
- Special guests
- Lifestyle quotient maintained by the business

Using Power BI, you want to import this SQL Server data in DirectQuery mode to generate a report that updates in real time and conveys the following:

- A comparison of year-wise performance input
- Which groups or categories have demonstrated the highest profit growth
- A cross-check of yearly distribution to improvise a sales index

How might you generate this report?

Practice questions

1. What are some key differences between import mode and DirectQuery mode?

2. Which mode ensures live data from the SQL Server database?

3. In which situations should you use import mode?

4. True or false: DirectQuery mode results in the creation of a Power BI model.

5. True or false: You can connect to multiple databases from the same Power BI server using DirectQuery mode.

6. How do you use an inline query to import SQL Server database data in import or DirectQuery mode?

7. How do you specify database authentication in Power BI?

8. How many rows can be loaded at one time with DirectQuery?

9. How do you configure a personal data gateway?

10. What is Row-Level Security (RLS)?

11. How do you assign a role to a user in Power BI?

12. How do you test whether RLS is working?

Develop Power BI reports from SSAS cube

In this chapter, you'll learn how to build a Power BI report that relies on data from a SQL Server Analysis Services (SSAS) cube. You'll also learn how to set up a data gateway to work with the SSAS cube. First, however, this chapter offers definitions of key terms that relate to SSAS cubes.

In this chapter:

- Basic terminology
- Import data from an SSAS cube into Power BI
- Create a Power BI report
- Set up and configure a data gateway

Practice files

As you work through this chapter, you'll use one practice file, which you can access from the book's companion website at *https://aka.ms/PowerBIDash/downloads* in the following folder: MSPBIDashboards\ch10. The file is as follows:

- **SSAS SampleCube.pbix** This file is a sample Power BI report generated from data in the Adventure Works cube. It consists of visuals for a reseller sales order. You'll use this report in the "Create a Power BI report" section later in this chapter.

Basic terminology

Before we get into the ins and outs of building a report from data from an SSAS cube, let's cover some basic terminology—specifically, let's define the terms SSAS cube, measure, and dimension.

A *SQL Server Analysis Services (SSAS) cube* consists of measures and dimensions for selecting data. These measures and dimensions are derived from tables and views in a data source such as a SQL Server database.

A *measure* is data returned from a numeric expression in a column. For example, the sum of an expression that represents total sales during a selected time period is a measure. Multiple measures sourced from columns within a table can be grouped together to form a measure group.

Dimension describes the attributes of the relationship between measures in a cube. These attributes are extracted from columns available from one or more tables containing the data. In other words, to quote Microsoft, a dimension is "a collection of all related objects called attributes which can be used to provide information about fact data in one or more cubes."

Import data from an SSAS cube into Power BI

There are two ways to import data from an SSAS database into Power BI:

- **Import mode** As with importing data from a SQL Server database, when you use import mode to import data from an SSAS cube, that data is cached from the database into Power BI. To ensure you are working with the latest data, you will need to refresh it on a regular basis.

- **Connect Live mode** This is a bit like DirectQuery mode, discussed in Chapter 9. With Connect Live mode, you do not explicitly import data into Power BI. Rather, you maintain a connection between Power BI and the SSAS cube. When you build a report in Power BI using this data, it will update in real time. Power BI interacts with the cube for every single user request for data.

If you opt to use Connect Live mode, here are a few points to keep in mind:

- You can use Connect Live mode for Analysis Services. There are two types of Analysis Services available: Tabular and Multidimensional.

- You can use Connect Live mode to directly access an OLAP cube. (An OLAP cube is a multidimensional database optimized for data warehouse and online analytical processing [OLAP] applications.)

- When you use Connect Live to connect Power BI with the SSAS cube, Power BI essentially acts as front-end visual component for the data in the cube. In other words, Power BI prepares the report directly from data in the cube.

- Connect Live allows for a direct connection with the enterprise model database. You need not copy or duplicate the data, and multiple users can access it.

- Because Connect Live mode does not actually import data into Power BI, no data model is created—meaning there is no option to change the model definition.

- Connect Live doesn't support the use of the Query Editor.

10

Import data using import mode

To import data from an SSAS cube into Power BI using import mode, follow these steps:

1. Click the **Home** tab in Power BI Desktop.

2. Click **Get Data**.

3. Choose **Database** and select **SQL Server Analysis Service**.

4. Click **Connect**.

    The SQL Server Analysis Services Database window opens. (See Figure 10-1.)

5. Type the name of the SSAS server from which you want to import data in the **Server** name box.

6. Type the name of the database from which you want to import data in the **Database** name box.

    The preceding step is optional. If you leave this box blank, you'll import all databases available in the server.

7. Select the **Import** option button.

8. Click **OK**.

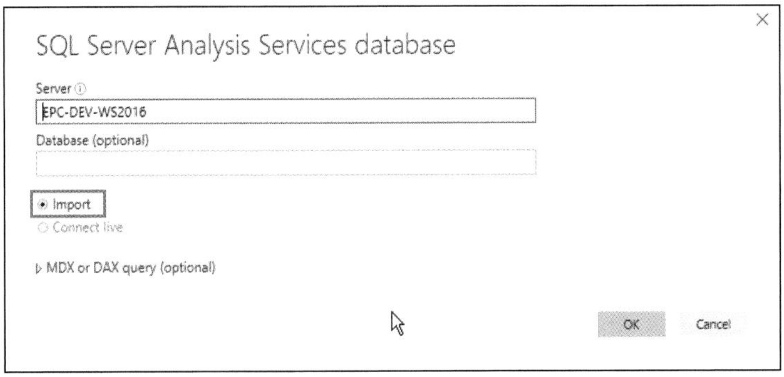

FIGURE 10-1 *Importing data from an SSAS cube using import mode.*

9. When prompted to select the authentication method, choose **Windows**.

10. Select the **Use My Current Credentials** checkbox, enter your Windows username and password, and click **Connect**. (See Figure 10-2.)

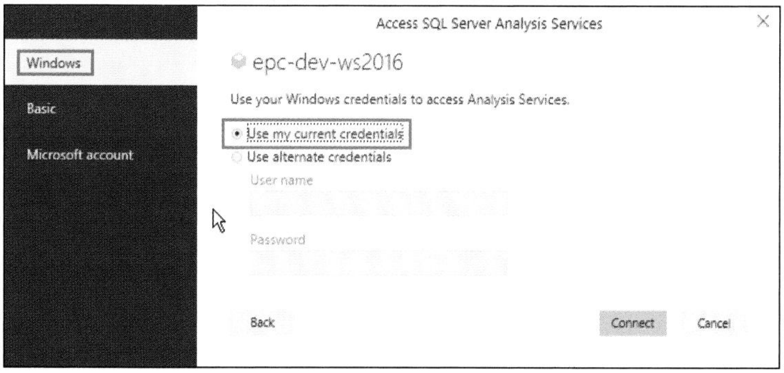

FIGURE 10-2 *Select the Windows authentication option and enter your credentials.*

A Navigator window opens. In the pane on the left is a list of all tables, cubes, measures, and dimensions in the SSAS database. You can click any of these to preview them in the pane on the right.

11. Open the cube that contains the measures and dimensions you want to include in your report (in this example, **Sales Targets**), select the desired measures and dimensions, and click the **Load** button. (See Figure 10-3.)

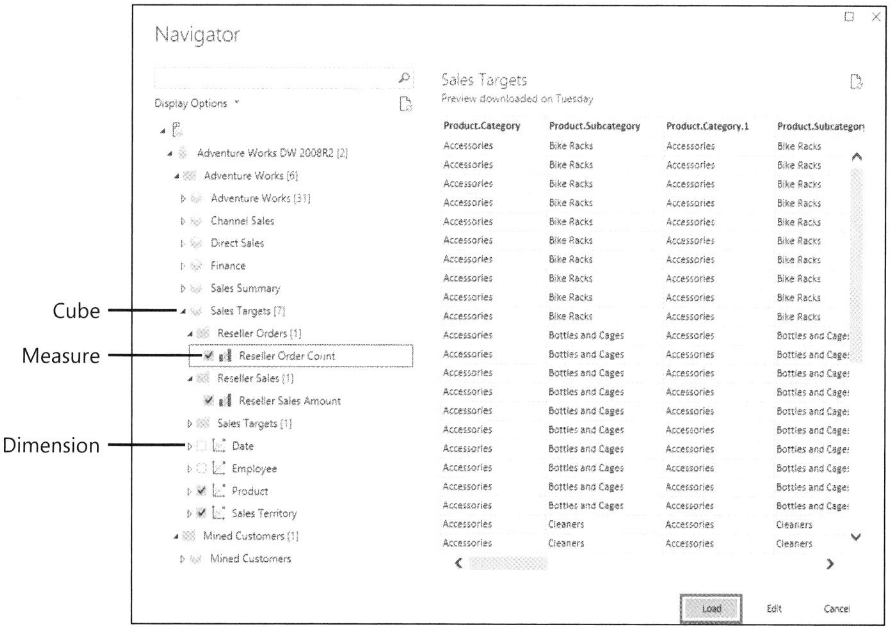

FIGURE 10-3 *The Navigator window lists all tables, cubes, measures, and dimensions in the selected database (left) and includes a preview (right).*

Power BI loads the selected measures and dimensions into a data model. Note that the Edit Queries button is active, indicating that when you obtain data using import mode, the Query Editor is available for your use. The Data and Relationships tabs are also visible. (See Figure 10-4).

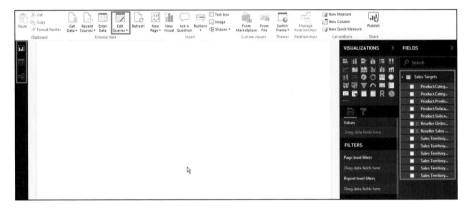

FIGURE 10-4 *Import mode shows the availability of Editing Queries and the Data and Relationships tabs.*

Connect with data using Connect Live mode

Here's how you connect with data in an SSAS cube from Power BI using Connect Live mode:

1. Repeat steps 1-6 from the previous section.

2. Select the **Connect Live** option button and click **OK**. (See Figure 10-5.)

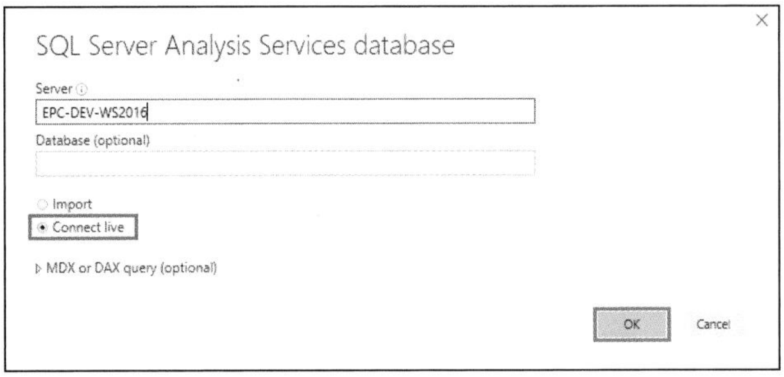

SQL Server Analysis Services database

Server ⓘ
EPC-DEV-WS2016

Database (optional)

○ Import
● Connect live

▷ MDX or DAX query (optional)

OK   Cancel

FIGURE 10-5 *Importing data from an SSAS cube database using Connect Live mode.*

3. When prompted to select the authentication method, choose **Windows**.

4. Select the **Use My Current Credentials** checkbox, enter your Windows user-name and password, and click **Connect**.

A Navigator window opens. In the pane on the left is a list of all cubes in the SSAS database. You can click any of these to preview its contents in the pane on the right.

5. Click the cube that contains the measures and dimensions you want to include in your report (in this example, **Sales Targets**) and click the **OK** button. (See Figure 10-6.)

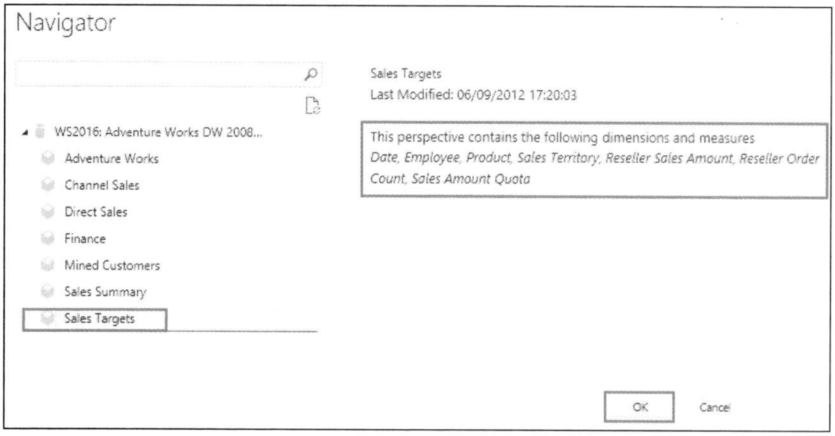

Navigator
WS2016: Adventure Works DW 2008...
Adventure Works
Channel Sales
Direct Sales
Finance
Mined Customers
Sales Summary
Sales Targets
Sales Targets
Last Modified: 06/09/2012 17:20:03
This perspective contains the following dimensions and measures
Date, Employee, Product, Sales Territory, Reseller Sales Amount, Reseller Order Count, Sales Amount Quota
OK
Cancel

FIGURE 10-6 *A list of all available cubes in the SSAS database (left) and the contents of the selected cube (right).*

Power BI Desktop connects to the cube, but unlike with import mode, it does not build a data model from it. This is because Power BI Desktop is connected directly to the data source. Note, too, that the Edit Queries option is not available, and that the Data and Relationships tabs no longer appear. (See Figure 10-7.)

Get Data
Recent Sources
Enter Data
Edit Queries
Refresh
External data
New Page
New Visual
Text box
Image
Shapes
Insert
From Store
From File
Custom visuals
Manage Relationships
Relationships
New Measure
New Column
Calculations
Publish
Share
FIELDS
VISUALIZATIONS
FILTERS
Search
Reseller Orders
Reseller Sales
Sales Targets
Date
Employee
Product
Sales Territory

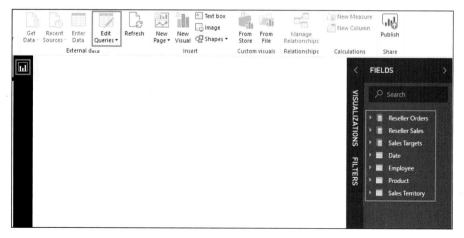

FIGURE 10-7 *Importing data from an SSAS cube using Connect Live mode.*

Create a Power BI report

In this section you'll create a Power BI report based on data from an SSAS database called Adventure Works, which you can download here: *https://github.com/Microsoft/ sql-server-samples/releases/download/adventureworks2008r2/adventure-works-2008r2-dw-full-database-backup.zip*.

The report will contain the following cube, dimensions, and measures:

- Sales Targets cube
- Product dimension
- Sales Territory dimension
- Reseller Sales Amount measure
- Reseller Order Count measure

Because earlier chapters, including Chapter 6, have discussed the ins and outs of creating reports—such as adding visuals, arranging visuals, preparing a report for mobile view, publishing and viewing the report, and preparing a dashboard from the report—I won't repeat that information here. Instead, I'll simply indicate which visuals to add, and show you the results in report, mobile, and dashboard form.

Let's start with the visuals. Add the following items to your report:

- **Slicer** You'll use a slicer to filter data by category.
- **Stacked bar chart** A stacked bar chart will show reseller sales amounts by sales category.
- **Map** A map will present reseller sales amounts by sales territory and region.
- **Multi-row card** You'll use a multi-row card to show information about related sales amounts and reseller order counts.
- **Treemap** A treemap will contain reseller order counts by product category.
- **Line chart** You'll use a line chart to show reseller sales amounts and reseller order counts by country.

After you add the visuals, you can arrange them as desired. (See Figure 10-8.)

> ⚠ **IMPORTANT** In case you didn't actually build the report, I provided a final version of it for your use: SSAS - SampleCube.pbix. As mentioned, you can access this file from the book's companion website.

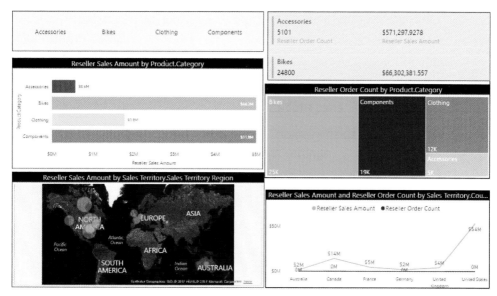

FIGURE 10-8 *Your Power BI report, complete with visuals.*

As you saw in previous chapters, you can also prepare the report for display on a mobile device. (See Figure 10-9.) (For more details, refer to Chapter 4.)

10

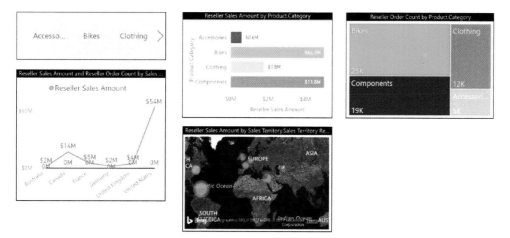

FIGURE 10-9 *Creating reports for mobile friendly layout.*

Figure 10-10 shows a dashboard generated from visuals from various reports, including the one you created in this chapter. (For more details, refer to Chapter 1.)

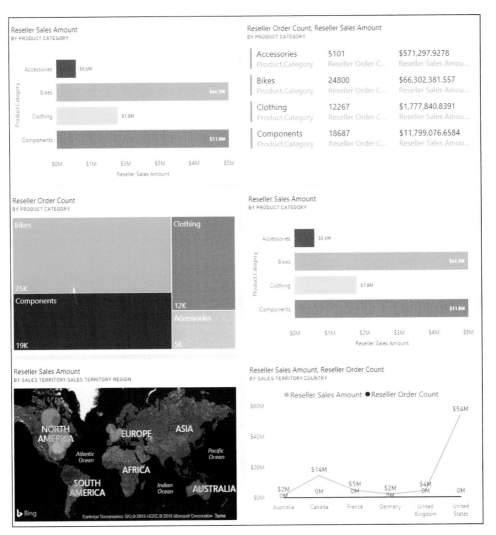

FIGURE 10-10 *Preparing a dashboard from different Power BI reports.*

Set up and configure a data gateway

As in previous chapters, you use a data gateway to establish a secure connection between the SSAS cube and Power BI. Through this secure connection, Power BI reports generated from the SSAS cube remain up to date. In essence, the gateway acts as a bridge between the SSAS cube and Power BI (as well as other Microsoft tools such as PowerApps, Logic Apps, and Microsoft Flow). Using this bridge, Power BI updates reports based on data on the SSAS cube.

Chapter 8 outlined the system requirements for a data gateway and explained what types of data gateways are available: shared and personal. It also stepped you through the procedure for setting up a shared data gateway. Chapter 9 explained how to set up a personal gateway. Please refer to those chapters for help setting up your gateway.

> ⚠ **IMPORTANT** Before you set up the data gateway, you must publish your report to Power BI service.

After your gateway is set up, you must configure it to use Power BI service. Follow these steps:

1. Log in to Power BI service.

2. Under **Datasets**, hover your mouse pointer over the report you created using data from the SSAS cube, click the ellipsis that appears, and click **Schedule Refresh**.

3. A Settings window for the report appears. Expand the **Gateway Connection** section and click the **Manage Gateways** link.

    The Gateway Cluster Settings window opens.

4. Click the **Add Data Sources to Use the Gateway** link.

5. The Manage Gateway Settings page opens. Click **Gateway Name** and then click **Add Data Source**.

6. Under **Gateway Clusters**, click **Live Data Connection**. (See Figure 10-11.)

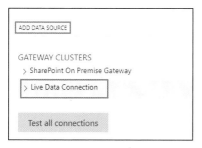

FIGURE 10-11 *Configuring a gateway in Power BI service to connect to an SSAS cube.*

    The Data Source Settings window opens. (See Figure 10-12.)

7. Type a name for the data source in the **Data Source Name** box.

8. Open the **Data Source Type** drop-down list and choose **Analysis Services**.

9. Type the name of the **SSAS server** to which you want to connect in the **Server** box.

10. Type the name of the **SSAS database** to which you want to connect in the **Database** box.

11. Type your SSAS server username in the **Username** box.

12. Type your password in the **Password** box.

13. Click **Add**.

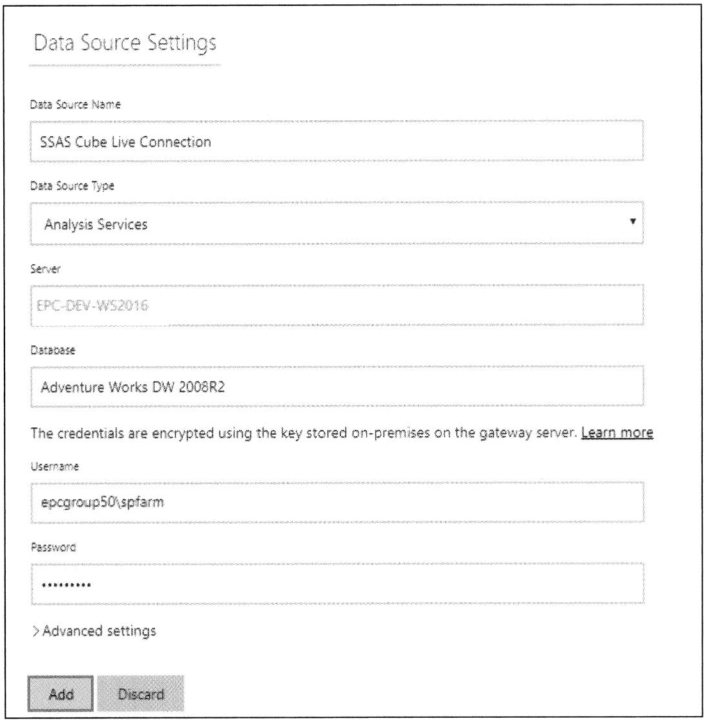

Data Source Settings

Data Source Name

SSAS Cube Live Connection

Data Source Type

Analysis Services ▼

Server

EPC-DEV-WS2016

Database

Adventure Works DW 2008R2

The credentials are encrypted using the key stored on-premises on the gateway server. Learn more

Username

epcgroup50\spfarm

Password

••••••••

> Advanced settings

Add   Discard

FIGURE 10-12 *Enter the requested information in the Data Source Settings window to configure the data gateway connection.*

The Data Source Settings window should indicate that the connection to the data gateway was successful.

14. In the report's Settings window, in the **Gateway Connection** section, select the **Use a Data Gateway** option button (see Figure 10-13) and click **Apply**.

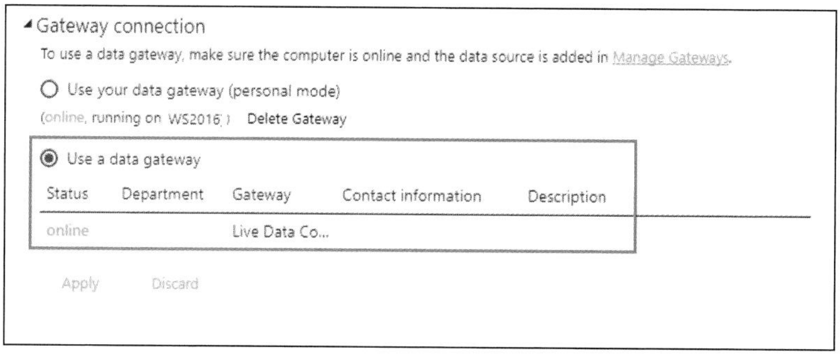

▲Gateway connection
To use a data gateway, make sure the computer is online and the data source is added in Manage Gateways.

○ Use your data gateway (personal mode)
(online, running on WS2016) Delete Gateway

⦿ Use a data gateway

Status	Department	Gateway	Contact information	Description
online		Live Data Co...		

Apply   Discard

FIGURE 10-13 *Select the Use a Data Gateway option button and click Apply.*

15. Expand the **Data Source Credentials** section of the same window to see the status of the connection.

Next, set up the report to refresh automatically through the data gateway.

16. Expand the **Scheduled Refresh** section of the same window and toggle the **Keep Your Data Up to Date** setting to **On**.

17. Open the **Refresh Frequency** drop-down list and select how often you want to refresh the data.

18. Open the **Time Zone** drop-down list and indicate your time zone.

19. Click **Apply**.

Skills review

In this chapter, you learned about:

- Basic terminology

- Importing data from an SSAS cube into Power BI

- Creating a Power BI report

- Setting up and configuring a data gateway

Practice tasks

This section provides a simple case study for you to study and solve using information from this chapter. This section also contains a series of practice questions for you to answer.

Case study

Suppose you work for a telecom group with offices all over the world. The company is well-established—it's been around for more than 20 years—and its network spans more than 75 countries. The company offers various products in different markets. These products include the following:

- Broadband/wireless connections
- Calling services for customers
- Hotspot/Wi-Fi connectivity
- Digital media services
- Fixed line and mobile phone connections
- Network security services
- Digital and Internet television connections

The organization would like to create Power BI reports from high volumes of existing historical data. This data is organized into SSAS cubes. To meet the organization's requirements, it's your job to:

- Extract the data from the SSAS cube and create a Power BI report from it
- Set up gateway connectivity
- Present the historical data in a more meaningful form
- Represent the data in visuals that best reflect your requirements

Specifically, your report should contain:

- An analysis of the popularity of services year by year, organized by region
- Achieved profit versus target profit, organized by year
- The services with the highest number of subscribers in historical yearly data
- The number of new subscribers this year versus last year
- A comparison of services to see the increase in sales percentage

How would you go about creating this report?

Practice questions

1. What is SSAS?
2. What is a measure?
3. What is a dimension?
4. What is a cube?
5. How do you import data from an SSAS cube?
6. What is the difference between import mode and Connect Live mode?
7. What are the benefits and limitations of using Connect Live mode?
8. True or false: Connect Live mode has a data option in Power BI Desktop.
9. How do you import data from an SSAS cube using import mode?
10. How do you configure a data gateway for an SSAS cube?

Develop Power BI reports from Azure SQL

In this chapter, you'll learn how to develop a Power BI report that relies on data from an Azure SQL database as its source. You'll also learn how to set up data refresh functionality for live data connectivity.

In this chapter:

- Overview of the Azure SQL portal
- Import data from an Azure SQL database into Power BI
- Create a Power BI report
- Set up a live data connection and data refresh functionality

Practice files

As you work through this chapter, you'll use one practice file, which you can access from the book's companion website at *https://aka.ms/PowerBIDash/downloads* in the following folder: MSPBIDashboards\ch11. The file is as follows:

- **SampleReportAzureSQL.pbix** This file is a sample Power BI report that consists of sales data for a product. You'll use this report in the "Create a Power BI report" section later in this chapter.

Overview of the Azure SQL portal

This section provides a basic overview of the Azure SQL portal, including how to access an Azure SQL database from the portal. In this example, we use the AdventureWorksLT database. If you have not yet deployed an Azure SQL database, please deploy this one. You can find this database here:

https://docs.microsoft.com/en-us/azure/sql-database/sql-database-get-started-portal

To explore the portal, follow these steps:

1. Type *https://portal.azure.com* in your web browser's address bar and enter your login credentials.

   After you log in, you'll see a Dashboard screen with various options and information about your Azure subscription. (See Figure 11-1.)

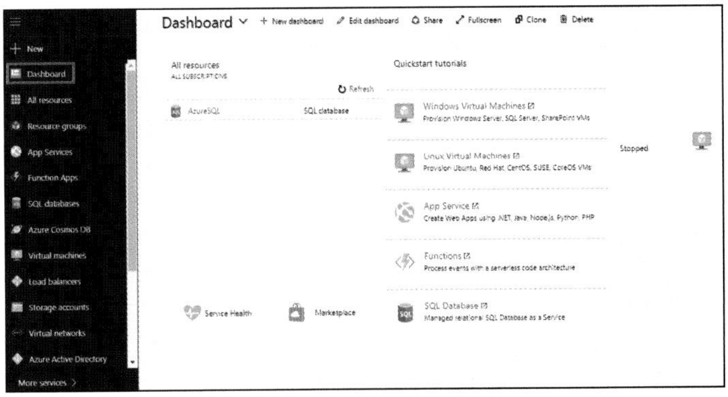

FIGURE 11-1 *The Dashboard screen in the Azure SQL portal.*

2. In the pane on the left, click the **SQL Databases** option. The pane on the right will display a list of all available SQL databases. (See Figure 11-2.)

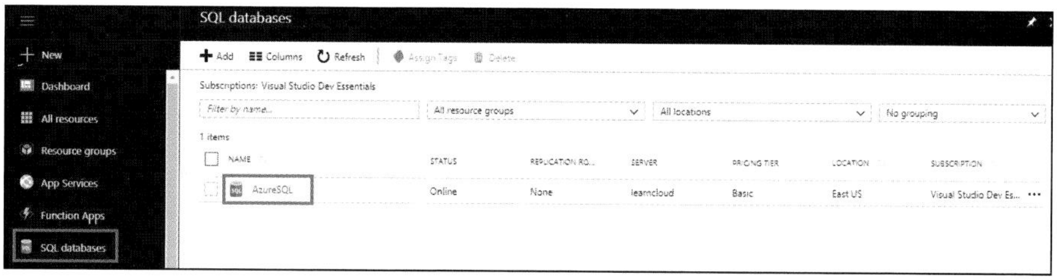

FIGURE 11-2 *Azure SQL databases list in Azure SQL dashboard.*

3. Click a database in the pane on the right—in this example, **AzureSQL**.

    Information about the selected database appears. Notice that Overview is selected in the middle pane. As a result, general information about the database appears in the right pane, including its server name. (See Figure 11-3.)

4. You'll need to know the server name later, when you prepare the report, so copy the name of the server, as shown in link form under the **Server Name** heading. Then click the link.

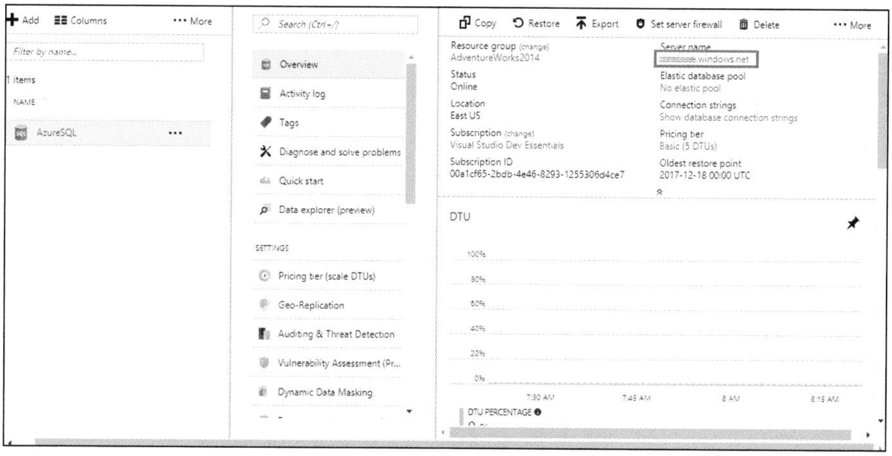

FIGURE 11-3 *Information about the selected Azure SQL database.*

Information about the server appears, including information about the server admin. (See Figure 11-4.)

5. You'll need to know the server admin later, when you prepare the report, so copy the admin name.

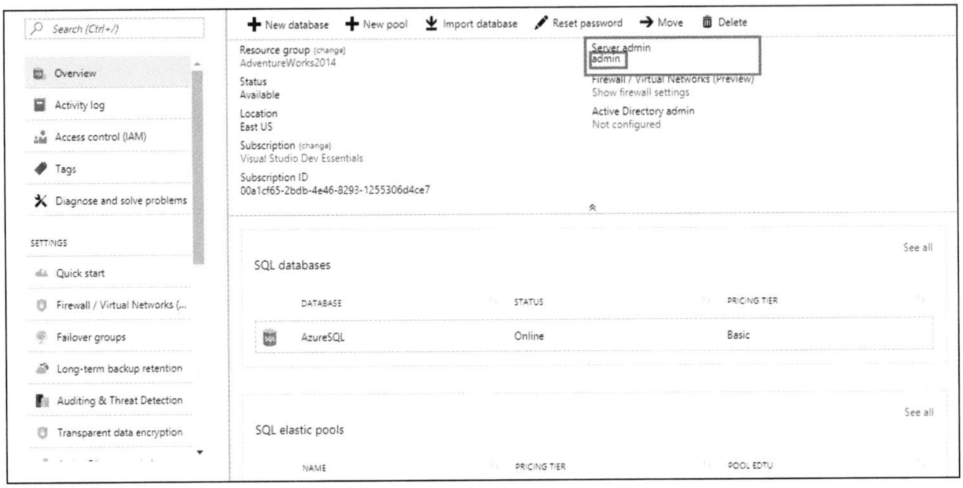

FIGURE 11-4 *Copy the server name and server admin information for later use.*

Import data from an Azure SQL database into Power BI

As with importing data from a SQL server into Power BI, there are two ways to import data from an Azure SQL database into Power BI:

- **Import mode** When you use import mode to import data, that data is cached from the database into Power BI. To ensure you are working with the latest data, you will need to refresh it on a regular basis.

- **DirectQuery mode** DirectQuery does not explicitly import data into Power BI. Rather, it maintains a connection between Power BI and the Azure SQL database. When you build a report in Power BI using this data, it will update in real time.

You'll review how to import data using both methods in this section.

> **TIP** For more information about these two modes, refer to Chapter 9.

Import data using import mode

To import data from an Azure SQL database into Power BI using import mode, follow these steps:

1. Click the **Home** tab in Power BI Desktop.

2. Click **Get Data**.

3. Choose **Azure** and select **Azure SQL Database**.

4. Click **Connect**.

   The SQL Server Database window opens. (See Figure 11-5.)

5. Type the name of the Azure SQL Server from which you want to import data in the **Server** name box. (Refer to step 4 in the preceding section.)

6. Type the name of the Azure SQL database from which you want to import data in the **Database** name box (in this case, **AzureSQL**).

7. Under **Data Connectivity Mode**, select the **Import** option button.

8. Click **OK**.

FIGURE 11-5 *The SQL Server Database window for connecting to an Azure SQL database.*

9. When prompted to select the authentication method (see Figure 11-6), choose **Database**.

10. In the **User Name** box, type the username for the Azure SQL database.

11. In the **Password** box, type the corresponding password.

12. Open the **Select Which Level to Apply These Settings To** drop-down list and choose from the available options.

13. Click **Connect**.

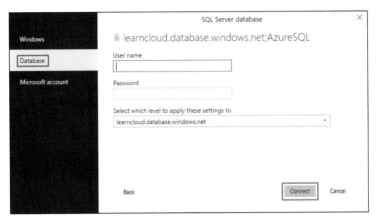

FIGURE 11-6 *Enter the username and password in the Database tab.*

You'll see a list of all the tables available in the Azure SQL database on the left, with a preview of the selected table on the right.

14. Select the tables you want to import and click **Load**.

Power BI Desktop imports the tables and builds a data model from them.

Connect with data using DirectQuery mode

Here's how you connect with data in an Azure SQL database from Power BI using DirectQuery mode:

1. Repeat steps 1–6 from the previous section.

2. Under **Data Connectivity Mode**, select the **DirectQuery** option button, and click **OK**.

3. When prompted to select the authentication method, choose **Database**.

4. In the **User Name** box, type the username for the Azure SQL database.

5. In the **Password** box, type the corresponding password.

6. Click **Connect**.

You'll see a list of all the tables available in the Azure SQL database, with a preview of the selected table.

7. Select the tables you want to connect to and click **Load**.

   Power BI Desktop connects to the tables, but unlike with import mode, it does not build a data model from it. This is because Power BI Desktop is connected directly to the data source. (See Figure 11-7.)

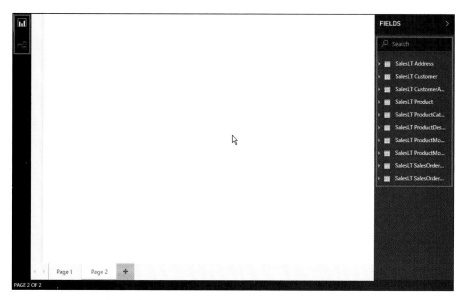

FIGURE 11-7 *Connecting to data in an Azure SQL database using DirectQuery mode.*

Import data using an inline query

You can also import data from an Azure SQL database into Power BI using an inline SQL query. Inline SQL queries can be used for both import mode and DirectQuery mode imports. These steps show you how to use an inline query to conduct an import mode operation:

> ⚠️ **IMPORTANT** If these seem familiar to you, it's because you followed similar steps in Chapter 9 to import data into a SQL Server database using an inline query.

1. Repeat steps 1–7 from the section "Import data using import mode."

2. Expand the **Advanced Options** section in the SQL Server Database window and type the following inline query:

```
SELECT Pr.[productid],Pr.[name],
        Pr.[productnumber],
        Pr.[color],
        Pr.[standardcost],
        Pr.[listprice],
        Pr.[size],
        Pr.[weight],
        Pr.[productcategoryid],
            PC.[name] AS ProductName,
        Pr.[productmodelid],
            PM.[name] AS ModelName,
        Pr.[sellstartdate],
        Pr.[sellenddate],
        Pr.[discontinueddate]
        FROM    [SalesLT].[product] AS Pr
        INNER JOIN [SalesLT].[productcategory] AS PC
                ON Pr.productcategoryid = PC.productcategoryid
        INNER JOIN [SalesLT].[productmodel] AS PM
                ON PM.productmodelid = Pr.productmodelid
```

3. Optionally, select the **Include Relationship Columns**, **Navigate Using Full Hierarchy**, and **Enable SQL Server Failover Support** checkboxes.

4. Click **OK**. (See Figure 11-8.)

5. When prompted to select the authentication method, choose **Database**.

6. In the **User Name** box, type the username for the Azure SQL database.

7. In the **Password** box, type the corresponding password.

8. Click **Connect**.

9. Preview the columns of data you specified for import and click **Load**. (See Figure 11-9.)

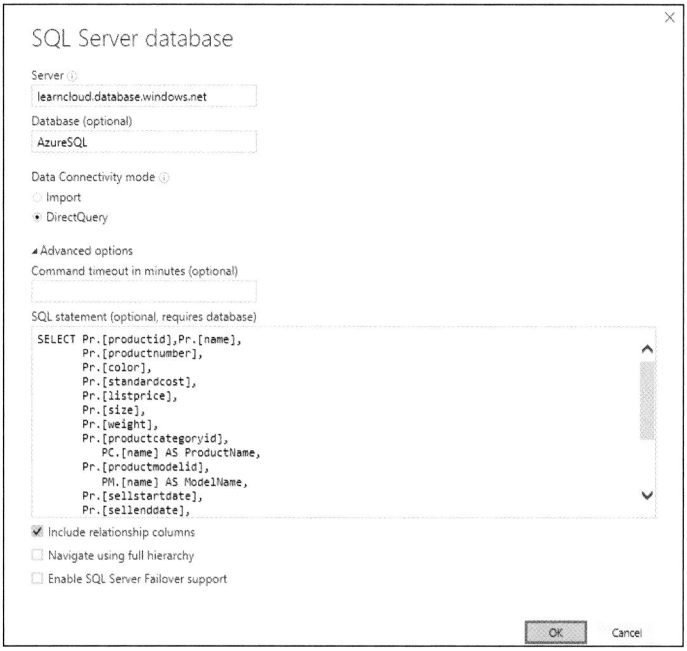

FIGURE 11-8 *Using an inline query to import from an Azure SQL database in import mode.*

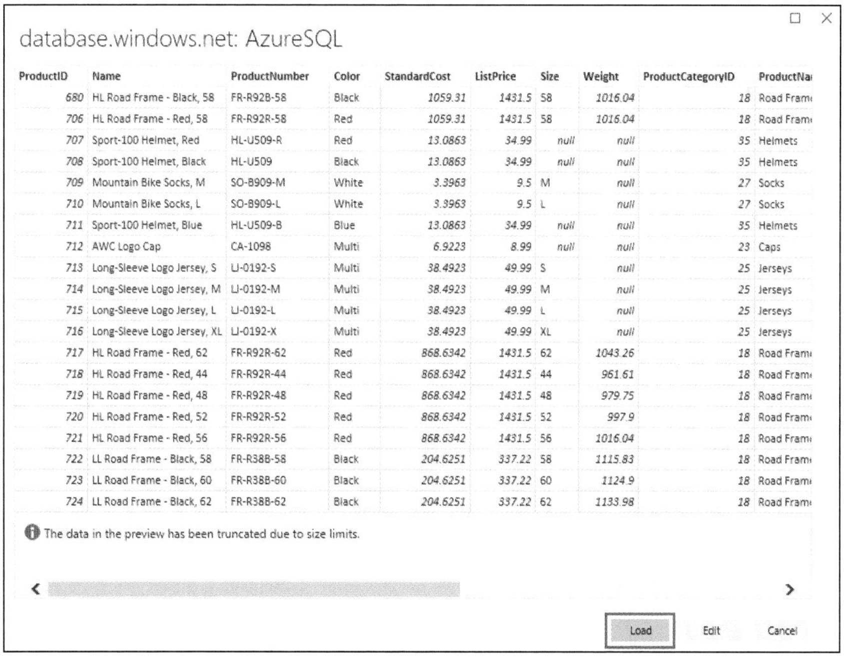

ProductID	Name	ProductNumber	Color	StandardCost	ListPrice	Size	Weight	ProductCategoryID	ProductNa
680	HL Road Frame - Black, 58	FR-R92B-58	Black	1059.31	1431.5	58	1016.04	18	Road Fram
706	HL Road Frame - Red, 58	FR-R92R-58	Red	1059.31	1431.5	58	1016.04	18	Road Fram
707	Sport-100 Helmet, Red	HL-U509-R	Red	13.0863	34.99	null	null	35	Helmets
708	Sport-100 Helmet, Black	HL-U509	Black	13.0863	34.99	null	null	35	Helmets
709	Mountain Bike Socks, M	SO-B909-M	White	3.3963	9.5	M	null	27	Socks
710	Mountain Bike Socks, L	SO-B909-L	White	3.3963	9.5	L	null	27	Socks
711	Sport-100 Helmet, Blue	HL-U509-B	Blue	13.0863	34.99	null	null	35	Helmets
712	AWC Logo Cap	CA-1098	Multi	6.9223	8.99	null	null	23	Caps
713	Long-Sleeve Logo Jersey, S	LJ-0192-S	Multi	38.4923	49.99	S	null	25	Jerseys
714	Long-Sleeve Logo Jersey, M	LJ-0192-M	Multi	38.4923	49.99	M	null	25	Jerseys
715	Long-Sleeve Logo Jersey, L	LJ-0192-L	Multi	38.4923	49.99	L	null	25	Jerseys
716	Long-Sleeve Logo Jersey, XL	LJ-0192-X	Multi	38.4923	49.99	XL	null	25	Jerseys
717	HL Road Frame - Red, 62	FR-R92R-62	Red	868.6342	1431.5	62	1043.26	18	Road Fram
718	HL Road Frame - Red, 44	FR-R92R-44	Red	868.6342	1431.5	44	961.61	18	Road Fram
719	HL Road Frame - Red, 48	FR-R92R-48	Red	868.6342	1431.5	48	979.75	18	Road Fram
720	HL Road Frame - Red, 52	FR-R92R-52	Red	868.6342	1431.5	52	997.9	18	Road Fram
721	HL Road Frame - Red, 56	FR-R92R-56	Red	868.6342	1431.5	56	1016.04	18	Road Fram
722	LL Road Frame - Black, 58	FR-R38B-58	Black	204.6251	337.22	58	1115.83	18	Road Fram
723	LL Road Frame - Black, 60	FR-R38B-60	Black	204.6251	337.22	60	1124.9	18	Road Fram
724	LL Road Frame - Black, 62	FR-R38B-62	Black	204.6251	337.22	62	1133.98	18	Road Fram

FIGURE 11-9 *Preview the columns you specified and click Load.*

11

Create a Power BI report

In this section you'll create a Power BI report based on data imported via import mode from the AdventureWorksLT Azure SQL database, which includes product and sales information. Because earlier chapters, including Chapter 6, have discussed the ins and outs of creating reports—such as adding visuals, arranging visuals, preparing a report for mobile view, publishing and viewing the report, and preparing a dashboard from the report—I won't repeat that information here. Instead, I'll simply indicate which visuals to add, and show you the results in report, mobile, and dashboard form.

Let's start with the visuals. Add the following items to your report:

- **Slicer** You'll use a slicer to filter data by product.

- **Line and clustered column chart** A line and clustered column chart will show order quantities by product.

- **Pie chart** A pie chart will show the customer count by country.

- **Donut chart** You'll use a donut chart to show customer count by salesperson.

- **Gauge chart** To show information related to total cities, total products, and total customers, you'll use a gauge chart.

- **Area chart** An area chart will show the customer count by city.

- **Stacked bar chart** A stacked bar chart will show the order quantity count by salesperson and product color.

- **Table** A table will contain informational data such as product name, list price, color, size, standard cost, and weight.

After you add the visuals, you can arrange them as desired. (See Figure 11-10.)

> ⚠ **IMPORTANT** In case you didn't actually build the report, I provided a final version of it for your use: SampleReportAzureSQL.pbix. As mentioned, you can access this file from the MSPBIDashboards\ch11 folder on the book's companion website.

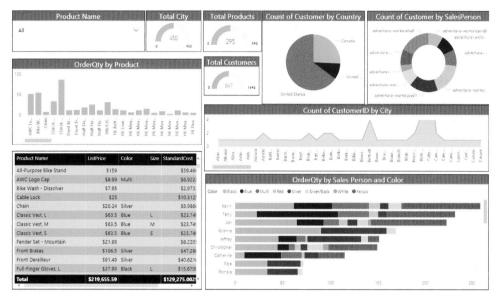

FIGURE 11-10 *Your Power BI report, complete with visuals.*

As you saw in previous chapters, you can also prepare the report for display on a mobile device. (See Figure 11-11.) (For more details, refer to Chapter 4.)

FIGURE 11-11 *Prepare the report for display on a mobile device.*

Finally, Figure 11-12 shows a dashboard generated from visuals from various reports, including the one created in this chapter. (For more details, refer to Chapter 1.)

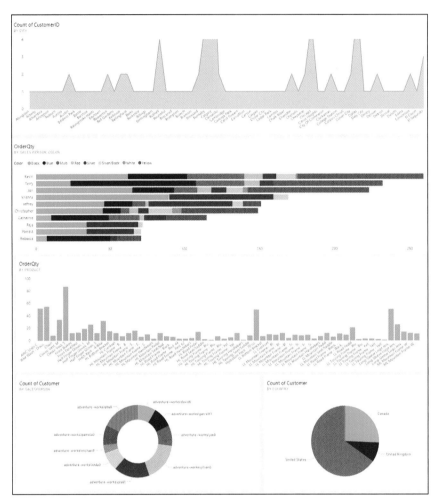

FIGURE 11-12 *Preparing a dashboard from different Power BI reports.*

Set up a live data connection and data refresh functionality

You can set up a live data connection between the Azure SQL database and Power BI. Through this connection, you can keep your Power BI reports up to date.

> ⚠ **IMPORTANT** Before you set up the live data connection, you must publish your report to Power BI service.

To configure a live data connection and set up your Power BI report to refresh on a schedule you select, follow these steps:

1. Log in to Power BI service.

2. Under **Datasets**, hover your mouse button over the report you created using data from the Azure SQL database, click the ellipsis that appears, and click **Schedule Refresh**. (See Figure 11-13.)

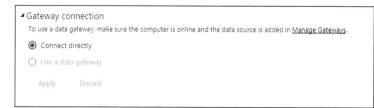

FIGURE 11-13 *Create a live data connection and set the refresh schedule.*

A Settings window for the report opens.

3. Expand the **Gateway Connection** section, click the **Connect Directly** option button, and click **Apply**. (See Figure 11-14.)

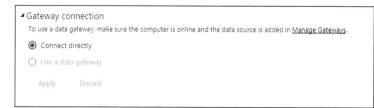

FIGURE 11-14 *Select the Connect Directly option button and click Apply.*

4. Expand the **Data Source Credentials** section of the Settings window and click the **Edit Credentials link**. (See Figure 11-15.)

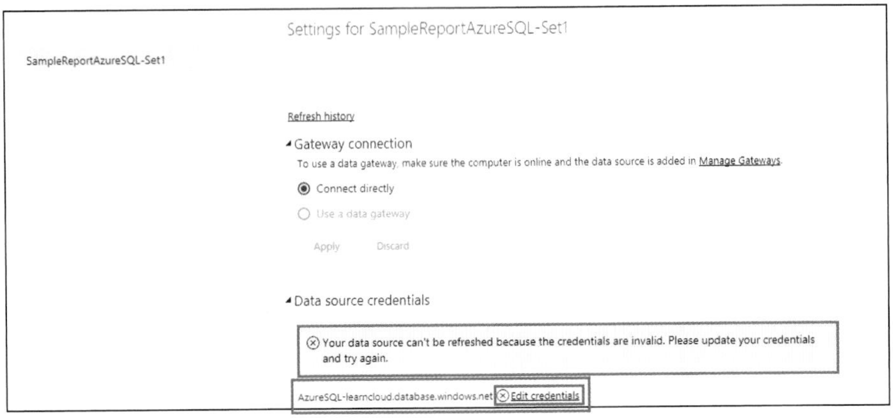

FIGURE 11-15 *Click the Edit Credentials link in the report's Settings window.*

A Configure window opens. (See Figure 11-16.)

5. In the **Server** box, type the name of the Azure SQL Server on which the database to which you want to connect lives. (Refer to step 4 in the section "Overview of the Azure SQL portal.")

6. In the **Database** box, enter the name of the database—in this case, **AzureSQL**.

7. Open the **Authentication Method** drop-down list and choose **Basic**.

8. Enter the username for the Azure SQL database to which you want to connect in the **User Name** box.

9. Type the corresponding password in the **Password** box.

10. Select the **End Users Use Their Own OAuth2 Credentials When Accessing This Data Source Via DirectQuery** checkbox.

11. Click the **Sign In** button.

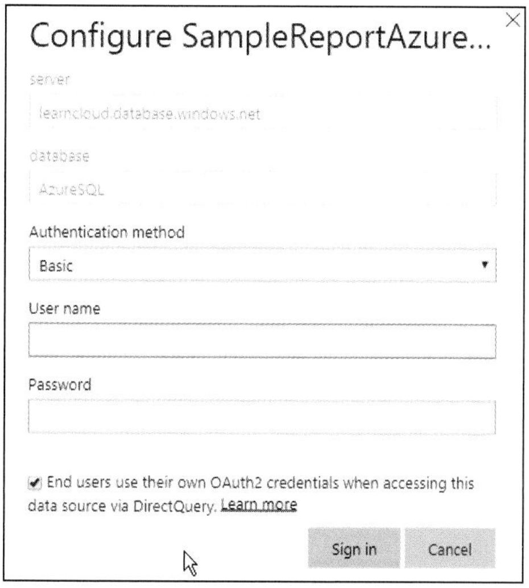

FIGURE 11-16 *You edit your credentials in the Configure window.*

12. Back in the Settings window for the report, expand the **Scheduled Refresh** settings.

13. Toggle the **Keep Your Data Up to Date** setting to **On**. (See Figure 11-17.)

14. Open the **Refresh Frequency** drop-down list and select how often you want to refresh the data.

15. Open the **Time Zone** drop-down list and indicate your time zone.

16. Optionally, select the **Send Refresh Failure Notification Email to Me** checkbox to receive an email in the event a refresh operation fails.

11

17. Click **Apply**.

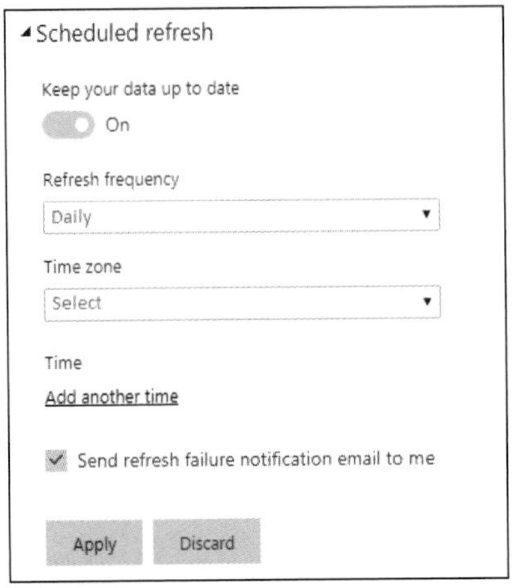

FIGURE 11-17 *Setting up scheduled refresh functionality.*

Skills review

In this chapter, you learned about:

■ The Azure SQL portal

■ Importing data from an Azure SQL database via import mode and DirectQuery mode

■ Creating a Power BI report

■ Setting up a live data connection and data refresh functionality

Practice tasks

This section provides a simple case study for you to study and solve using information from this chapter. This section also contains a series of practice questions for you to answer.

Case study

Suppose you work for a forensics lab that deals with medical assessments. You deal with different ratios of data across distinct research fields and several parameters on your Power BI platform. You draw your data from an Azure SQL database. Most of this data belongs to the research and analysis department.

Your mission is to convey the following data to extend the yearly analysis:

- The number of drugs researched

- The probability of patients encountering death organized by cause of death

- The number of food samples taken for further observation and reported appropriate versus inappropriate

- The count of human blood samples and their associated deficiencies

- The number of studies conducted to analyze the health of accident patients

- Cumulative data for animal diseases and their after-effects

- An analysis of the number of cases involving malnutrition or deficiency disorders

To achieve this, you'll need to do the following:

- Prepare the report from data on the Azure SQL database.

- Set up a live data connection to fetch data from the Azure SQL database at a refresh rate of your choice.

Using this report, decision-makers can come to a definite conclusion on the overall quality of the forensic research performed on distinct categories. By analyzing any faults, an improvement in the overall success ratio becomes possible.

Practice questions

1. How do you connect with an Azure SQL database using Power BI Desktop?

2. What is the difference between using import mode and using DirectQuery mode to obtain data from an Azure SQL database?

3. How can you find out the server name and database name from the Azure portal?

4. True or false: You can see available data options when you connect to the Azure SQL database using DirectQuery mode.

5. How do you set up scheduled refresh functionality in Power BI?

Develop Power BI reports from Oracle

In this chapter, you'll learn how to build a Power BI report that relies on data from an Oracle database. Like several other data sources, you can obtain data from an Oracle database by importing it using import mode or DirectQuery mode. You'll also learn how to set up a data gateway to work with the Oracle database. This data gateway will be configured with Oracle Data Access Components (ODAC).

In this chapter:

- Import data from an Oracle database into Power BI
- Create a Power BI report
- Set and configure a data gateway

Practice files

As you work through this chapter, you'll use one practice file, which you can access from the book's companion website at *https://aka.ms/PowerBIDash/downloads* in the following folder: MSPBIDashboards\ch12. (I recommend you save this file to your system before you proceed.) The file is as follows:

- **SampleReport - Oracle.pbix** This file is a sample Power BI report generated from data in an Oracle database. It consists of HR information. You'll use this report in the "Create a Power BI report" section later in this chapter.

Import data from an Oracle database into Power BI

There are two ways to import data from an Oracle database into Power BI:

- **Import mode** When you use import mode to import data, that data is cached from the database into Power BI. To ensure you are working with the latest data, you will need to refresh it on a regular basis.

- **DirectQuery mode** DirectQuery does not explicitly import data into Power BI. Rather, it maintains a connection between Power BI and the Oracle database. When you build a report in Power BI using this data, it will update in real time.

You'll learn how to import data using both methods in this section.

> **TIP** For more information about these two modes, refer to Chapter 9.

> **IMPORTANT** To import data from an Oracle database into Power BI Desktop, the Oracle client software must be installed on the computer running Power BI Desktop. For more information, see *https://docs.microsoft.com/en-us/power-bi/desktop-connect-oracle-database*.

> ⚠️ **IMPORTANT** The steps in this section are simply for your edification. In fact, you'll access the Oracle database from which you will build a Power BI report from one of the following links:
>
> *https://docs.oracle.com/database/121/COMSC/installation.htm#COMSC001*
>
> *https://github.com/oracle/db-sample-schemas.*

Import data using import mode

To import data from an Oracle database into Power BI using import mode, follow these steps:

1. Click the **Home** tab in Power BI Desktop.

2. Click **Get Data**.

3. Choose **Database**, select **Oracle Database**, and click **Connect**. (See Figure 12-1.)

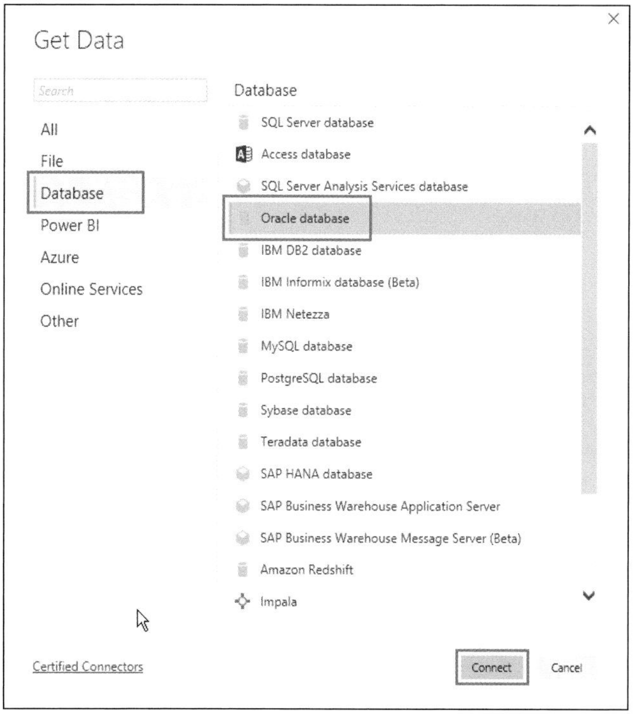

FIGURE 12-1 *Select Oracle Database from the Database options in the Get Data window.*

The Oracle Database window opens. (See Figure 12-2.)

4. Type the name of the Oracle server from which you want to import data in the **Server** box.

5. Under **Data Connectivity Mode**, select the **Import** option button.

6. Click **OK**.

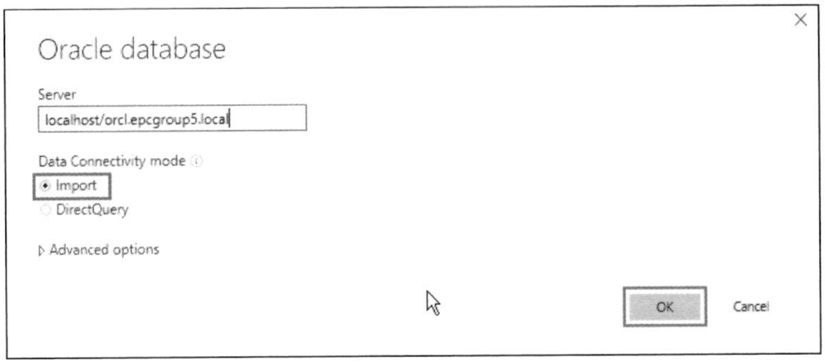

FIGURE 12-2 *The Oracle database window for connecting to an Oracle database.*

7. When prompted to select the authentication method (see Figure 12-3), choose **Database**.

8. In the **User Name** box, type the username for the Oracle database.

9. In the **Password** box, type the corresponding password.

10. Click **Connect**.

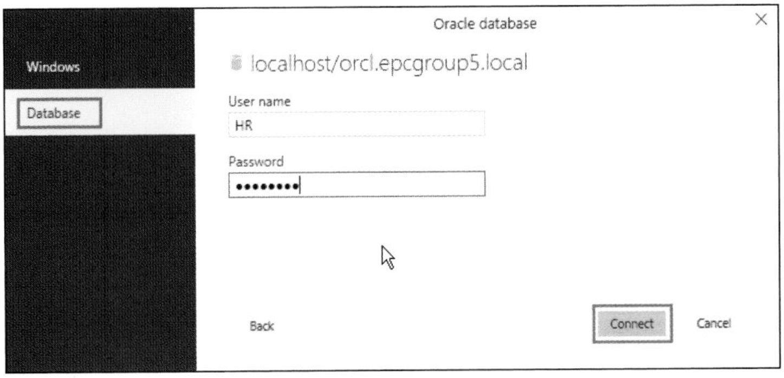

FIGURE 12-3 *Selection of authentication method for Oracle database.*

You'll see a list of all the tables available in the Oracle database on the left, with a preview of the selected table on the right. (See Figure 12-4.)

11. Select the tables you want to import and click **Load**.

Power BI Desktop imports the tables and builds a data model from them.

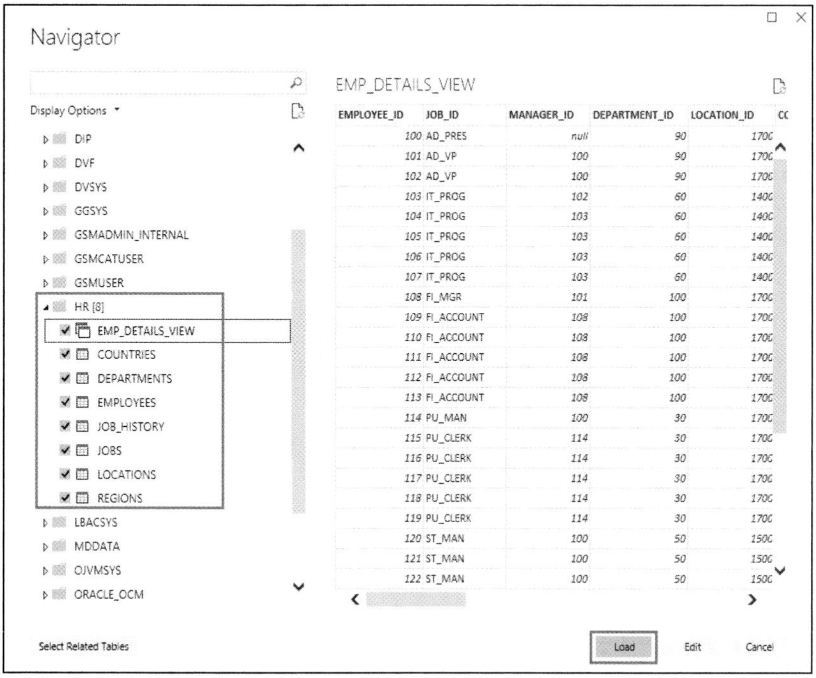

FIGURE 12-4 *Select the tables you want to import from the Oracle database.*

Connect with data using DirectQuery mode

Here's how you connect with data in an Oracle database from Power BI using DirectQuery mode:

1. Repeat steps 1–4 from the previous section.

2. Under **Data Connectivity Mode**, select the **DirectQuery** option button, and click **OK**. (See Figure 12-5.)

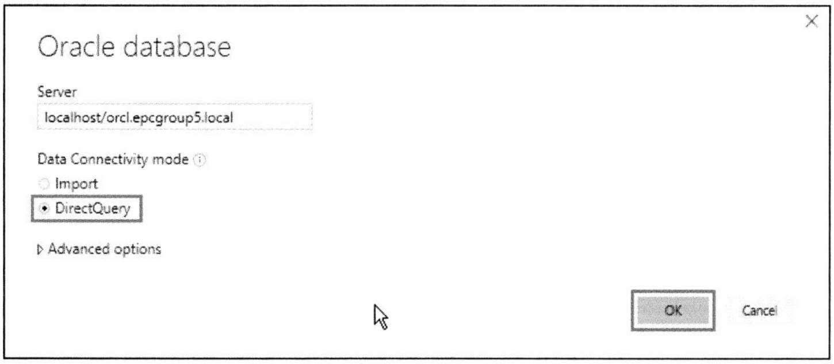

FIGURE 12-5 *Select DirectQuery under Data Connectivity Mode and click OK.*

3. When prompted to select the authentication method, choose **Database**.

4. In the **User Name** box, type the username for the Oracle database.

5. In the **Password** box, type the corresponding password.

6. Click **Connect**.

    You'll see a list of all the tables available in the Oracle database, with a preview of the selected table.

7. Select the tables you want to connect to and click **Load**.

    Power BI Desktop connects to the tables, but unlike with import mode, it does not build a data model from it. This is because Power BI Desktop is connected directly to the data source. (See Figure 12-6.)

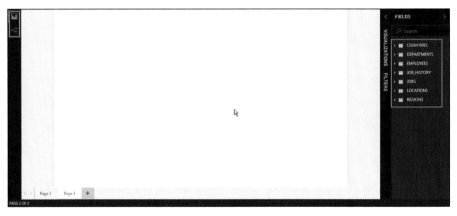

FIGURE 12-6 *Connecting to data in an Oracle database using DirectQuery mode.*

Import data using an inline query

You can also import data from an Oracle database into Power BI using an inline query. Inline queries can be used for both import mode and DirectQuery mode imports. These steps show you how to use an inline query to conduct an import mode operation:

⚠️ **IMPORTANT** If these seem familiar to you, it's because you followed similar steps in Chapter 9 and Chapter 11 to import data into an Oracle database using an inline query.

1. Repeat steps 1-5 from the section "Import data using import mode."

2. Expand the **Advanced Options** section in the Oracle Database window and type the following inline query (see Figure 12-7):

```
SELECT* from Employees
```

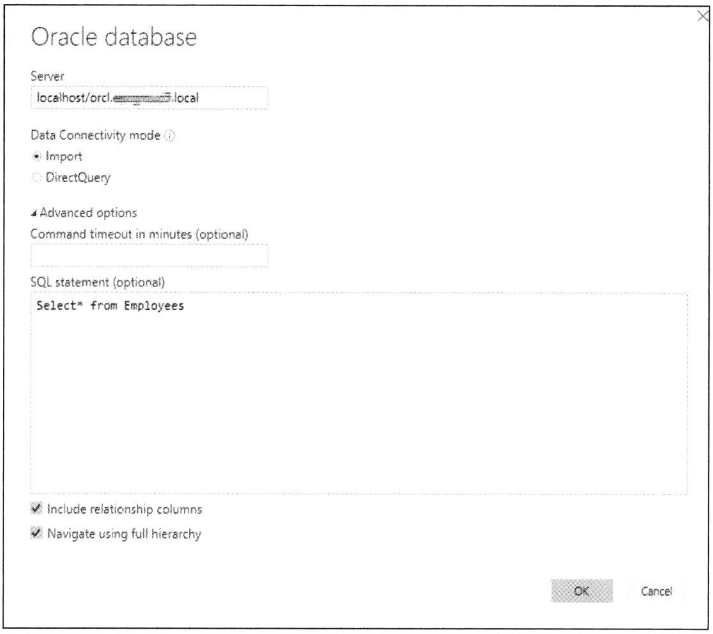

FIGURE 12-7 *Using an inline query to import from an Oracle database in import mode.*

3. Optionally, select the **Include Relationship Columns** and **Navigate Using Full Hierarchy** checkboxes.

4. Click **OK**.

5. When prompted to select the authentication method, choose **Database**.

6. In the **User Name** box, type the username for the Oracle database.

7. In the **Password** box, type the corresponding password.

8. Click **Connect**.

9. Preview the columns of data you specified for import and click **Load**. (See Figure 12-8.)

12

localhost/orcl.epcgroup5.local

EMPLOYEE_ID	FIRST_NAME	LAST_NAME	EMAIL	PHONE_NUMBER	HIRE_DATE	JOB_ID	SALARY	COMMISSION_PCT
100	Steven	King	SKING	515.123.4567	6/17/2003 12:00:00 AM	AD_PRES	24000	
101	Neena	Kochhar	NKOCHHAR	515.123.4568	9/21/2005 12:00:00 AM	AD_VP	17000	
102	Lex	De Haan	LDEHAAN	515.123.4569	1/13/2001 12:00:00 AM	AD_VP	17000	
103	Alexander	Hunold	AHUNOLD	590.423.4567	1/3/2006 12:00:00 AM	IT_PROG	9000	
104	Bruce	Ernst	BERNST	590.423.4568	5/21/2007 12:00:00 AM	IT_PROG	6000	
105	David	Austin	DAUSTIN	590.423.4569	6/25/2005 12:00:00 AM	IT_PROG	4800	
106	Valli	Pataballa	VPATABAL	590.423.4560	2/5/2006 12:00:00 AM	IT_PROG	4800	
107	Diana	Lorentz	DLORENTZ	590.423.5567	2/7/2007 12:00:00 AM	IT_PROG	4200	
108	Nancy	Greenberg	NGREENBE	515.124.4569	8/17/2002 12:00:00 AM	FI_MGR	12008	
109	Daniel	Faviet	DFAVIET	515.124.4169	8/16/2002 12:00:00 AM	FI_ACCOUNT	9000	
110	John	Chen	JCHEN	515.124.4269	9/28/2005 12:00:00 AM	FI_ACCOUNT	8200	
111	Ismael	Sciarra	ISCIARRA	515.124.4369	9/30/2005 12:00:00 AM	FI_ACCOUNT	7700	
112	Jose Manuel	Urman	JMURMAN	515.124.4469	3/7/2006 12:00:00 AM	FI_ACCOUNT	7800	
113	Luis	Popp	LPOPP	515.124.4567	12/7/2007 12:00:00 AM	FI_ACCOUNT	6900	
114	Den	Raphaely	DRAPHEAL	515.127.4561	12/7/2002 12:00:00 AM	PU_MAN	11000	
115	Alexander	Khoo	AKHOO	515.127.4562	5/18/2003 12:00:00 AM	PU_CLERK	3100	
116	Shelli	Baida	SBAIDA	515.127.4563	12/24/2005 12:00:00 AM	PU_CLERK	2900	
117	Sigal	Tobias	STOBIAS	515.127.4564	7/24/2005 12:00:00 AM	PU_CLERK	2800	
118	Guy	Himuro	GHIMURO	515.127.4565	11/15/2006 12:00:00 AM	PU_CLERK	2600	
119	Karen	Colmenares	KCOLMENA	515.127.4566	8/10/2007 12:00:00 AM	PU_CLERK	2500	

ⓘ The data in the preview has been truncated due to size limits.

Load   Edit   Cancel

FIGURE 12-8 *Preview the columns of data you specified for import and click Load.*

Create a Power BI report

In this section you'll create a Power BI report based on data imported via import mode from the Oracle database, which contains HR information. Because earlier chapters, including Chapter 6, have discussed the ins and outs of creating reports—such as adding visuals, arranging visuals, preparing the report for mobile view, publishing and viewing the report, and preparing a dashboard from the report—I won't repeat that information here. Instead, I'll simply indicate which visuals to add, and show you the results in report, mobile, and dashboard form.

Let's start with the visuals. Add the following items to your report:

- **Attribute slicer** You'll use an attribute slicer to filter data by department name.
- **Slicer** You'll use a slicer to filter data by job title, salary, and hiring date.
- **Funnel chart** A funnel chart will show employee count by region.
- **Pie chart** A pie chart will show the employee count by country and region.
- **Line and stacked column chart** You'll use a line and stacked column chart to show the employee count by department and job title.
- **Gauge chart** To show total employee count, you'll use a gauge chart.
- **Table** A table will contain informational data such as employee first name, last name, phone number, salary, and job title.

After you add the visuals, you can arrange them as desired. (See Figure 12-9.)

> ⚠ **IMPORTANT** In case you didn't actually build the report, I provided a final version of it for your use: SampleReport - Oracle.pbix. As mentioned, you can access this file from the MSPBIDashboards\ch12 folder on the book's companion website.

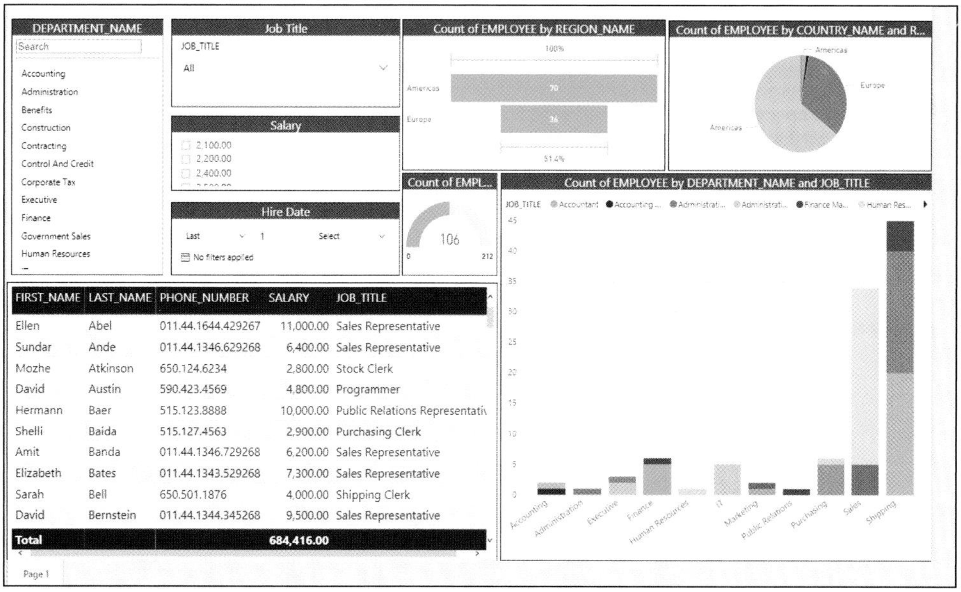

FIGURE 12-9 *Your Power BI report, complete with visuals.*

As you saw in previous chapters, you can also prepare the report for display on a mobile device. (See Figure 12-10.) (For more details, refer to Chapter 4.)

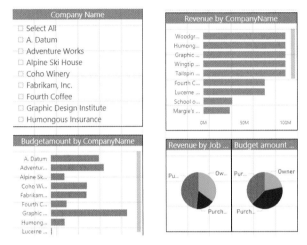

FIGURE 12-10 *Prepare the report for display on a mobile device.*

Finally, Figure 12-11 shows a dashboard generated from visuals from various reports, including the one created in this chapter. (For more details, refer to Chapter 1.)

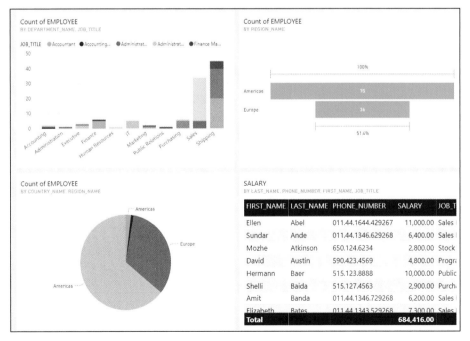

FIGURE 12-11 *Preparing a dashboard from different Power BI reports.*

Set up and configure a data gateway

As in previous chapters, you use a data gateway to establish a secure connection between the Oracle database and Power BI. Through this secure connection, Power BI reports generated from data in the Oracle database remain up to date. In essence, the gateway acts as a bridge between the Oracle database and Power BI. Using this bridge, Power BI updates reports based on data on the Oracle database.

Chapter 8 outlined the system requirements for a data gateway and explained what types of data gateways are available: shared and personal. It also stepped you through the procedure for installing a shared data gateway. Chapter 9 explained how to install a personal gateway. Please refer to those chapters for help installing your gateway. (This chapter assumes you set up a shared gateway.)

> ⚠ **IMPORTANT** Before you set up the data gateway, you must publish your report to Power BI service.

After your gateway is installed, you must configure it to use Power BI service. Follow these steps:

1. Log in to Power BI service.

2. Under **Datasets**, hover your mouse pointer over the report you created using data from the Oracle database, click the ellipsis that appears, and click **Schedule Refresh**. (See Figure 12-12.)

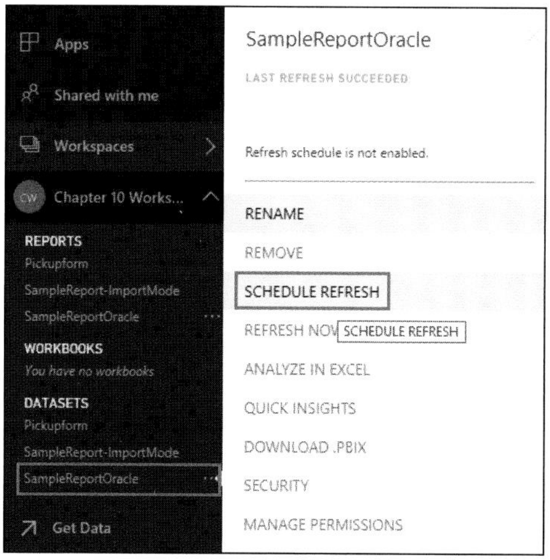

FIGURE 12-12 *Configuring the data gateway.*

3. In the Settings window that opens, select the Datasets tab and expand the **Gateway Connection** section. (See Figure 12-13.)

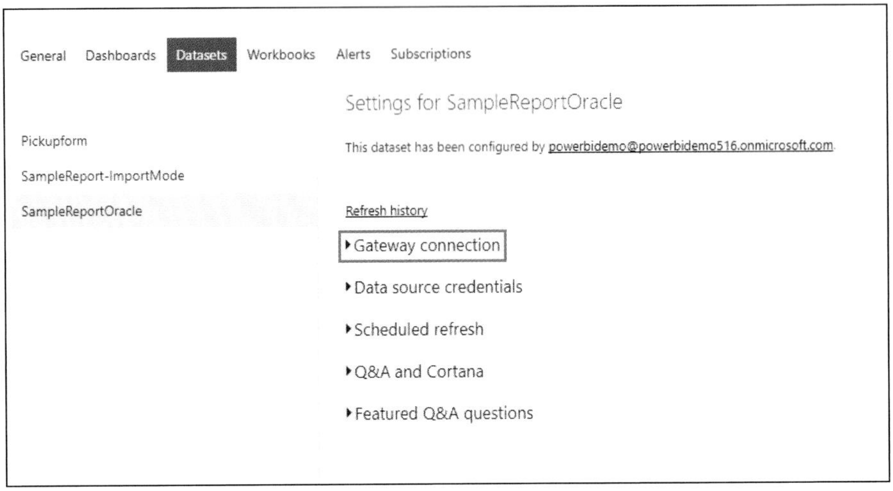

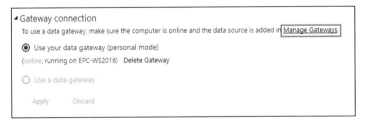

FIGURE 12-13 *Expand the Gateway Connection settings.*

4. Click the **Manage Gateways** link. (See Figure 12-14.)

FIGURE 12-14 *Click the Manage Gateways link.*

The Gateway Cluster Settings window opens. (See Figure 12-15.)

5. Click the Oracle Data Gateway option in the left pane.

6. Click the **Add Data Sources to Use the Gateway** link in the right pane.

FIGURE 12-15 *The Gateway Cluster Settings window.*

The Data Source Settings window opens. (See Figure 12-16.)

7. Type a name for the data source in the **Data Source Name** box.

8. Open the **Data Source Type** drop-down list and choose **Oracle**.

9. Type the name of the Oracle server to which you want to connect in the **Server** box.

10. Open the **Authentication Method** drop-down list and choose **Basic**.

11. Type your Oracle username in the **Username** box.

12. Type your password in the **Password** box.

13. Click the **Add** button.

12

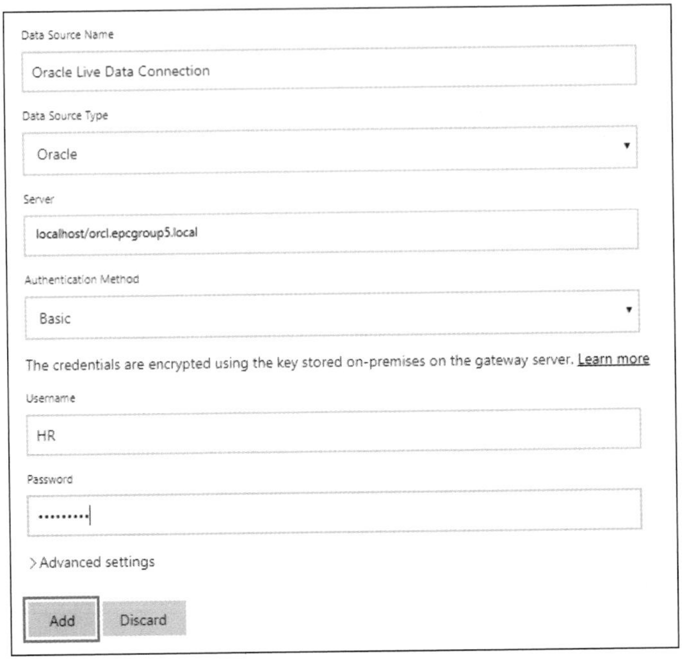

Data Source Name

Oracle Live Data Connection

Data Source Type

Oracle ▾

Server

localhost/orcl.epcgroup5.local

Authentication Method

Basic ▾

The credentials are encrypted using the key stored on-premises on the gateway server. Learn more

Username

HR

Password

•••••••••

> Advanced settings

[Add] [Discard]

FIGURE 12-16 *Enter the requested information in the Data Source Settings window to configure the data gateway connection.*

The Data Source Settings window should indicate that the connection to the data gateway was successful. (See Figure 12-17.)

14. To enable other users to use the connection, click the **Users** tab in the Data Source Settings window.

Data Source Settings   Users

✓ Connection Successful

ⓘ Next Step: Go to the Users tab above and add users to this Data Source

FIGURE 12-17 *The connection was successful.*

15. To allow someone permission to use the data gateway, type that person's email address in the **People Who Can Publish Reports That Use This Data Source** box and click **Add**.

16. In the Settings window for the report, under **Gateway Connection**, select the **Use a Data Gateway** option button, select the gateway (or gateways, if there are more than one), and click **Apply**. (See Figure 12-18.)

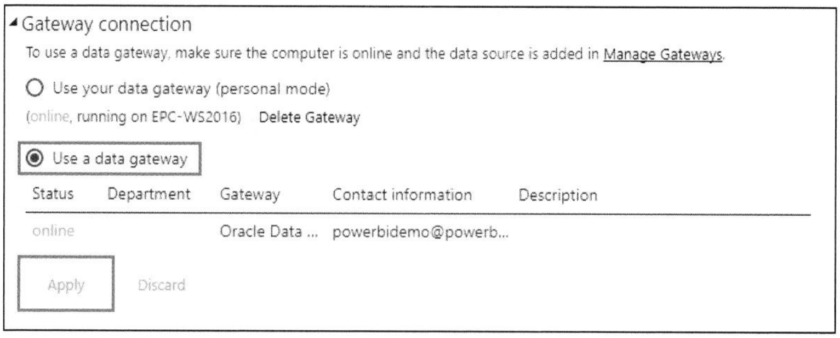

FIGURE 12-18 *Gateway connection setting option in Power BI.*

You'll see a Connection Updated message.

As a final step, you need to set up the report to refresh automatically through the data gateway.

17. Expand the **Scheduled Refresh** section in the Settings window. (See Figure 12-19.)

18. Toggle the **Keep Your Data Up to Date** setting to On.

19. Open the **Refresh Frequency** drop-down list and select how often you want to refresh the data.

20. Open the **Time Zone** drop-down list and indicate your time zone.

21. Select the **Send Refresh Failure Notification Email to Me** checkbox.

22. Click **Apply**.

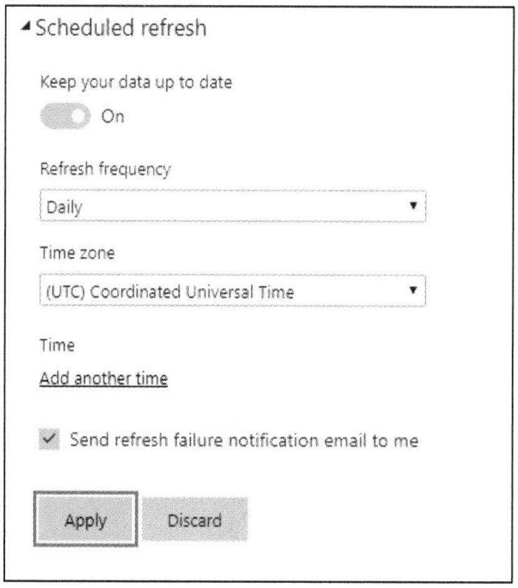

12

FIGURE 12-19 *Setting up scheduled refresh functionality.*

Skills review

In this chapter, you learned about:

- Importing data from an Oracle database via import mode and DirectQuery mode

- Creating a Power BI report

- Setting up and configuring a data gateway

Practice tasks

This section provides a simple case study for you to study and solve using information from this chapter. This section also contains a series of practice questions for you to answer.

Case study

Suppose you work for an ice-cream manufacturing company. The company has existed for more than 50 years and has a worldwide presence.

The manufacturer offers different products, such as the following:

- Hard ice-creams, which generally contain milk or cream with added ingredients for flavoring, such as candies and nuts

- Smooth ice-creams, which are generally frozen with cones

- Light ice-creams, which contain fat-free stabilizers and milk

- Organic ice-creams made from organically produced milk and other ingredients

- Dessert ice-creams, which generally include brownies or cookies

Sales data for all these product types over the last 50 years is stored in an Oracle database. You want to organize this data and present it in a series of Power BI reports for analysis by upper management, including the organization's chief financial officer (CFO). Specifically, you want the report to include the following information:

- A comparison of the sales of hard ice-cream with their smooth ice-cream counterparts during the previous year

- Region-specific sales for all product types

- Profits and losses per year during the previous 10 years

- Improvements to achieve target sales and reduce latency, filtered by product category

- Total revenue distribution across all products for the previous year

- A comparison of marketing channels and their success ratio

- A historic trend analysis using a growth graph to reflect actual growth percentage

How would you go about creating these reports?

Practice questions

1. How do you import data from an Oracle database?

2. What are the two modes of connection for obtaining data from an Oracle database?

3. How do you import data using an inline query?

4. True or false: You can see the data option when you connect to an Oracle database using DirectQuery mode.

5. How do you install a data gateway in personal mode and configure it with Power BI Online?

6. How do you set up the report to refresh automatically on a schedule you specify?

Develop Power BI reports from Dynamics 365

In this chapter, you'll learn how to develop a Power BI report that relies on data from Dynamics 365 as its source. In addition to learning how to import data from Dynamics 365 into Power BI Desktop, you'll learn how to import it into Power BI service. You'll also learn how to embed Power BI reports in a Dynamics 365 dashboard page and to set up data refresh functionality.

In this chapter:

- Import data from Dynamics 365 into Power BI Desktop

- Create a Power BI report

- Import data from Dynamics 365 into Power BI service

- Embed a Power BI dashboard into a Dynamics 365 dashboard

- Set up a live data connection and data refresh functionality

Practice files

As you work through this chapter, you'll use one practice file, which you can access from the book's companion website at *https://aka.ms/PowerBIDash/downloads* in the following folder: MSPBIDashboards\ch13. The file is as follows:

- **Sample-Dynamics 365 Sales Report.pbix** This file is a sample Power BI report that consists of organizational information, like total revenue, employee information, and so on. You'll use this report in the "Create a Power BI report" section later in this chapter.

Import data from Dynamics 365 into Power BI Desktop

To connect to Dynamics 365 using Power BI Desktop, you must obtain an OData endpoint URL from Dynamics 365. (This is also referred to as a Web API.) You'll use this URL to connect to Dynamics 365.

Obtain the OData endpoint URL

To obtain the OData endpoint URL, follow these steps:

1. Log in to your Dynamics 365 environment.

2. Click the **Settings** option.

3. In the **Customization** category, click **Customizations**. (See Figure 13-1.)

FIGURE 13-1 *Click the Customizations option under Customization in the Dynamics 365 Settings page.*

A Customization page opens. (See Figure 13-2.)

4. Click **Developer Resources**. These resources enable you to view information or download files to develop applications and extensions for Dynamics 365.

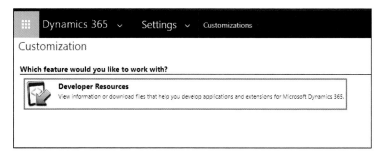

FIGURE 13-2 *Click Developer Resources in the Customization page.*

The Developer Resources window opens.

5. Copy the URL in the Service Root URL box in the **Instance Web API** section under **Connect Your Apps to This Instance of Dynamics 365**. (See Figure 13-3.) You'll refer to this URL in the next set of steps.

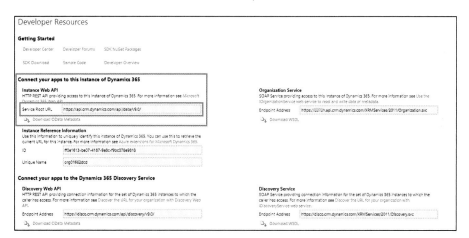

FIGURE 13-3 *The Developer Resources page.*

Connect to Dynamics 365

After you obtain the OData endpoint URL, you're ready to connect to Dynamics 365 to obtain the desired data for your Power BI report. Follow these steps:

1. In Power BI Desktop, click the **Home** tab.

2. Click **Get Data**.

3. Choose **Online Services** and select **Dynamics 365 (Online)**. (See Figure 13-4.)

4. Click **Connect**.

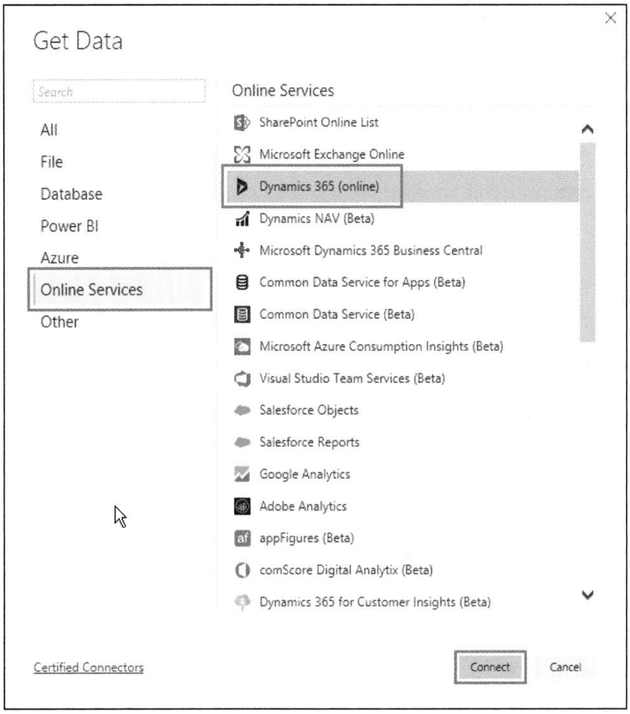

FIGURE 13-4 *Connect to Dynamics 365 in Power BI Desktop.*

A Dynamics 365 (Online) dialog box opens. (See Figure 13-5.)

5. Select the **Basic** option button.

6. In the **Web API URL** box, enter the URL you obtained in step 5 in the previous section.

> ⚠️ **IMPORTANT** In this example, I typed v8.1 at the end of the URL rather than v.9.0. This is because v8.1 is more stable. It's also the version used in the official Microsoft blog, as shown here: *https://technet.microsoft.com/en-us/library/dn708055.aspx.*

7. Click **OK**. Power BI Desktop will use this URL to connect to Dynamics 365.

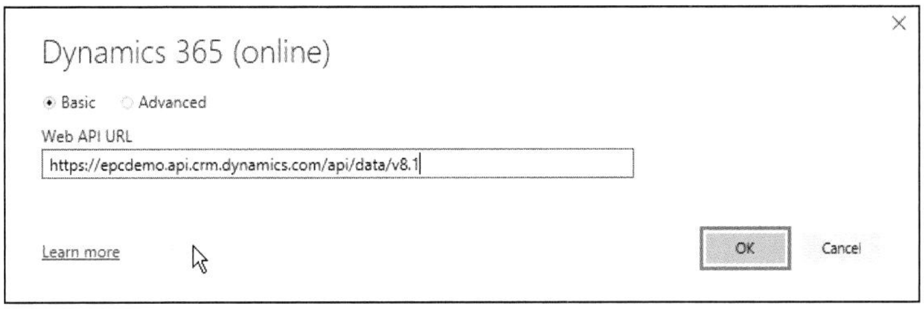

FIGURE 13-5 *Enter the Web API URL in the Dynamics 365 Online dialog box.*

URL syntax

Generally, the syntax for Web API URL is as follows:

https://OrganizationName.api.crm.dynamics.com/api/data/v8.1

where OrganizationName is the name of your organization. In this example, the organization's name is xyz, so its Web API URL is as follows:

https://xyz.api.crm.dynamics.com/api/data/v8.1

13

8. Power BI Desktop prompts you to choose from several authentication methods. In this example, select **Organizational Account**.

9. Enter your Dynamics 365 username in the **Username** box.

10. In the **Password** box, type the corresponding password.

11. Click **Connect**.

   After you connect, you'll see a list of all the tables available in Dynamics 365 on the left, with a preview of the selected table on the right.

12. Select the tables you want to import and click **Load**.

   Power BI Desktop imports the tables and builds a data model from them.

Create a Power BI report

In this section you'll create a Power BI report based on data imported from Dynamics 365 using OData endpoints. Because earlier chapters, including Chapter 6, have discussed the ins and outs of creating reports—such as adding visuals, arranging visuals, preparing the report for mobile view, publishing and viewing the report, and preparing a dashboard from the report—I won't repeat that information here. Instead, I'll simply indicate which visuals to add, and show you the results in report, mobile, and dashboard form.

Let's start with the visuals. Add the following items to your report:

- **Slicer** You'll use a slicer to filter data by company name.

- **Funnel chart** A funnel chart will show employee counts by job title.

- **Pie chart** Pie charts will show the revenue by job title and budget by job title.

- **Clustered bar chart** You'll use clustered bar charts to show revenue by company name and budget by company name.

After you add the visuals, you can arrange them as desired. (See Figure 13-6.)

> ⚠ **IMPORTANT** In case you didn't actually build the report, I provided a final version of it for your use: Sample - Dynamics 365 Sales Report.pbix. As mentioned, you can access this file from the MSPBIDashboards\ch13 folder on the book's companion website.

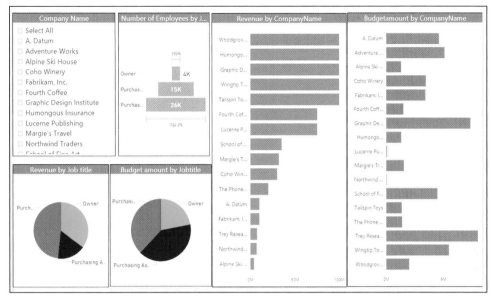

FIGURE 13-6 *Your Power BI report, complete with visuals.*

As you saw in previous chapters, you can also prepare the report for display on a mobile device. (See Figure 13-7.) (For more details, refer to Chapter 4.)

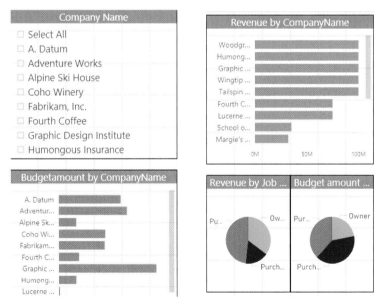

FIGURE 13-7 *Prepare the report for display on a mobile device.*

13

Finally, Figure 13-8 shows a dashboard generated from visuals from various reports, including the one created in this chapter. (For more details, refer to Chapter 1.)

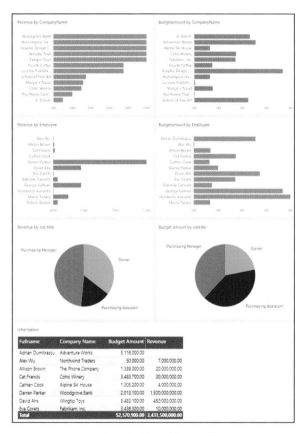

FIGURE 13-8 *Preparing a dashboard from different Power BI reports.*

Import data from Dynamics 365 into Power BI service

In addition to importing Dynamics 365 data into Power BI Desktop, you can import it into Power BI service. You can then use this data with content packs to create custom dashboards in Power BI service.

To import Dynamics 365 data into Power BI service, follow these steps:

1. In the Power BI service portal, click the **Get Data** option.

2. Under **Microsoft AppSource**, in the **Services** section, click the **Get** button. (See Figure 13-9.)

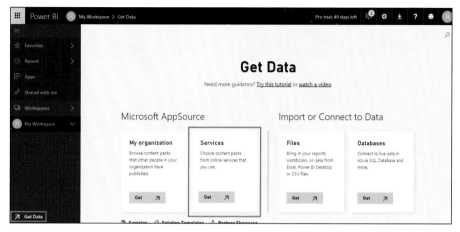

FIGURE 13-9 *Click the Get button under Services in Power BI service.*

The Apps for Power BI Apps screen opens, with various content packs.

3. Click the **Sales Analytics for Dynamics 365** content pack to access historical analytics and performance data. (See Figure 13-10.)

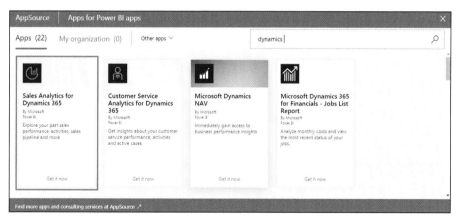

FIGURE 13-10 *Select the Sales Analytics for Dynamics 365 option.*

A Connect to Sales Analytics for Dynamics 365 dialog box opens. (See Figure 13-11.)

4. In the **Dynamics CRM Online 2016 Service** box, enter the URL that corresponds to your Dynamics CRM Online Service.

5. In the **Fiscal Year End Month Number**, enter the number that represents the last month of your fiscal year (in this example, I entered **8**, for August).

6. Click **Next**.

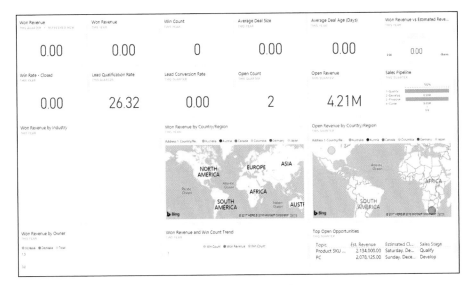

FIGURE 13-11 *Connecting to sales analytics data for Dynamics 365.*

7. When prompted, enter your username and password in the appropriate boxes.

A Power BI dashboard opens showing the data you specified. (See Figure 13-12.)

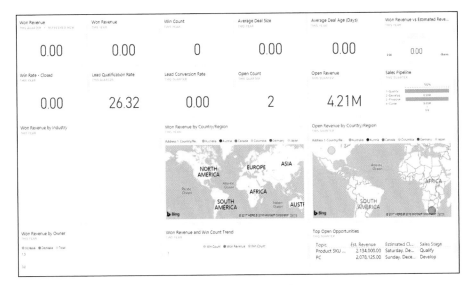

FIGURE 13-12 *A Power BI dashboard showing Dynamics 365 data.*

Embed a Power BI dashboard into a Dynamics 365 dashboard

In addition to generating Power BI dashboards from Dynamics 365 content packs, you can embed a Power BI dashboard into a Dynamics 365 dashboard. This way, you can access the information directly within Dynamics 365.

Enable the embed feature

Before you can embed a Power BI dashboard in a Dynamics 365 dashboard, you must enable the embed feature. Follow these steps:

1. Log in to your Dynamics 365 environment.

2. Click the **Settings** option.

3. In the **System** category, click **Administration**. (See Figure 13-13.)

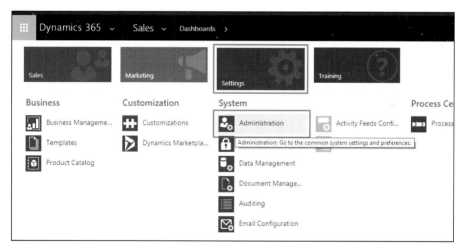

FIGURE 13-13 *Click the Administration option under System in the Dynamics 365 Settings page.*

An Administration page opens. (See Figure 13-14.)

4. Click **System Settings**. This will enable you to set tracking, marketing, and custom settings.

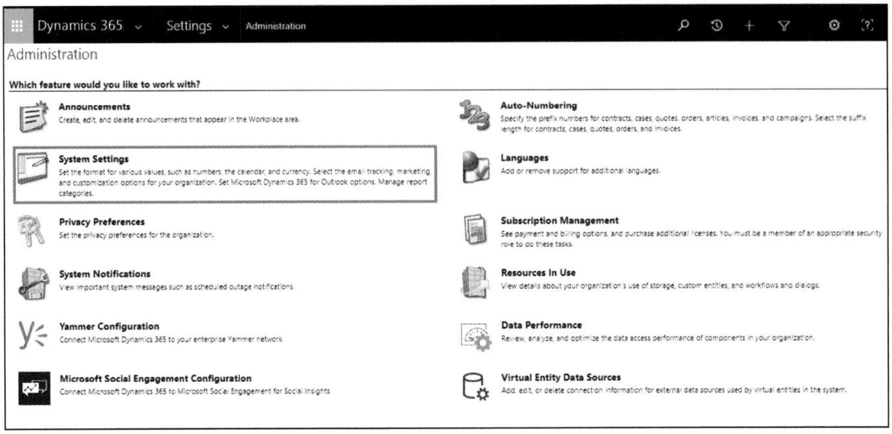

FIGURE 13-14 *Click System Settings in the Administration page.*

> ⚠ **IMPORTANT** You must have administrator privileges to change the system settings.

5. Select the **Yes** option button to the right of **Allow Power BI Visualization Embedding** and click **OK**. (See Figure 13-15.)

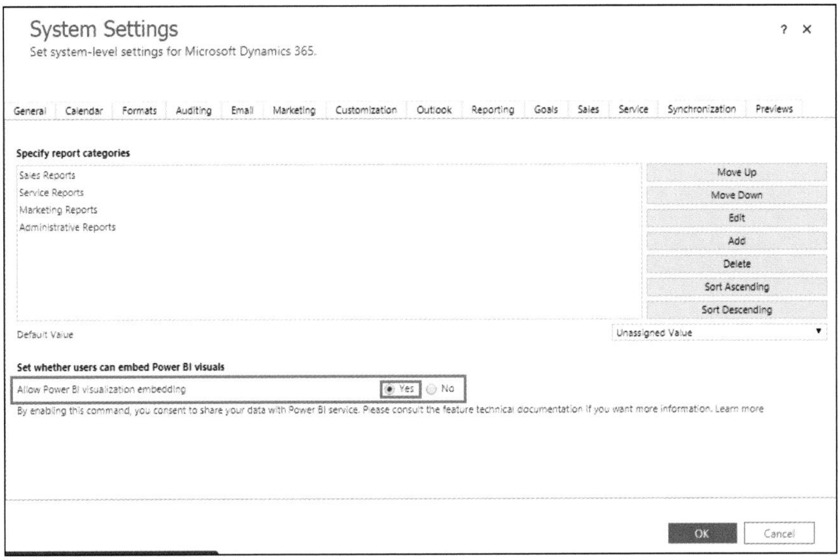

FIGURE 13-15 *Enable the embed feature.*

Embed the dashboard

Now that you've enabled the embed feature, you're ready to embed a Power BI dashboard into a Dynamics 365 dashboard. Follow these steps:

1. Open the Dynamics 365 Sales Dashboard.

2. Click **New** and choose **Power BI Dashboard**. (See Figure 13-16.)

FIGURE 13-16 *Click the New button and choose Power BI Dashboard.*

The Add Power BI Dashboard dialog box opens. (See Figure 13-17.)

3. Click the **Workspace** drop-down list and choose the workspace on which your Power BI dashboard is saved.

4. Open the **Dashboard** drop-down list and choose the dashboard you want to embed.

5. To enable mobile viewing of the embedded dashboard, select the **Enable for Mobile** checkbox. Then click **Save**.

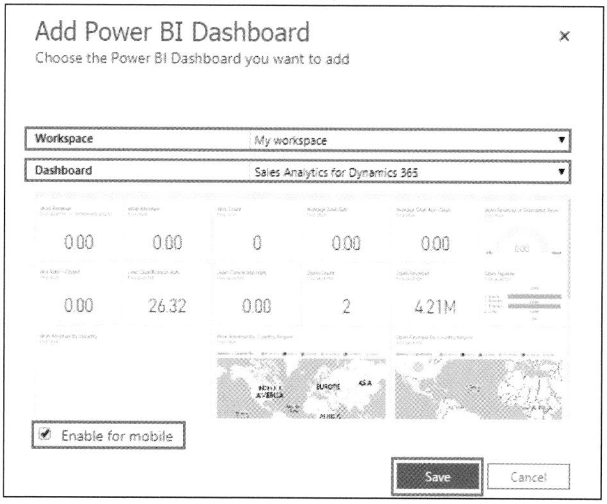

13

FIGURE 13-17 *Embed a Power BI dashboard into Dynamics 365.*

The Power BI dashboard is embedded in the Dynamics 365 dashboard. (See Figure 13-18.)

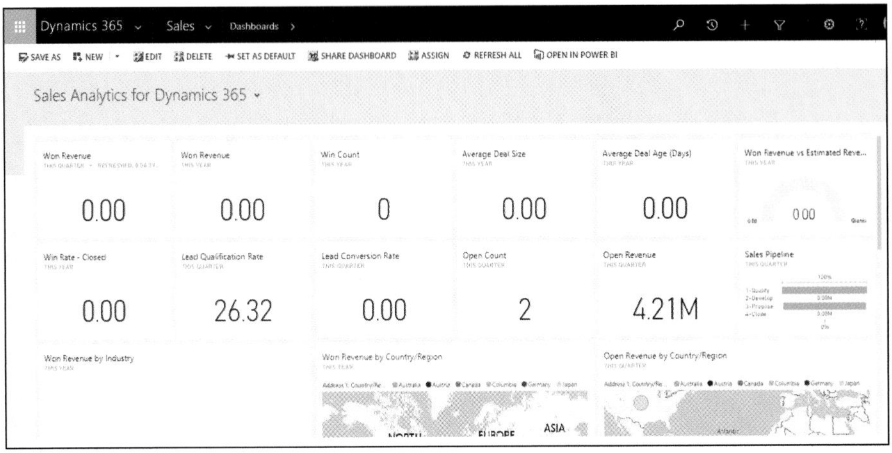

FIGURE 13-18 *The Power BI dashboard is embedded in the Dynamics 365 dashboard.*

Set up data refresh functionality

You can set up a schedule refresh between Dynamics 365 and Power BI. In this way, you can keep your Power BI reports based on Dynamics 365 data up to date.

> ⚠️ **IMPORTANT** Before you set up data refresh functionality, you must publish your report to Power BI service.

To configure a live data connection and set up your Power BI report to refresh on a schedule you select, follow these steps:

1. Log in to Power BI service.

2. Under **Datasets**, hover your mouse pointer over the report you created using data from Dynamics 365, click the ellipsis that appears, and click **Schedule Refresh**. (See Figure 13-19.)

Recent
Apps
Shared with me
Workspaces
Chapter 12 Works...
DASHBOARDS
Chapter 12 Dashboard
REPORTS
Sales-DSales
WORKBOOKS
You have no workbooks
DATASETS
Sales-DSales
Get Data
Sales-DSales
LAST REFRESH SUCCEEDED
Mon Jan 08 2018
Refresh schedule is not enabled.
RENAME
REMOVE
SCHEDULE REFRESH
REFRESH NOW
ANALYZE IN EXCEL
QUICK INSIGHTS
DOWNLOAD .PBIX
SECURITY
MANAGE PERMISSIONS

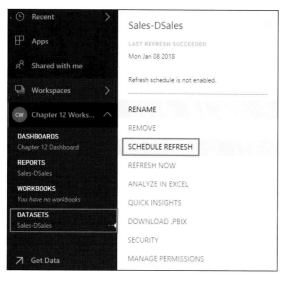

FIGURE 13-19 *Create a live data connection and set the refresh schedule.*

3. A Settings page opens for the selected data source. Select the Datasets tab and expand the **Data Source Credentials section**. (See Figure 13-20.) Then click **Edit Credentials**.

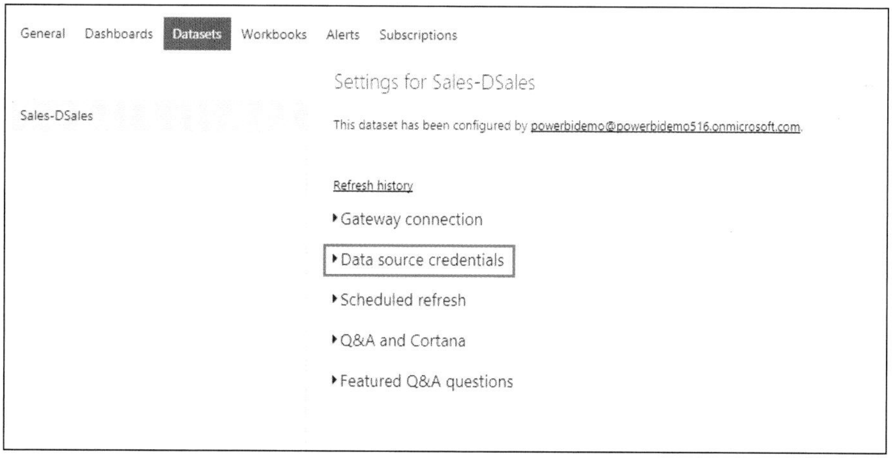

General
Dashboards
Datasets
Workbooks
Alerts
Subscriptions
Settings for Sales-DSales
Sales-DSales
This dataset has been configured by powerbidemo@powerbidemo516.onmicrosoft.com.
Refresh history
Gateway connection
Data source credentials
Scheduled refresh
Q&A and Cortana
Featured Q&A questions

FIGURE 13-20 *Current data source setting showing Data source credentials.*

A Configure dialog box for the selected data source opens. (See Figure 13-21.)

4. Open the **Authentication Method** drop-down list and choose **OAuth2**.

5. Click the **Sign In** button.

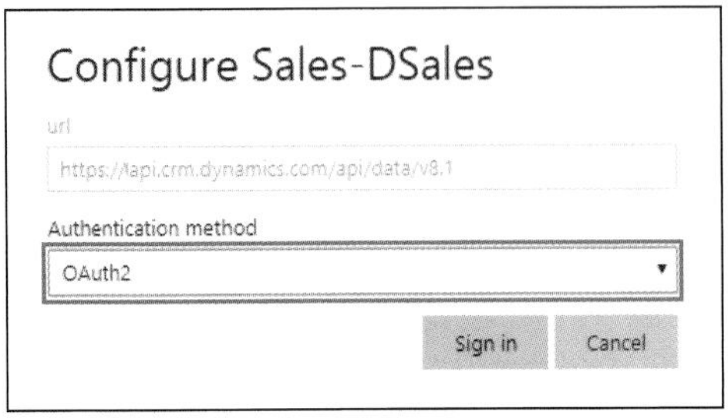

FIGURE 13-21 *Configure your data source credentials.*

6. When prompted, enter your Dynamics 365 username and password.

7. Expand the **Scheduled Refresh** section in the Settings window. (See Figure 13-22.)

8. Toggle the **Keep Your Data Up to Date** setting to **On**.

9. Open the **Refresh Frequency** drop-down list and select how often you want to refresh the data.

10. Open the **Time Zone** drop-down list and indicate your time zone.

11. Optionally, select the **Send a Refresh Failure Notification Email to Me** checkbox to receive an email in the event a refresh operation fails.

12. Click **Apply**.

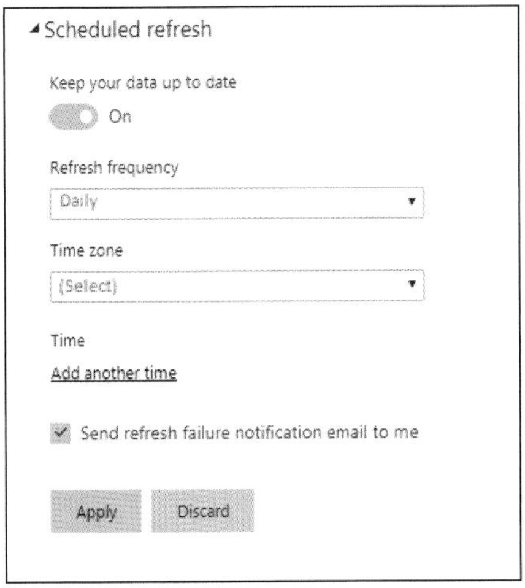

FIGURE 13-22 *Setting up scheduled refresh functionality.*

Skills review

In this chapter, you learned about:

- Importing data from Dynamics 365 into Power BI Desktop

- Creating a Power BI report

- Importing data from Dynamics 365 into Power BI service

- Embedding a Power BI dashboard into a Dynamics 365 dashboard

- Setting up a live data connection and data refresh functionality

13

Practice tasks

This section provides a simple case study for you to study and solve using information from this chapter. This section also contains a series of practice questions for you to answer.

Case study

Suppose you work for an online shipping organization. The company is three years old and already has a global presence. It manages an extremely large database. For all packages delivered, the company tracks the following information in a Dynamics 365 environment:

- Existing customers, including their contact information

- Prospective customers, including their contact information

- Package pick-up points across different regions

- Delivery points across different regions

- Order delivery dates for the previous three years

- E-commerce organizations, including their contact information

- Orders shipped by e-commerce organizations for the previous three years

- Delivery status of all shipments to date

- Monitoring of shipments through freight, warehouse distribution, lead logistics, and temperature-controlled spaces

- Export and import organizations involved

You want to present this data in Power BI report form to analyze profits and losses, and to obtain an overview of the company's growth around the globe. You also want to find out the following:

- Data on all shipments on a specific date

- The number of shipments by category, such as supply chain, logistics, warehouse, etc.

- The success ratio for deliveries (to identify and rectify delays)

- The number of prospective customers including their contact details, from the previous year

- A comparison of existing and new customers year by year over the previous three years

- The number of shipments completed by quarter

- The number of shipments by region

How would you go about creating these reports?

Practice questions

1. How do you connect with Dynamics 365 using Power BI Desktop?

2. How do you connect with Dynamics 365 using Power BI service?

3. How do you prepare an OData endpoint URL to connect with Dynamics 365?

4. How do you enable Power BI reporting in Dynamics 365?

5. How do you embed a Power BI dashboard in a Dynamics 365 dashboard?

Index

parent and child functions, 120–121
PATH function, 120
PATHITEM function, 120–121
PATHITEMREVERSE function, 121
PATHLENGTH function, 121
POWER function, 119
RELATED function, 115
REPLACE function, 122–123
ROUND function, 120
statistical functions, 122
SUM function, 118
SUMX function, 118–119
SWITCH function, 118
syntax of expressions, 109–110
text functions, 122–123
TIME function, 113
time intelligence functions, 114–115
TODAY function, 113
TOTALMID function, 114–115
TOTALQTD function, 115
TOTALYTD function, 115
TRIM function, 123
UNION function, 123
UPPER function, 123
WEEKDAY function, 113
YEAR function, 113
deleting
custom visualizations, 44
relationships for Desktop reports, 88
Desktop. *See* Power BI Desktop
developer settings, Admin Portal, 41
DirectQuery mode
Azure SQL database, 228–229
Oracle databases, 245–246
SQL Server, 188–189, 191–192, 203
donut charts, 65–66, 232–234
drill-through filters, applying to reports, 74
Dynamic datasets, 5
Dynamics 365
clustered bar charts, 264–266
data refresh functionality, 272–274
embedding dashboards, 269–272
funnel charts, 264–266
importing data from, 260–264
importing into Power BI service, 266–268
OData endpoint URL, 260–261
pie charts, 264–266
reports, 264–266
slicers, 264–266
Web API URL, 263

E
embed codes, Admin Portal, 42
embed feature, using with dashboards, 269–272
Embedded feature, 7
End User BI, 4
Excel, using, 40
Excel workbooks. *See also* Workbooks screen
importing data from, 128–129
measures and calculated columns, 129–131
EXCEPT function, DAX (Data Analysis Expressions), 123
export and sharing settings, Admin Portal, 37–38. *See also* sharing with others

F
FACT function, DAX (Data Analysis Expressions), 119
File data sources, 82
filled maps, 68–69
FILTER function, DAX (Data Analysis Expressions), 115–117
filters, applying in reports, 73–74. *See also* slicers
function, AND DAX (Data Analysis Expressions), 117–118
funnel charts
Dynamics 365, 264–266
reports and SharePoint Online lists, 150
using, 65–66

G
gateway. *See* data gateway
gauge charts
Azure SQL database, 232–234
SQL Server database, 193
using, 65–66
GCD function, DAX (Data Analysis Expressions), 119
General formatting, applying in Power BI Desktop, 93
Global Search, using, 40
group dashboards, reports, and datasets, 33–34

H
historical growth data, viewing, 3